EXPLORING THE
UNHEIMLICH

STUDIO AS BOOK
N0.12

SERIES INTRODUCTION

Studio as Book is a series of publications that tender the extraordinary creative work undertaken in the School of Architecture + Cities design studios – in detail. Each book in the series covers the work of a single design studio, either undergraduate or graduate, and sometimes both, over the course of at least two years. Its objectives are:

- To record, archive, and present the pedagogical programme and creative student outputs of a design studio.
- To position the work of a design studio within a broader intellectual, scientific or aesthetic field.
- To advance the design driven research being undertaken in the School's design studios.
- To provide a reference for future iterations and variations of a design studio.

Compressing the creative output of a multi-year design studio into a single volume, using a pre-designed book template is no easy undertaking, and it is necessarily selective. At the same time, it provides a consistent, sure platform for the wide range of approaches to the discipline of teaching architectural design which characterise the school.

Each Studio as Book has been peer-reviewed on the basis of a proposal submitted by the studio's tutors to an editorial committee. In addition to studio briefs and student work, each book includes content that draws out the studio's research and pedagogical agenda. The format that this takes varies from book to book – reflective essays by tutors or past students, interviews, theoretical essays from parallel fields, and so forth.

I wish to acknowledge the contribution of the following in bringing this project to fruition: Lindsay Bremner, Director of Research and Knowledge Exchange, who was the driving force behind the series when it was launched in 2016; Mark Boyce, author of Sizes May Vary, A workbook for graphic design (Lawrence King, 2008) – and the designer of Studio as Book; Filip Visnjic and Mirna Pedalo, who have given the books a presence on OpenStudiowWestminster: http://www.openstudiowestminster.org/studio-as-book/; and the design tutors and students who have given of their time and energy to collate and edit the books into this unique series.

Harry Charrington
Former Head of the School of Architecture + Cities
University of Westminster

EXPLORING THE
UNHEIMLICH

DS3.1
EDITED BY JANE TANKARD
+ JAKE PARKIN

STUDIO AS BOOK
N0. 12

SCHOOL OF ARCHITECTURE + CITIES
UNIVERSITY OF WESTMINSTER

PREFACE BY JANE TANKARD + JAKE PARKIN

DS3.1 has been exploring the architectural, political and social contexts to notions of the 'overlooked' for over a decade. As the studio has evolved, we have focused on a central concern with the interstitial, the liminal and the marginal through explorations of the *Unheimlich* or uncanny. In this context, the notion of the uncanny resides in the thresholds, not just between architectural space, but between self and other, social norms and transgression.

The studio (previously DS3.7) became DS3.1 in 2015 and since then has been led by Jane Tankard with three key studio contributors, Alicia Pivaro (2015-2018), Thomas Grove (2018-2024) and Jake Parkin (2024-present). Over the past 25 years, we have had the pleasure of working with a long lineage of previous students, two of whom, Mark Rowe and Chris Hartiss, have been part of the collaboration since being Part 2 students of Jane's at South Bank Polytechnic in the 1990s.

The influence and legacy of Kevin Rhowbotham and Kath Shonfield's teaching, writing and inspiration have permeated the studio's life throughout. Adopting an experimental and interrogative position using creative and analytical processes, our methodology is designed as a mechanism with which to mine the rich seam of creativity and potentiality that exists within the uncanny. The reframing of historical and cultural events described through text (for example, Paris 1871 and 1968) and film (for example In the Mood for Love, Fish Tank and The Florida Project), are positioned as the location and identities of the marginal, the liminal and the collective. Using analytical representations in two and three dimensions, in analogue, digital and composite form, we investigate the mechanisms of palimpsest, imprint and superimposition, making work that layers spatial narratives, memory, diversity and inclusivity into speculative concepts for the city. Architecture is conceived not as a static object but as an active, critical participant in rewriting shared urban narratives. This methodology aligns closely with the reimagined notion of the uncanny in contemporary art and architectural theory. By '(re)enacting' moments of historical and cultural intersectionality, our practice deliberately estranges the familiar, revealing hidden structures, suppressed narratives and overlooked spaces.

We reference artists who deliberately curate, rather than resolve, the uncanny, challenging normalisation, hegemony and accepted social hierarchies and orders. The notion of the palimpsest, of layering, addition and memory in opposition to the tabula rasa is a tool for establishing temporalities, provoking the interstitial as a site for dislocating the normative and choreographing the experience of estrangement. In this sense, our speculative projects treat the uncanny not as a symptom in need of analysis, but as a generative condition, a critical mode through which architecture confronts the politics of memory, the complexity of collective identity and the possibilities of a more inclusive urban future.

The relationship between the built and the unbuilt is a territory that is both ambiguous and yet deeply significant in architectural educational discourse; it is the spectre under the bed, the ghost in the wings, La Passante's 'tap on the shoulder'. In the studio we are thinking speculatively about the future yet somehow attempting to prepare Part 1 architectural students for the profession as it exists now, a context that is deeply flawed, bound by the conditions of colonisation, commodity and capitalism. We work to identify a space between binary worlds as an interstitial cultural landscape where a polemical, transient creativity can be found; one that challenges established hierarchies and resists fixed categorisation.

Using filmic mechanisms, projection (both real and other) and adapted orthographic drawing (the latter enabling the unfolding of temporality, sequence and series/duplicate), our methodology shifts between the macro and the micro.

We use a palimpsest of actions and prompts, from Kevin Rhowbotham's post-structuralist actions to the visions of Orhan Pamuk, the writings of Bachelard, Marx and Benjamin and the challenges of conscious intersectionality (hook, Lorde, Freire). The Architect's role is privileged for we have the education and sometimes the resources to act, to oversee, manifest; but our privilege brings responsibilities to listen and more importantly, to hear and dissolve the hierarchies hegemony has constructed around us. Every testimony is real, every experience and response valid and valued.

CONTENTS

FOREWORD 009
Mark Rowe

PAST / FUTURE TEMPORALITY, TABULA RASA 021
Victoria Watson

CHALLENGING THE TABULA RASA: 045
IN SEARCH OF THE *UNHEIMLICH*
Jane Tankard

BRIAN ENO: BETWEEN PORTRAIT AND LANDSCAPE 059
GHOSTS, BELLS, AND THE SONIC CARTOGRAPHY OF SUFFOLK
Steve Bowkett

SAME, SAME BUT DIFFERENT 073
Jake Parkin

AN ARCHITECTURAL AUTOPSY: 087
'DISSECTING THE EXQUISITE CORP(U)SE'
Peter J. Baldwin

SECTIONING THE *UNHEIMLICH* 099
Jane Tankard

SPECULATIVE CITY: 123
TWO ISTANBUL TYPOLOGIES FOR URBAN COLLECTIVISM
Deniz Çetin + Çağda Özbaki

SPECULATIVE CITY: CASE STUDIES 133
Jane Tankard

APPROPRIATE, RECONFIGURE, MAKE DO AND MEND 213
Alicia Pivaro

MAKE DO AND MEND: ON TECHNOLOGY AND THE *UNHEIMLICH* 229
Jane Tankard

BROTHER HOUSES, KOSOVO 243
Anesa Cana

SERIES, EVENT 253
Jake Parkin

I FALL IN BETWEEN 267
Celo Grassi

ACKNOWLEDGEMENTS 275
Jane Tankard + Jake Parkin

JANE TANKARD
ARB RIBA FHEA BA(Hons) PGDIP

Jane is an Architect and Senior Lecturer at the University of Westminster, where she has been employed for over 26 years. She studied for her Part 1 at the University of Manchester in the early 1980s, where she became immersed in the counterculture scene in Hulme and Moss Side. Her Masters studies were at South Bank Polytechnic, which for one year was under the inspirational guidance of Kevin Rhowbotham. His departure from the institution precipitated a radical educational moment in time when, along with Tonia Carless and others, Jane co-led an architectural education collective for the final master's year, which resulted in Tonia winning the RIBA Silver Medal. (01) Jane has taught at a number of institutions, including the AA and the Bauhaus-Universität Weimar, and has collaborated on a number of experimental architectural and art interventions. She is currently teaching MArch design studio 17 with Jake. Her research focuses on cross-disciplinary practice and intersectionality. Jane is also a Director of Tankard Bowkett Architects, who work on private and community projects.

JAKE PARKIN
AA Dipl. MArch ARB

Jake is an Architect and Lecturer at the University of Westminster. He studied Object and Spatial Design at the Leeds College of Art before receiving a five year scholarship to study at the AA School of Architecture, where he was nominated for Diploma Honours and awarded the William Glover Prize. He has worked internationally, most notably at Bureau Spectacular in California on projects for the Museum of Modern and Contemporary Art in Seoul, the Chicago Architecture Biennial, and the Taiwan Academy in Hollywood. In the UK, he has contributed to projects at practices such as Foster + Partners and Farshid Moussavi Architecture. Since 2022 he has taught at the University of Westminster, where he co-leads design studio 17 on the MArch course with Jane Tankard. He has also taught at the AA, the Leicester School of Architecture, the Leeds School of Architecture, and the RIBA Studio programme at Oxford Brookes University. He has held guest critic roles at UCLA, UNM, CPP, the Bartlett and at the AA. He has taught on the AA Summer School and Media Studies programmes and co-founded the AA Visiting School in Los Angeles with Jimenez Lai. In 2024 he established Jake Parkin Studio.

MANY THANKS TO OUR CONTRIBUTORS

Peter J. Baldwin ARB RIBA SF-HEA
Head of Department, Architecture and Built Environment, Birmingham City University

Steve Bowkett BA (hons) MA (RCA)
SL London South Bank University, Director Tankard Bowkett Architects

Anesa Cana BA (hons) RIBA Part 1
Masters student and Architectural Assistant

Assistant Professor Dr Deniz Çetin
Faculty of Engineering and Architecture, Altinbas University Istanbul

Celo Grassi BSc (LSE)
International Social & Public Policy, Monitoring & Evaluation, Social Impact Research

Dr Maria Faraone MArch, OAA
Associate Professor. Programme Director RIBA Studio, Oxford Brookes University

Assistant Professor Dr Çağda Özbaki
Faculty of Engineering and Architecture, Altinbas University Istanbul

Alicia Pivaro BSc (hons) PG Dip Arch MSc Urban Studies
Climate and Community Activist, Educator, Artist

Mark Rowe ARB RIBA

Studio Juggernaut
An open research group, led by Jane Tankard, exploring intersectionality in architectural education and beyond.

Dr Victoria Watson
Senior Lecturer in Architecture, University of Westminster

NOTES

(01) Jane Tankard, "*A Few People, a Brief Moment in Time: Architectural Education Experiments 1987-91*," AAE Charrette no. 6 (2020)

FOREWORD

MARK ROWE

FOREWORD BY MARK ROWE

'Architecture for the age of doom: There is only the *Unheimlich* to look forward to now'

At some point towards the end of the Twentieth Century I was fortunate enough to complete my Part 2 academic architectural education under the radical guidance of Jane Tankard, alongside Sherry Bates and Kath Shonfield at South Bank University and then Katerina Rüedi and Sarah Wigglesworth at Kingston University. Through projects as diverse and whimsical as Ideal Home for a Serial Killer, Vitrine for a Whopper, a field trip to survey the then militarised fault lines of Belfast, and a dissertation focussed on the writings of Manfredo Tafuri, we explored the political context of both architecture and architectural graphic production in a way that felt inspiring, exciting and necessary to someone who up until that point had only been exposed to narratives of function, space, light, form and damp proof courses.

During subsequent working life in practice, as I played my part in generating hundreds of thousands of tonnes of planet-warming CO_2 emissions through the relentless specification of concrete, aluminium, glass and steel, I have sought to keep a grounding foot in that vital academic world through occasional visits as critic, tutor, or observer to Jane's evolving units at Westminster University, most recently and with increasingly regularity, through DS3.1 which clearly retains the theoretical rigour with which I was already familiar, albeit in very different and shifting times, during which notions of the uncanny have become a particularly useful prism through which to view our current moment.

(right) Limehouse Archive, Rania Elkharim, DS3.1

Perhaps within the demanding hothouse of day-to-day life in the construction industry it has been too easy for many of us to fail to fully comprehend the concurrently accelerating crises of climate breakdown, techno-surveillance, wealth concentration, political authoritarianism and ethno-racial supremacism (the reader should feel free to speculate on the various overlapping chicken-and-egg scenarios which have delivered this polycrisis during the span of our lifetimes), but however daunting the work of the academy, and for all of us within the profession, remains to ask what might ethical propositions for appropriately responsive architectural programmes, forms or actions look like within this seemingly death-spiralling situation?

The students, tutors and work of DS3.1 have shown me that the next generation is already feeling its way towards answers, or at least hints of answers or maybe new questions, and has in no small part informed my own prognosis on where our collective focus should lie.

CONCENTRATIONS OF ATMOSPHERIC CARBON

As our home, this planet, begins to change irrevocably, everywhere we know begins to become *Unheimlich*, superficially recognisable but clearly different and sometimes even horrific at a primal level; we may be walking through the streets of London in the late afternoon, but the experience of darting for shade, gasping in forty degree temperatures is only recognisable from youthful dulled memories of the Mediterranean at the height of summer.

Clearly our architectural responses are duty-bound to mitigate these changing local climates, and to accept where they are inevitably heading in the longer term however effective society's actions going forwards from today, but we must be similarly obligated to do no further harm in the context of the carbon releasing, material extracting, habitat destroying orgy with which the contemporary development and construction industry, and by extension the general architectural profession, has been engaged with since the Industrial Revolution as it plays out its growth fixated dogma. Whilst we await the arrival of magical techno-solutions (or not), we can only mitigate further harm by developing an architecture of resource sufficiency, necessarily focussing on the optimal re-use of the buildings and infrastructure which we already have, rather than the erection of new structures.

Consequently, this requires a relative sublimation of the creative ego, a willingness to maintain, a loosening of ideas of control, eschewing the idea of the Architect as dramatic urban sculptor. Perhaps even a readiness to sometimes do nothing, so antithetical to the dynamic and active ideal of the hero Architect which persists to this day. Such an architecture of care, repair, retrofit and modest extension will itself still need to pay heed to our meagre and diminishing remaining carbon budgets, and by implication be focussed on low embodied carbon strategies; the scaling up of the use of natural materials that we are more used to seeing in rural, one-off or vernacular buildings allied with the reuse of our existing materials bank, true front-end circularity not the green-washing gloss of future potential demountability at a point when the planet may already be cooked.

(right) Refuge for the Homeless, Yara Samaha, DS3.1

The aesthetic result of such a formula will clearly be lumpier, rougher, more collage based, serendipitous, and evolving in real time, than those clean, sleek forms which modernism championed and which have persisted through the various orthogonal and biomorphic post-modernisms that have followed in its wake. Just as the geographical home is becoming unrecognisable, so too our professional home will become unfamiliar. It is incumbent for this future to be explored within the academy if young practitioners are to be ready for this new world in which they will work, particularly at a time when contemporary professional practice, with several notable but small-scale exceptions, seems so unready, unwilling and ill-equipped to grapple with this moment of universal change and challenge. But as we face up to that existential challenge of architecture's centrality to the civilizational overshoot driving the climate and ecological crises, we should not lose sight of those concurrent societal traumas which also proscribe our field of operations and might be easily overlooked given the scale of this central climatic preoccupation.

CONCENTRATIONS OF WEALTH

It has remained the case during the modern period that significant architectural interventions generally require substantial capital; from those individuals, companies, financial entities or government bodies able to access this, directly or via debt markets, and that Architects must ultimately heed the instructions of those that provide this capital funding. Socially progressive architecture has sought to channel that capital for the benefit of the wider population where it is able to.

Despite steady progress in the methods of community stakeholder engagement over this period, the shots are still ultimately called by capital and such engagement processes often merely grease the progress of capital's demands through obligatory semi-democratic regulatory procedures. So little fundamentally new here since Tafuri's time. But since the late 1970's, and despite the globally diminishing percentage of the population deemed to be in abject poverty, the benefits of fossil fuel driven economic growth have been increasingly delivered and concentrated within a small global elite, often referred to colloquially as the One Percent, all the while as low tax, high debt government has progressively sought to transfer its own capital programmes over to private finance. Whether in vanity projects, luxury resorts, high end residential or the speculative investments of data centres, PFI projects, crammed co-living, or now blooming laboratories (sometimes researching drugs to prolong human life on a planet increasingly unable to support it), these are the people who generally dictate what gets built, where, and to some degree what it looks like.

Within the academy we have often deluded ourselves that the establishment will magically support our altruistic briefs and programmes. However our politico-economic system offers little hope of communities controlling either the capital, or means of production, that would give them any meaningful power beyond merely paying lip service to ideas of democratic input.

Should our projects accept the realities of the current paradigm as a fait-accompli?

(right) Billingsgate Raft, Munira Osman, DS3.1

Or might we, by mapping out the lived realities of those (often currently without voices) in the communities in which we site our projects, by developing projects with them that reflect their needs and desires, be ready for the future crumbling or overthrow of the tyranny of extreme wealth, irrespective of whether architecture is able to play any direct role in that demise?

CONCENTRATIONS OF POWER

The concentration of wealth has inexorably led us to further concentrations of political power, through old fashioned lobbying and corruption fuelled by burgeoning capital, and the almost total capture of old media to set agendas, and new media algorithms to fuel them, and occasionally visa-versa. Again, the current moment appears uncanny and frightening in the context of the liberal certainties of the past; in the UK, mainstream politicians calling for forced remigration, pensioners sent to prison for peaceful protest against genocide, human rights for trans people being removed, nationalist flag waving and explicitly racist ideas endorsed as 'common sense' within government and our national broadcaster. With the US simply a step or two ahead down this path. All of this makes sense in one scenario as the pitch-rolling for a Rand-ian climate breakdown fascist future in which the strategy is to bet everything on AI-driven economic growth, burning through all of our outstanding fossil fuel reserves, surfing the wave of extreme temperature and sea level rises, with the richest optimistically insulated somehow from its worst effects, whilst we watch (or more likely, our media looks away from) the deaths of billions in the global South following their successful othering and the turning of the global North into a walled authoritarian fortress.

Just as Engineers and Architects drafted the blueprints for the Nazi's concentration camp gas chambers in the past, and are working up the plans for Trump and Netanyahu's New Gaza Riviera today, so our profession will be asked to enact the infrastructure of this dystopian future. Within the academy we have rare opportunities (perhaps only shared with science fiction in literature and film) to step into these futures and help others imagine them, we are able to speculate on them, the current tendencies leading towards them, and lay bare those real and potential structures of power through satire, caricature or simple direct representation.

CONCENTRATIONS OF DATA

Concentration of power and wealth is further catalysed by, and in turn supportive of, a US based technology complex which seeks to know everything about almost every aspect of our lives, ostensibly to drive ad revenue, but as likely to end up assisting state or military monitoring. A shadowy company like Palantir can sift through the entirety of our NHS datasets whilst simultaneously providing targeting information via facial recognition software direct to Israeli sniper drones in Gaza.

Predictive AI algorithms literally holding the power of life and death within the context of a genocide, or a missed cancer screening appointment. Seemingly benign accurate digital twin building models crafted by our industry within Revit software provide the perfect backdrop to future ever more accurate geo-location tracking, the surveillance capabilities of our own carried and worn devices complemented by those of the oft-touted all-seeing smart building.

(right) Microbrewery for Southwark, Alexander Donov, DS3.1

Within our industry, innovation and technology are routinely and naively viewed as positive with little questioning of whom they benefit and to what ends. Whether that is in the practice studio where the roles of marketing assistants or Part I graduates are increasingly usurped by ChatGPT or Midjourney AI software (all of course linked to the wider implications of AI's energy demands, water demands, copyright infringements, and safety concerns - all too deep to unpack in the space of this essay); on site where repeatedly eulogised robotic technologies may leave tradespeople redundant; or completed smart buildings where our every movement and interaction is tracked and harvested. Again, within the academy we are able, through our hypothetical projects, to critique this present and future on the level of the actual and the imagined. To ask is it the future we want? What might a different tech future look like?

And critically as the Luddites once asked (enroute to birthing the labour movement); for whose benefit are these machines being deployed?

THERE IS ONLY THE *UNHEIMLICH* TO LOOK FORWARD TO NOW

As Freud sets out, the *unheimlich* provokes the deep and constant desire to seek out the *heimlich*. One only needs to survey contemporary right wing discourse, and to a lesser extent unreformed productivist leftist thought or Modern Monetary Theory proponents, to see that nostalgic ideas of a safe home, a pure homeland, a muscular working-class, a benign climate or steady growth economy are gaining in popular resonance at a time when a return to those imagined sanctuaries is becoming a near impossibility.

If we are to play our part as a discipline in finding a way through this civilizational polycrisis it becomes incumbent on us as practitioners, educators and students to evolve a field of ideas, of a transformed architecture within the already arriving climate, political, economic and professional *unheimlich* rather than embracing the understandable, instinctual desire to deny, ignore or flee it.

Over the last decade or so, DS3.1 has grappled with all of these preoccupations, either explicitly or tangentially, harnessing the idea of the uncanny to excavate and inhabit the interstitial zones within our cities, both physical and abstract, which will inevitably become more pervasive during this age of amplifying contextual change. For that reason, the writing, images and projects which follow should be of interest to all of us as we search for our own individual and collective analyses and responses.

(right) Theatre of the Moon, Olha Petrachkova, DS3.1

NOTE

Mark's 'Ideal Home for a Serial Killer' project can be found on page 206.

PAST / FUTURE TEMPORALITY, TABULA RASA

VICTORIA WATSON

PAST / FUTURE TEMPORALITY, TABULA RASA BY VICTORIA WATSON

'The purposes for which a building is used are constantly changing and we cannot afford to tear down the building each time'

This essay is a reflection on a drawn and modelled proposition by the famous twentieth century Architect Ludwig Mies van der Rohe, for a 'future-proof' microcosm of sustainable intervention for the City of London. To begin with it is necessary to dispel some misconceptions about Mies. Just like many others of the avant-garde artists and Architects of his generation, Mies held the view that technology and progress, taken together, were negative and destructive forces that ought to be resisted. Mies invented his own project of resistance, he conducted a campaign against technological progress by adopting a strategy of neutralisation, which he approached from two directions: ornament and program.

Mies' tactics for neutralising ornamentation are well recorded in histories of the Modern Movement in Architecture, which examine the way he reduced the appearance of his buildings to mute, unadorned parallelepiped structures with gridded facades woven out of optically scintillating tapestries of steel and glass. Mies' tactic of weaving facades guaranteed a distinct similarity between his buildings, to the extent that some people claim the buildings all look the same. In fact, with a modicum of attention, it is possible to see how, by varying the proportions and materiality of the weave, Mies was able to make his buildings quite different.

(upper right) Plan diagram showing the principles of Mies revision of Sullivan's formula, Sullivan on the left, Mies on the right.

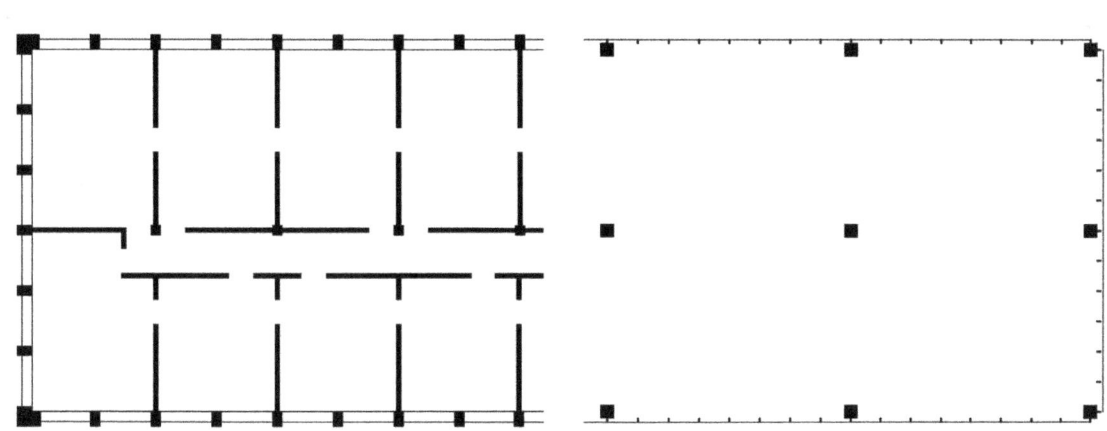

What is more, the reflective and refractive properties of the glass facades meant that a Mies, wherever it is located, maintains a certain distance from its surroundings, while at the same time mirroring the local environment in scintillating imagery. This is because light bounces around between the surfaces of the glass and is picked-up and interpreted by the perceptual apparatuses of the viewing subject, i.e., people like you and me, as we move around and about the building. As for Mies' tactics for neutralising the building program, these continue to generate confusion and for that reason it is necessary to consider them in some detail. In an interview with Christian Norbert-Schulz, published in the journal *Baukunst und Werkform* in 1958, Mies was attempting to clarify his approach when he stated:

"The purposes for which a building is used are constantly changing and we cannot afford to tear down the building each time. That is why we have revised Sullivan's formula 'form follows function' and construct a practical and economical space into which we fit the functions." (01)

Here, Mies was referring to Louis Sullivan's essay from 1896 about office buildings. In his essay Sullivan set out his parameters for the 'true normal type' of the tall office building. Based on his observations of natural structures, Sullivan postulated a direct relationship between 'life' and 'form.' He thought man-made, artificial forms, when they were not overly constrained by theoretical speculation, also conformed to the natural model and hence produced a sure fit between form and function. In the case of tall office buildings, Sullivan thought the horizontal and vertical divisions of the bulk of the structure should be based on what he called the 'office unit,' that being 'a room of comfortable area and height.' This basic cell, explained Sullivan, is 'similar to a cell in a honey-comb, merely a compartment, nothing more.'

If we turn to Sullivan's Wainwright Office Building, built in St Louis, Missouri between 1890 - 1891, we can see his cellular theory reflected in the look and organisation of the design. The cells are repeated and lined up, side by side, to form a single, typical floor arrangement, with corridor connections, which are in turn repeated and stacked up, tier upon tier, to 'form [...] the true basis of the external development of the exterior'. (02) Turning now to Mies' designs for tall office buildings, we can see how he revised Sullivan's principles by eliminating the cell, and hence the corridors, to produce the floor plan-type of the clear, uncluttered expanse, marked only by the grid of the supporting structural frame and the service cores, with their clusters of stairs, lifts, rest-rooms and rising ductwork.

Mies' neutralising approach to program did not arise simply out of practical considerations, it was a realistic critique of the obvious fact of life's subjection to temporal change, which, as Mies once remarked, 'even Plato recognised'. (03) For Mies, adopting a realist attitude to time meant facing up to the fact that everything present in life is only transitory, including plans for the future. Plans are doomed to fail because they run out of time, the people who devise them pass away and those who follow have no grasp of the urgency that once made those plans so compelling. Mies believed it was a mistake for Architects to propose forms for buildings based on preconceived notions about how they would be used, which, even with swift procurement, could be no more than a projection into the future.

For Mies, the real challenge for the aspiring Architect was to leave the use of the building open to the future. It can help to understand Mies' avant-garde attitudes through a metaphor invented by Walter Benjamin in his famous evocation of Paul Klee's painting, Angelus Novus.

(top right) Paul Klee, Angelus Novus, 1920

It was a painting which Benjamin owned, having bought it in 1921. In his writings, Benjamin often referred to the Angel, likening it to his avant-garde friends and acquaintances, one of whom was Mies. In his posthumously published essay, *Theses on the Philosophy of History*, Benjamin reflected on the significance of the Angel and on what it told him about human history. We can see from the image shown, the Angel looks as if it is suspended in a space without gravity, hovering with open eyes and mouth and with outstretched wings and dangling legs and toes. The Angel's posture is reminiscent of Robin Evan's description of Mies' tall buildings, that appear in Evan's influential essay *Mies van der Rohe's Paradoxical Symmetries*. The essay was first published in AA Files in 1990 and had a profound effect on many young Architects, including the founders of DWA, at the time. Evans commented on the way tall Miesian structures:

"...do not rise against the pull of gravity; gravity does not enter into it. They make you believe, against reason, that they do not partake of that most pervasive and relentless of all natural forces. So the result is not the exhilarating levitation of an object, a familiar effect, but a gentle, dreamy disorientation in the observer". (04)

Benjamin describes the Angel as facing toward the past and moving backwards into the future. It's gaze rests upon the traces of the past that are piling up behind. The Angel sees the wreckage of history as a single catastrophe, rather than a chain of events, a disorganised heap that just keeps on getting bigger!

In Mies' well known text of 1924, *Baukunst und Zeitwille* (Building Art and the Will of the Epoch), he made a statement that is plausibly a reference to Benjamin's Angel:

"We find again and again that excellent building masters fail because their work does not serve the will of the epoch... it is the essential that matters. One cannot walk forward while looking backward, and one cannot be the instrument of the will of the epoch if one lives in the past". (05)

Baukunst and Zeitwille was published in the avant-garde Journal *Der Querschnitt* (The Cross Section), known at the time for its unorthodox literary and graphic style (Mies' sometime colleague, the Dada artist and film maker, Hans Richter referred to Der Querschnitt as:

"a very successful operation performed on the corpse of a present-day life." (06)

At a first reading, Mies seems to have been admonishing his fellow Architects for facing the wrong way, as if he did not want them to be Angels. However, an equally legitimate and perhaps more accurate, reading suggests it was not the direction Mies was criticising but the mode of perambulation: Mies had no objection to facing backwards, it was walking backwards that troubled him. And, given Mies' aversion to living in the past, what better assurance could there be than to face it in opposition, keeping it firmly in sight as you turned your back to the future.

(bottom right) Mies van der Rohe, Mansion House Square and Office Tower, collage view of model and photograph (you can recognise the Mansion House by its pedimented portico, the office tower is facing parallel to the side elevation of that building, the plaza stretches between them)

Thought about in this way, Mies' preferred architectural posture might be described as that of suspended, backward-facing, immobility, as if it were possible to maintain a mobile equilibrium, held in a state of relative stability, by pushing-back against the temporal flow. Mies' London design consisted of a small office tower, placed opposite to the Mansion House, with the two buildings connected by a large open plaza. It conforms to his avant-garde outlook, but the histories that tell of it have tended to overlook that aspect of Mies' proposal. Sometimes the history is written in terms of architectural style and Mies' design is described as futuristic, reductive and unadorned, with the idea of the large open space seen both as a solution to problems of congestion and as a potential place for events.

Under the style category, Mies' use of rectangular geometries and the organising principle of the grid is seen as corresponding to the use of those same forms in modernist painting. Or the history may be told as a battle between progressive and conservative forces, wherein property developers and their Architects are pitted against amenity societies, activist groups and members of the royal family, such as the Victorian Society, SAVE Britain's Heritage and HRH the Prince of Wales. In the developer versus conservationist histories, special attention is given to the two sensational planning inquiries, both of which ended up before the secretary of state for the environment. Each inquiry served as a platform for the conservationists to argue for the rights of the listed Victorian buildings that were to be demolished to make way for Mies' design. The conservationists portrayed the Victorian buildings as massively popular and exemplary of the architectural preferences of ordinary people. On the other hand, they portrayed Mies' design as standing for the power and greed of wealthy elites. A further point of antagonism for this kind of history is the Victorian buildings' sympathetic relationship to the patchwork urbanism of the City's built fabric, as opposed to the formal clarity of Mies' design.

A third kind of history, one that has only recently begun to acknowledge Mies' London design, belongs to the tradition of the architectural monograph.

In histories of this type, the design is framed within an evolutionary history of the Architect's intellectual life and practice. In an essay of 2004, *Mies Immersion*, Phyllis Lambert categorised the London design as a carefully worked out but unbuilt 'stand-alone high-rise'. [07] More recently, in 2014, a monographic treatment by Detlef Mertins traced the formal lineage of Mies' London design back to the Seagram Building in New York, completed in 1958. Mertins explains how Mies' design of the Seagram Building set the precedent for the architectural type of the combined office tower and open plaza development, which after its construction 'triggered a change in the zoning by-law' of New York City and indirectly 'encouraged the construction of more public plazas'. Mertins read Mies' London design as having failed because the urban typology of the office tower and open plaza was 'too controversial in its modernity to be realised in that city'. [08] His assessment is partially correct, because the modernity of Mies' design did contribute to its eventual rejection, but that was not the reason the project failed. The reason the project failed was due to the quite considerable delay in the procurement process, during which the flow of time crept up on Mies' proposal and engulfed it!

It was in June 1962, when Mies was in the last phase of his career, that the property developer and art collector, Peter Palumbo, commissioned him to propose a design for the development of a large plot of land to the west of the Mansion House in the City of London.

Mies' proposal was granted outline planning permission in May 1969. In those days it was not necessary to actually own the property rights in order to apply for planning permission and it was understood that full permission would be granted at a later date, when Palumbo had acquired all properties on the site. It took Palumbo about twenty years and it cost him £10 million to acquire the twelve freeholds and 245 leaseholds necessary to be in a position to realise Mies' design. So it was not until January 1982, by which time Mies was dead (he passed away in August 1969) that Palumbo could apply for full planning permission. On doing so, permission was refused, it was refused on the grounds that:

(top right) Plan diagram showing the expanded conservation area boundary between 1971 (dashed line) & 1981 (dot-dashed line) and listed buildings on Palumbo's site (pale grey fill)

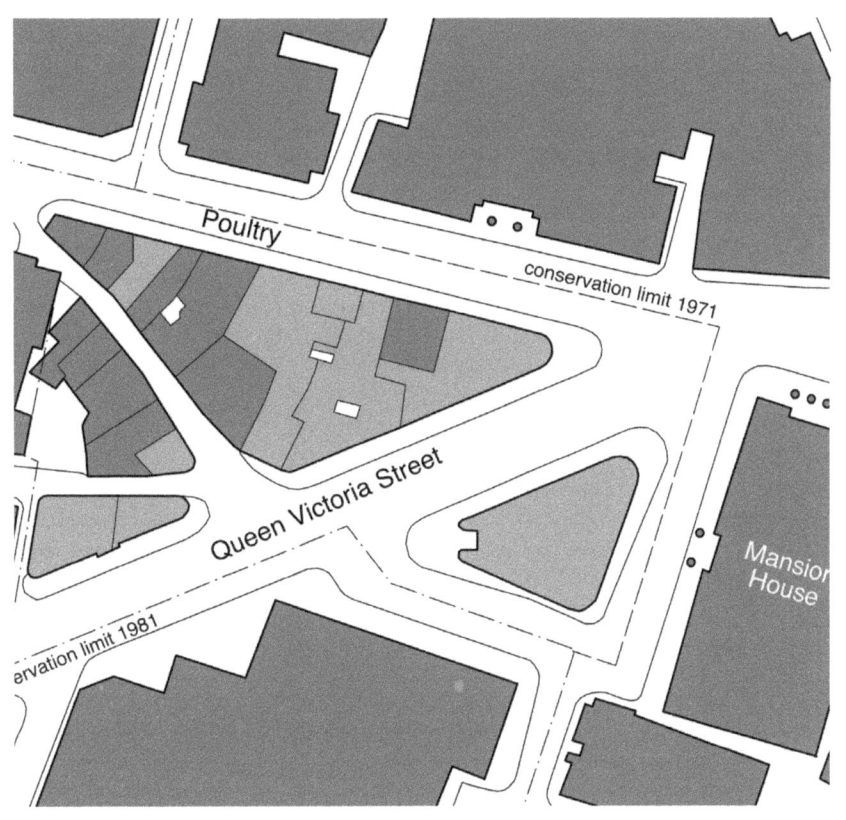

"The proposed development…would not accord with the special architectural and visual qualities of the Bank Conservation Area, and would be seriously detrimental to its character and appearance…to the setting of nationally known historic buildings and other listed buildings in the locality…" (09)

The refusal was based on conservationist principles. Between 1969 and 1982, as Palumbo was acquiring the property rights, the site had become incorporated into the Bank Conservation Area, including the listing of some of the incumbent buildings. The slow listing process began as early as 1971, but Palumbo's plot was not incorporated into the conservation area until December 1981, just a month before Palumbo applied for planning permission. And perhaps it was the fear of increasing conservation pressures that prompted Palumbo to apply when he did. Palumbo appealed against the refusal on the grounds he already had outline permission and had acquired the necessary property holdings in good faith. The appeal led to a public inquiry, launched by the British Government in May 1984, the proceedings of which were long and protracted but the outcome was no different and again permission was refused. The grounds for refusal were again essentially conservationist, the inspectors report noticed, quite correctly, how obtrusive the proposed tower would be and how it would 'affect significant local views… draw attention away from the present central area and its civic buildings and dominate the whole of the space between it and the Royal Exchange'.

The report also noted how the proposed square would 'eliminate the central focus served by the radiating roads signalling the heart of the City' and, contrary to the claims of the applicants, would 'not enhance the setting of the principal listed buildings facing the square'. (10) It is hard to think of a counter argument to rebuff the inspectors objections, because the Mies was indeed, in true avant-garde spirit, intended to offer a radical alternative to the extant urban form. It was not that Mies was intending to shock the City by eradicating its historically evolved forms, rather it was because he could see little point in preserving them. Because, regardless of what he or anyone else might wish, modernity's faith in the march of progress meant all such forms were anyway destined to perish. By 1982 there was little sympathy, or awareness, of Mies' radical urbanism, not even his most avid supporters seemed to be able to follow his logic in this regard. As a result of the inquiry it became obvious to everyone, including those who supported the Mies, that his approach to urban design and architecture had completely lost its appeal. Palumbo must have been disappointed, he seems to have been quite genuine in his admiration for the Mies and judging by his publicity statements, looked upon it as a kind of gift from himself, as patron, to the City, rather in the way private collectors give artworks to public museums, as something to remember them by. And maybe, it was because the secretary of state realised the economy of gift-giving had become entangled in that of property development that the DOE letter, sent to Palumbo's solicitors, included the following conciliatory passage:

(upper right) Palimpsest meets Tabula Rasa, One, Declan Slonim, DS3.1

"The fact that a building is listed or is within a Conservation Area does not necessarily mean that it will be preserved. The secretary of state does not rule out redevelopment of this site if there are acceptable proposals for replacing the existing buildings. He does not consider that the buildings are of such overriding importance that their preservation should outweigh all other considerations." (11)

The passage was qualified and reinforced with the following, distinctly progressivist, anti-conservationist, proclamation:

"The secretary of state takes the view that, for the City to continue to function efficiently as a world financial centre, it needs to adapt to the requirements of the modern commercial world. It needs to attract high quality, efficient, modern buildings… It would be wrong to attempt to freeze the character of the City of London." (12)

Quite soon after the decision, Palumbo announced his intention to go ahead with a new proposal for the site, one that would take into consideration the comments and recommendations of the DOE letter and of the new patterns in international finance that were transforming the way the City imagined itself.

THE BIG BANG

When Palumbo first approached Mies back in the early 1960s, the City still saw itself as the international clearing-house of what was known as the 'sterling area'.

(A group of countries, mainly part of the commonwealth, pegging their currencies to the pound sterling or actually using the pound as their currency).

But by the 1980s, sterling's reserve currency status was no longer credible and the clearing function was pretty well over. By the time of the Mansion House Square public inquiries the City had completely changed its character, it was now a key hub in the vast new global capital marketplace and the key driver for its success was no longer the old Commonwealth connections but the ability to capture a huge share of the business associated with the rapid growth of the Eurobond market. At a more local level and perhaps of greater consequence for the imagination of the City, the British government were in the process of instituting the legislation necessary to trigger what came to be known as the 'Big Bang.' By abolishing the minimum fixed fee on trades, Big Bang legislation aimed to encourage greater competition in financial trading. By putting an end to the separation between dealers in stocks and shares and investment advisors, it aimed to encourage mergers and take-overs and, by allowing foreign firms to own UK brokers, it aimed to open up London's market to international banks. All this was to be accompanied by a switch from traditional, face-to-face share dealing, to electronic trading.

These immanent changes generated an atmosphere of anticipation and excitement in the City, one with architectural consequences. One consequence was an attack on the kind of conservationist attitudes that had led to the listing of so many buildings on Palumbo's plot.

(bottom) Palimpsest meets Tabula Rasa, Two, Declan Slonim, DS3.1

Within the culture of the Big Bang sensibility, conservationist attitudes were heavily criticised as an attempt to turn the City into a museum. And, for the same reasons, Palumbo's gifting approach to development seemed inappropriate. Increasingly, the City Corporation came under pressure to respond to a perceived future need for 'Vast, open-plan, high-tech trading floors where all the different arms of the new securities conglomerates could be housed under one roof.' Such trading floors were not compatible with narrow Victorian frontages. As early as January 1985 a poll by Savills of 251 City occupiers revealed that more than two-thirds of respondents expected to be looking for large, open-plan areas, with nearly half feeling the floor sizes of over 10,000 square feet were 'most suited to their needs'. (13)

The Mies, it should be noted, had been designed with a single occupancy user in mind, that being Lloyds Bank. At the time Lloyds had a 'sterling area' outlook and were planning to use the tower as their Overseas Head Office. Mies even went so far as to prepare layouts for each floor-level, corresponding to Lloyd's specified requirements. According to Palumbo, Lloyds waited for 12 years, but eventually pulled out of the deal. Assuming that 12 year period began at the time of outline planning permission, which, again according to Palumbo, coincided with Mies completion of the detail design process, then Lloyds would have dropped out around 1980, just 2 years before full planning permission was applied for and refused. However, thanks to Mies' neutralising attitude to the building program, the bias of the design in favour of a single, specified occupant had only a negligible impact on the form.

It was only the location of partition walls and furniture that qualified each floor layout and those could be removed without making any difference to the design.

As we have already seen, it was an inherent principle of Mies' approach that the interior layout of a building was merely contingent, not an essential, formative principle and could always be changed, or even removed, without detriment to the design. The notion of changeability as an essential principle can be traced back to a time in Mies career, long before he made his comments on Louis Sullivan. Infact it had been a key tactic in his avant-garde approach since the 1920s. Changeability was already present as a principle in Mies design for the Weissenhof apartment block, part of the German Werkbund exhibition, *Die Wohnung*, that opened in Stuttgart in July 1927 (for which Mies served as artistic director). The sketches Mies made of the interior layout of his Weissenhof block are evidence of his fascination with the different spatial possibilities inherent in the same basic structural system. In a short text written at the time, Mies justified the principle of changeability by balancing the notion of 'rational construction' against that of 'programmatic freedom,' he stated:

"Economic reasons today necessitate rationalisation and typification in the construction of apartment buildings. The increasing differentiation of our housing needs, however, demands on the other side an ever greater freedom of usage..."

And he went on to identify what he called 'skeleton structure' as the key devise for achieving just such a balance:

(top) Mies van der Rohe, Weissenhof Apartment House, 1926-'27. Sketch by Mies exploring the different spatial possibilities inherent in the basic structural organisation of the block

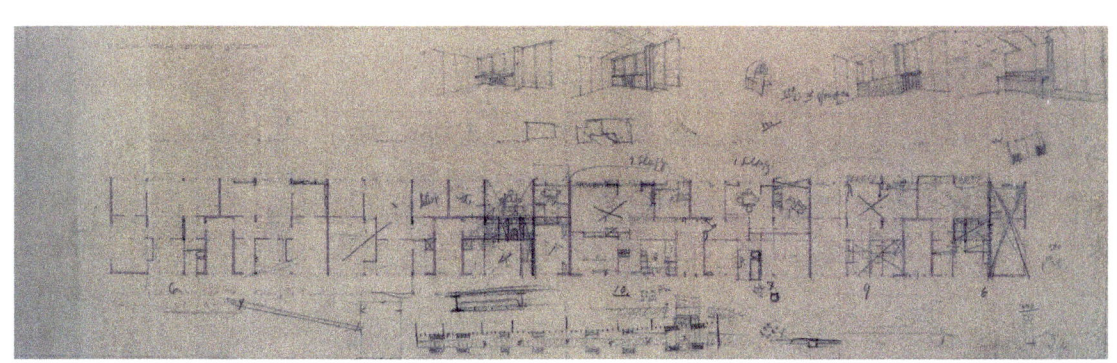

"For this purpose the skeleton structure is the most suitable system of construction. It makes a rational production possible and yet permits total freedom of disposition of the interior. If one limits oneself to the predetermination of kitchen and bath locations on account of the required installations and if one divides the other space by movable walls, I feel that all legitimate living purposes can be accommodated." (14)

The Weissenhof apartment block was the first opportunity Mies had to actually work with a rational building frame, in assessing the project today, it is important not to lose sight of the strategic value, signalled in the text, that he attached to the idea of skeletal structure. When the trajectory of Mies' career moved from Europe to North America, there were greater opportunities to test his permanent-change/skeleton-structure approach.

In America, Mies was invited to design high-rise apartment and office blocks, many of which were realised (although by no means as many as Mies' critics might lead us to suppose - according to the records Mies built only seven high-rise office developments and sixteen high rise residential developments, although some of both types involved groups of towers). All of Mies' American high rise structures demonstrate the permanent-change/skeleton-structure idea. In each case, the skeleton structure is a three-dimensional lattice of horizontal and vertical members that punctuate the entire built volume with the regular rhythm of their order. The London Mies was no different, it too had a skeleton structure, a frame of horizontal and vertical members, organised as a regular lattice with a measure of 26 x 36 feet between the vertical members and 13 feet between the horizontals.

So far as the floor-layouts of the London Mies were concerned, the design could easily have been adapted to suit the new kinds of open-plan space desirable to the 1980s Big Bang sensibility. But it wasn't the principle of permanent change that stood in the way of the Mies, it was the medium of expression that was the problem, i.e., the skeletal structure, which sounded the death knell for the design. One of the arguments put forward in favour of the Mies was the way the Architect had adjusted the dimensions of the skeleton structure so that the proportions of the new tower would harmonise with those of the Lutyens building flanking it to the North. As we have noted, Mies spaced the vertical members 13 feet apart, which corresponded to a floor-to-floor height of the same dimension. Unfortunately, the new Big Bang craze for minimum open-plan spaces of 10,000 square feet was coupled to a stipulated minimum floor-to-floor height of 15 feet. The new, increased floor-height, meant the Mies was out by 2 feet. It would have been possible to readjust the design to accommodate the new height, but that would have negated the argument about harmonising with the Lutyens and, perhaps more to the point, it would no longer have been possible to claim the design was authored by Mies! A second problem relating to the skeleton structure concerned the notion of open-plan. Although the floors of the Mies would be spacious and clear, they would not, strictly speaking, have been open-plan. The vertical members of the skeleton structure would have formed a grid of columns on each floor, interrupting the spatial field and making each floor more like a hyper-style hall than an uninterrupted flow of space. Mies had already begun to experiment with, what he called, clear-span structures long before he began work on the London design.

(top right) Mies' Westmount Square development (Montreal, 1965-'68), Note the four hyper-style spaces of Mies design, three are high-rise buildings, one a low-level structure.
(top left) the Achaemenid City of Persepolis (from 515 BC). The two dominant hyper-style spaces shown on the Persepolis plan are the Hall of 100 columns, on the left, and the Great Palace of Xerxes, on the right.

(bottom right) Comparison of the relative plan footprint of three clear-span structures and the Mansion House skeleton-structure: right, Chicago Convention Hall (project); smaller drawing to its top left, Crown Hall, IIT; middle left, New National Gallery, Berlin. Bottom left, Office Tower, Mansion House Square, London (unbuilt).

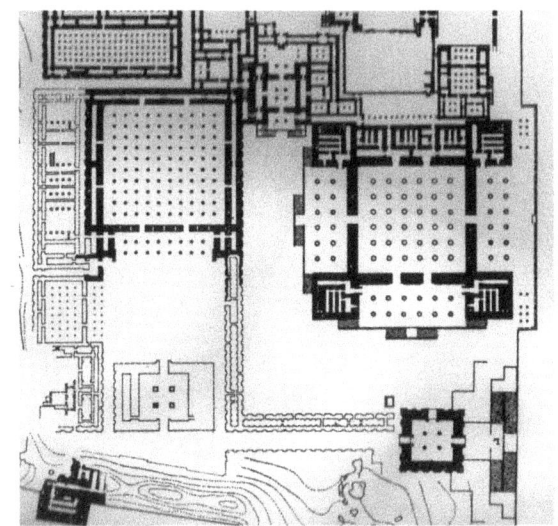
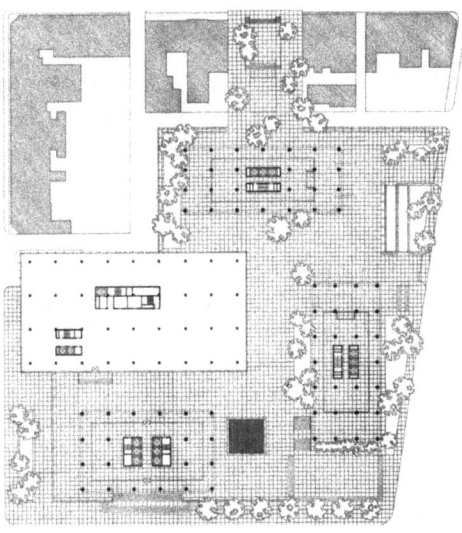
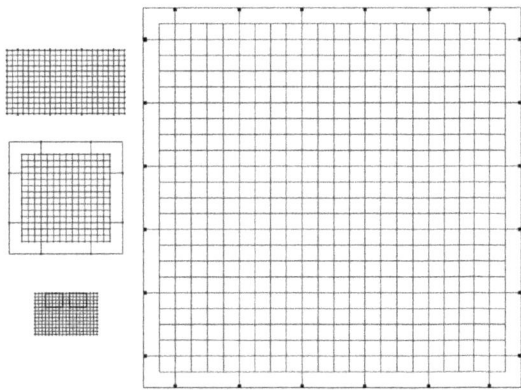

Perhaps his most extraordinary clear-span proposition was the Chicago Convention hall of 1953-4, a remarkable 720 square feet of interior space, sheltered under an enormous canopy and supported on perimeter columns but with no interior supports to interrupt the continuity, sadly it was never built. Mies' first realised clear-span structure of considerable size was the Crown Hall at IIT, work on the project began in 1950. The building was not completed until 1960, it contains a remarkable 262 x 524 feet of uninterrupted space. In the same year he first met with Palumbo, 1962, Mies began work on the New National Gallery for the city of Berlin, an amazing 214 square feet of uninterrupted space. The building opened to the public in 1968. Yet all Mies' clear-span structures were conceived as single-storey buildings, it never seems to have occurred to him to stack the clear-spans up on top of one other. The habits of the building industry in the 1950s and '60s were perhaps not yet ready to realise the idea of the stacked clear-span; and perhaps Mies' avant-garde spirit prevented him from proposing anything whose technical challenge might encourage, progressive, anti avant-garde attitudes.

The decision to reject the Mies eventually led Palumbo to develop the site on the basis of a low-level urban infill block design by the British Architect James Stirling, then at the height of his career. Stirling's Poultry design, in striped shades of pink and buff stonework, with an embedded circular atrium, open to the sky, was reminiscent of his Neue Staatsgalerie in Stuttgart. Stirling completed the Stuttgart building in 1984, at the time it was thought to exemplify the new, postmodern attitudes to form and space in architecture and urbanism that had been emerging in the international architecture culture of the 1970s.

Postmodern Architects had a different, if no less idiosyncratic, view of temporality than did their modernist predecessors. To the postmodernist, the architectural past was a repository of formal possibilities, rather than a testament to impermanence and change. For these Architects, past forms could be adapted and utilised in the present to make new combinations. Stirling's buildings, with their profusion of obsessively repeated forms and motifs are symptomatic of this postmodern outlook.

His obsession with the device of the embedded circular atrium, for example, references a number of historic buildings: the Maritime Theatre of Hadrian's Villa at Tivoli, the house of Mantegna in Mantua and Vignola's circular courtyard at the Farnese Villa at Caprarola. Just like at Stuttgart, Stirling's Poultry building had an interiorised, yet open, rotunda, with an urban route cutting through a substantial building mass. Reciprocally, just like No1 Poultry, the Stuttgart building displayed amusing architectural motifs, including fake Cyclopean walls in stripy stonework with garishly coloured handrails. In the mid 1980s, Palumbo could rely on the success of Stirling's Stuttgart project to persuade the City authorities and arbiters of taste, that his design for No1 Poultry was of sufficiently high quality, modern in outlook and acceptable as a replacement for the existing buildings on the site. But perhaps the most important thing to note about the design is the 15 foot floor-to-floor dimension. For all that the massing of the Stirling looks like it is composed of several different spatial volumes, on the inside we see it is nothing of the kind. It is a block, striated with evenly spaced floor plates, 15 feet apart. Each floor is a single volume of space with minimal interruptions.

(top right) Plan diagram showing the site layout of James Stirling's No1 Poultry.

(bottom left) No1 Poultry, plan diagram showing the open field of columns of a typical office floor.

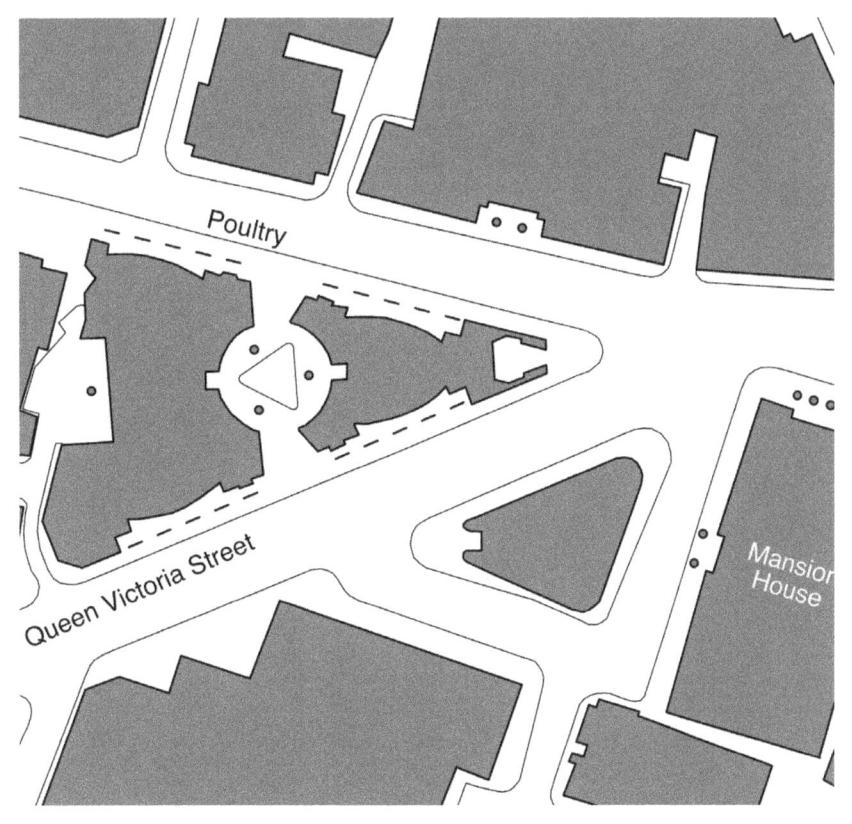

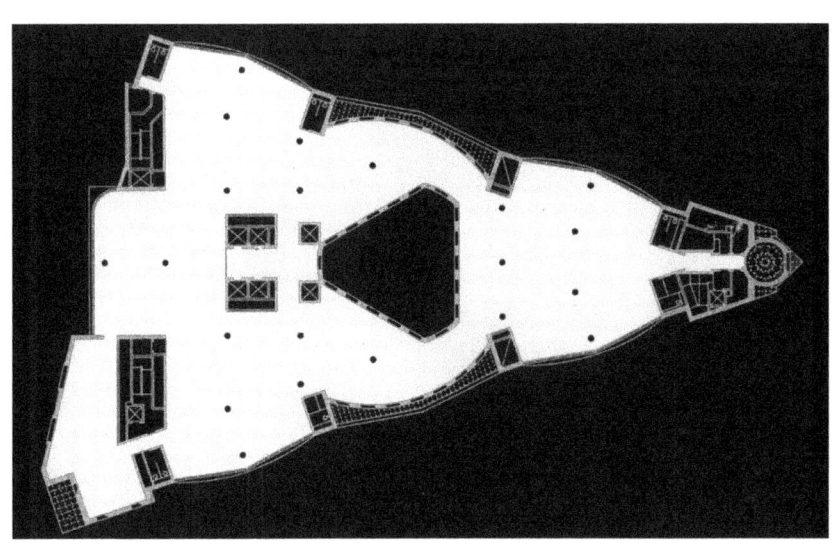

These are, first, in the middle of the block, where the figure of the atrium penetrates the floor-plate, second, the service cores and third, the distribution of columns, not on a regular grid like the Mies,' but still, an orderly interruption of the spatial flow. At first glance, Stirling's design does not look anything like the Mies, which might have stood in its place, and yet, on closer inspection we see a spirit of continuity between the two. First, notice the way Stirling's design reverses the figure/ground relations of Mies' design. Second, notice how each Architect has mused on the past and kept it at arms length. Mies' musings led him to position his architecture as conspicuously uninvolved in the past, where Stirling's led him to use the past almost like a huge toy-box, to rummage about inside, looking for forms he could use in the present. There is a third kind of temporal conundrum related to the Mansion House saga, it concerns another event of Mies' posthumous career.

THE RECONSTRUCTION OF THE BARCELONA PAVILION

At more or less the same time as Mies' design was being scrutinised by hostile conservationists and City planners in London, in Barcelona the City Hall was setting up the Fundacio Mies van der Rohe (Mies van der Rohe Foundation). The Foundation's first project was the reconstruction of the Pavilion, designed by Mies and his partner Lilly Reich, as a temporary structure to represent the Weimar Republic at the Barcelona International Exhibition of 1929. The project was entirely successful and the reconstructed Pavilion was opened to the public in 1986, since then, it has served as an attractive destination for architectural tourism and events and been the subject of revisionist interpretations of Mies. (15)

But, of equal importance, the reconstructed Pavilion became the Foundation's symbolic home-base for its long term mission, which is to foster debate on modern and contemporary architecture and urban planning in Europe. As well as the pavilion building itself, the most potent instrument at the disposal of the Foundation is the joint organisation, along with the European Commission, of the European Union Prize for Contemporary Architecture, otherwise known as the EU Mies Award.

One aim of the Award is to 'highlight the European City as a model for the sustainably smart city, contributing to a sustainable European economy;' another is to draw attention to 'the involvement of the European Union in supporting architecture as an important element that reflects both the diversity of European architectural expression and its role as a unifying element to define a common European culture'. (16) By linking it to economics and sustainability, the first objective makes the idea of something traditional - the European City - appear to be progressive and forward-facing. The second objective reflects the more general aspiration of the European Union to represent unification through diversity. Given their EU context, there is nothing surprising about either of these objectives, what is strange is find a Miesian building, symbolically acting as their home. Because it is evident, both from the things Mies said and from the buildings he designed, he would not have been sympathetic to the kind of architectural and urbanist rhetoric the EU Mies Award currently promotes in his name. Mies' designs never were intended to sympathise with the context in which they were placed (be it the European City or otherwise), nor to add scenographically to the formal diversity of some particular portion of the built environment.

(top right) Barcelona Pavilion, reconstruction, 1986, Birds Eye View from Google Earth.

Rather, Mies' designs aimed to create a new kind of space, one that turned away from the traditional forms of architecture that had shaped the cities of Europe and looked, instead, to the truthful expression of prevalent structural conditions, which, for him, meant the worldwide influence of science and technology, as he expressed it:

"I think there will be certain influences, climatic influences, but that will only colour what is done. I think a much greater influence is the influence of science and technology that is worldwide and that will take all these old cultures away and everybody will do the same. Just this light coloration." (17)

(right) Mies van der Rohe Foundation, Barcelona Pavilion, reconstruction, 1981-1986, Barcelona. A selection of photographs taken by DWA on a visit to the pavilion in 2018, including close-up shots of some of the stone surfaces that sub-divide the spaces

NOTES

(01) Fritz Neumey, *The Artless Word: Mies van der Rohe on the Building Art*, trans. Mark Jarzombek (Cambridge, MA, and London: MIT Press, 1991), 339.
(02) Louis Sullivan, "The Tall Office Building Artistically Considered," *Lippincott's Magazine*, March 1896, https://ocw.mit.edu/courses/architecture/4-205-analysis-of-contemporary-architecture-fall-2009/readings/MIT4_205F09_Sullivan.pdf. (All quotations from Sullivan are from this article; there are no page numbers.)
(03) Neumeyer, *The Artless Word*, 252.
(04) Robin Evans, "Mies van der Rohe's Paradoxical Symmetries," in *Translations from Drawing to Building and Other Essays* (London: Architectural Association, 1997), 233–276, 246.
(05) Neumeyer, *The Artless Word*, 245.
(06) Detlef Mertins and Michael W. Jennings, eds., *G: An Avant-Garde Journal of Art, Architecture, Design and Film, 1923–1926* (London: Tate Publishing in association with the Getty Research Institute, 2010), 173.
(07) Phyllis Lambert, "Mies Immersion," in *Mies in America*, ed. Phyllis Lambert (Montreal and New York: Canadian Centre for Architecture, Whitney Museum of American Art, and Harry N. Abrams, 2001), 192–589, 512 (note 89).
(08) Detlef Mertins, *Mies* (London and New York: Phaidon Press, 2014), 423.
(09) Quoted in *Architects' Journal*, "City Rejects Mies," *AJ*, 29 September 1982, 29.
(10) Quoted in *Architects' Journal*, "Highlights from the Inspector's Report," *AJ*, 29 May 1985, 25.
(11) Ibid., 24.
(12) Ibid.
(13) David Kynaston, *The City of London, Volume IV: A Club No More, 1945–2000* (London: Pimlico, 2001), 700–701.
(14) Neumeyer, *The Artless Word*, 259.
(15) For example, see K. Michael Hays, "Critical Architecture: Between Culture and Form," *Perspecta* 21 (1984); or Evans, "Mies van der Rohe's Paradoxical Symmetries."
(16) EUmiesaward, "About the Prize," https://www.miesarch.com, accessed 23 June 2019.
(17) Moisés Puente, ed., *Conversations with Mies van der Rohe* (New York: Princeton Architectural Press, 2006), 47.

CHALLENGING THE TABULA RASA: IN SEARCH OF THE *UNHEIMLICH*

JANE TANKARD

CHALLENGING THE TABULA RASA: IN SEARCH OF THE *UNHEIMLICH* BY JANE TANKARD

'We may understand the uncanny as simultaneously a symptom of the limits of rationality and a site where rationality seeks to extend its control.'

In *Modern Architecture: A Critical History*, Kenneth Frampton cites Hannes Meyer who, in reference to his and Hans Wittwer's entry for the 1927 League of Nations competition, stated:

"our building symbolises nothing." [01]

Frampton, while critical of the Architects' 'scientific' solution (from which one might infer rational, modern, broken with the past), describing their building as amongst other things, 'picturesque', explains their claim could be understood as 'tenable' due to standard prefabricated modularisation and an indifference to site beyond aesthetic evaluation. The notion that architecture should or could be without symbolism or reference to the past is one the architectural profession knows only too well: a concept that informed much of the European local, and eventually global, architecture of the 20th century. The notion of a reductivist, rationalist and purely objective response to programmatic requirements, form follows function and a spatial and theoretical tabula rasa became the raison d'être of the modernist style.

This notion precipitated both the demonisation of modernist architecture as materially and spatially mean and mechanistic and the ultimate recuperation of radical 20th century ideas of socialism and equity into an ameliorated 21st century post-liberal commodity politics. Yet, a number of significant 20th century Architects, for example Carlo Scarpa, have created work that embeds many of the fundamental ingredients of modernism: form follows function, truth to materials, the free plan, whilst creating an architecture of palimpsest, designing buildings saturated with history, memory and metaphor. While Mies van der Rohe is often framed as the embodiment of modernist reductionism with his 'less is more' mantra read as a commitment to the tabula rasa, his work, as Dr Watson's essay *Past/Future Temporality* [02] addresses, makes no sense if interpreted through the clichéd notion of form follows function. Projects such as the Barcelona Pavilion and the Neue Nationalgalerie reveal a layering of material, spatial and cultural registers: veined onyx, travertine and marble carry geological and historical memory; shifting planes and carefully staged vistas produce sequential spatial experiences that unfold over time. As Watson outlines, the pavilions act as spaces of 'neutralised programme' becoming receptive frameworks for new layers of use, occupation and meaning. [03]

In this sense, Mies's apparent minimalism conceals a more complex engagement with time and memory, where architecture operates as a device for the accumulation and revelation of successive narratives.

(top right) AA School of Architecture Cross Crit, Inaaya Amer, DS3.1, photograph by Jake Parkin

This rereading of notions of reductivist modernism asks questions of the opportunities inherent in considering what has been obscured and overlooked in design studio discourse; ideas revealed and framed by exploring the notion of the *Unheimlich*. Exploring the uncanny in theoretical terms is also dependent on the Situationist Internationale's theory of Recuperation. (04)

The term describes the process by which radical, subversive or oppositional ideas and practices are absorbed, repackaged and neutralised by the dominant culture or capitalist system, stripping them of their revolutionary potential. This can be read as an attempt to dilute the radical palimpsest in favour of a politically stable and recuperated tabula rasa - a space where all that went before is dissolved and erased from the collective narrative. This process of what might be described as cultural domestication (05) operates through the marginalisation and silencing of those groups and voices who challenge the status quo, often depicting them in popular media as irrational, out of control or even dangerous. Sigmund Freud's 1919 essay *Das Unheimlich* defines the *Unheimlich* not simply as the unfamiliar, or 'unhomely,' but as the strange within the familiar:

"that class of the frightening which leads back to what is known of old and long familiar." (06)

"What a view, it's not far from the water. I wonder what it used to be before, a warehouse on the water, when transport was key. A proper French door, a Juliette balcony, surely lots of rats. The swans are heading back now. Can you go upstream on a canal? They create their own waves. They're scrounging for food and sleeping in the reeds. Swans are counted for the Queen. Some die, some are born, you can't see the atrophy or growth when you're up close; it takes distance." (07)

This notion of the return of the repressed often involves the exposure of something that should have remained hidden, the reanimation of what should be inert, or the doubling of the self.

Classical examples include the automaton, the doppelgänger and disquieting repetitions of events. For Freud, these phenomena are symptoms of unresolved psychic conflict, generating mental anxiety that psychoanalysis seeks to interpret and resolve. Freud situates the uncanny primarily in relation to repressed elements of the psyche, often those linked to taboo, forbidden desires or socially unacceptable impulses and the notion arises when these repressed or disavowed elements surface in disguised or doubled forms. Many of Freud's examples of uncanny phenomena can be read as manifestations of deviance, challenging normative boundaries of self-hood, identity and social order. The uncanny in Freud's terms, it could be argued, can be understood as a negative affective state, destabilising, uncomfortable, demanding a return to psychological equilibrium. Freud embodies a modernist faith in reason and cure: by uncovering and interpreting the repressed, the uncanny can be tamed through objectivity, restored to the symbolic order and equilibrium. If we turn a critical lens on the uncanny, in particular towards the patriarchal hegemony of 20th-century Western European thinking, we see Freud's framework is embedded in the modernist project of rationality, scientific inquiry and the attempt to render the unconscious knowable and treatable.

(top) Convoys Wharf Settlement, Declan Slonim, DS3.1

The uncanny, in Freud's view, produces anxiety because it undermines the reassuring binaries that modernist rationality relies on: subject/object, living/dead, animate/inanimate, self/other. (08) In this sense, we may understand the uncanny as simultaneously a symptom of the limits of rationality and a site where rationality seeks to extend its control.

Twentieth and twenty first century art and architectural theory often reframes this disturbance not as a pathology to be cured, but as a fertile critical and creative resource. In this alternate reading, the uncanny is valued precisely for its ability to unsettle, to estrange the everyday and to provoke new ways of perceiving both material culture and spatial environments. Hélène Cixous observes:

"the uncanny is not simply a feeling but a mode of knowledge." (09)

This offers insights into what is repressed, overlooked, or unacknowledged in the familiar fabric of the everyday. In these terms, identifying the uncanny is a means to reveal something hidden that disrupts the familiar, exposing the 'shadow' of social constructs, of what society tries to repress or exclude. The notion is often linked to social deviance, the forbidden, the abject and the marginal. In these terms, the uncanny serves as a destabilising mechanism, subverting accepted norms by surfacing what capitalism and patriarchy prefer to remain hidden, whether suppressed desires, unacceptable social behaviours or political resistance. (10) Anthony Vidler's *The Architectural Uncanny* (11) makes this theoretical shift between the uncanny as psychological 'failure' and creative knowledge-forming within the context of the built environment.

Vidler appropriates Freud's concept but relocates it from the clinical setting of the psychoanalytic couch to the cultural space of architecture. For Vidler, the uncanny in architecture is not a matter of pathology but of modernity's disorienting conditions: alienation, estrangement and the fragmentation of memory. He identifies sites and architectural forms that generate this estrangement: abandoned buildings, empty urban sites, labyrinthine spatial arrangements and the inversion of interior and exterior conditions. Importantly, Vidler treats these conditions as revelatory, exposing the fractures of modern experience and the suppressed histories and cultural conditions embedded in architectural form. (12) In this sense, the uncanny becomes a critical lens through which to read the material and cultural residues of the city. Hal Foster extends this reorientation into contemporary art in *The Return of the Real*. (13) Drawing on Lacanian psychoanalysis, Foster frames the uncanny not simply as the return of the repressed but as an encounter with the Real, that which resists symbolic assimilation. In an interview with Wired magazine Brian Eno explores the idea that:

"art is a kind of rehearsal space in which one can practice acts of counter-culture with impunity, that this is the role of art, a safe place where you can have quite extreme and rather dangerous feelings… like a plane simulator… art is a little world where you can crash and then get out and laugh." (14)

In art, this engagement with danger and counter-culture often appears as the staging of traumatic memory, repetition or estrangement, not to be 'worked through' towards closure, but to hold the viewer in a suspended state of confrontation.

(top) Theatre of the Moon, Olha Petrachkova, DS3.1

In Situationist terms, recuperation is the process by which radical gestures are appropriated and rendered harmless by the dominant order. (15) In Foster's account of the uncanny Real, a related dynamic occurs when the repressed or disruptive returns not as raw political truth but as a mediated, aestheticised form. Foster's return of the Real, is not simply an unfiltered eruption of the authentic, it often arrives already framed, curated and thus partially neutralised, echoing the Situationist concern that subversive energies can be absorbed into the cultural spectacle. (16) Both frameworks expose how systems metabolise rupture: in recuperation, the insurgent act is domesticated into 'style'; in the uncanny Real, the traumatic or politically charged content re-emerges in forms that both disturb and reassure, destabilising while still being containable within art or culture. Together they illuminate the paradox that critical interventions, whether in politics or aesthetics, are shadowed by the possibility of their own assimilation. Identifying the liminal or interstitial in the design studio requires the careful study of process precedents. The work of British artists Cornelia Parker and Rachel Whiteread are among a number of artists whose work mines the creative seam of a generative uncanny and have been central to early studio thinking. Both artists manipulate the familiar matter of everyday life, be it architecture, everyday objects or making processes, to produce disquieting estrangement. Parker's Cold Dark Matter (17) reconstructs the remains of a garden shed detonated by the British Army, suspending its fragments in a gallery space and illuminating them from a central lightbulb. The garden shed, a domestic structure and archetype of *heimlich* security, is rendered alien through its disarticulation, yet paradoxically preserved in a moment of perpetual suspension.

Parker's work manifests Vidler's 'architectural fragment', offering viewers a frozen instant between destruction and order. The piece stages an uncanny temporality: we are both before and after the moment of rupture, caught in a space of impossible stasis. Rachel Whiteread's House (18) project operates through a different but related inversion. By casting the interior void of a condemned Victorian terrace in concrete, Whiteread solidifies absence, rendering the negative space of domestic life as a monumental presence. Here, the familiar geometry of staircases, windows, and doorways is visible only in reverse, as protrusions rather than recesses.

Similarly in her 2016 project Cabin, (19) Whiteread locates the humble garden shed as a permanent monument to domesticity on New York's Governor's Island and in so doing challenges our perception of the island's history as militarised zone of governmental control and power.

The uncanny resides in this inversion of solid and void, interior and exterior, domesticity and powerlessness and in the work's confrontation with loss, both of the individual home and of a disappearing socio-historical terrain. As in Foster's notion of 'traumatic realism', (20) Whiteread preserves the disturbance rather than resolving it; the uncanny is not neutralised but maintained as part of the work's meaning. The strategies of Parker and Whiteread resonate with other artists and theorists who embrace the productive potential of the uncanny. Gordon Matta-Clark, another key figure in the studio's analytical and creative explorations, uses architectural 'cuts' to slice through abandoned buildings, revealing unfamiliar cross-sections of domestic space, destabilising architectural conventions while inviting alternative readings of form and function.

(left) New York Cabin, Rachel Whiteread, photograph by Jane Tankard

(right) Cold Dark Matter, Cornelia Parker, photograph by Jane Tankard

His process employs a broad spectrum of media to document and reposition his work, including film, video, architectural drawing, performance art and photography. [21] Similarly, artists associated with critical spatial practice, [22] use the uncanny to disrupt conventional relationships between bodies and space, highlighting the political and historical conditions embedded in the built environment. In literature, this aligns with Viktor Shklovsky's concept of ostranenie (defamiliarisation), [23] in which art's task is to make the familiar strange so that perception is renewed, a concept that resurfaces in David Byrne's True Stories, [24] a film examined regularly in the studio, that delves into the uncanny every day of small-town American life. These opportunities for theoretical and methodological discourse have also been employed in architectural phenomenology. Juhani Pallasmaa, for instance, in his seminal book *The Eyes of the Skin* [25] acknowledges that architecture can elicit unsettling affective states, but sees these as essential for engaging the imagination and deepening existential experience. Rather than avoiding the uncanny, his approach argues for its capacity to connect occupants with time, memory and the layered meanings or palimpsest of place.

The historical and cultural shift from Freud's negative construct to a recognised mode of critical engagement is a location of a creative 'other.' Where psychoanalysis aims to translate the uncanny into meaning, to render it safe within the symbolic and rationalised order, artists and Architects can deliberately identify, sustain and respond to its strange disquiet. This suspension allows for a heightened awareness of the historical, emotional and political forces that shape our physical environment and contexts.

The work of DS3.1, particularly in semester 1, focuses on identifying and acting upon the spaces and locations of the uncanny, be they literal or metaphorical. Forensic forms of analysis and re-representation, particularly through filmic mechanisms and the notion of social, historical and cultural re-enactment, manifest as a series of 'choreographic' drawings that, similar to Eyal Weizman's work with Forensic Architecture, [26] uses conventional orthographic systems and modes of representation to reveal what has been overlooked, marginalised, or suppressed, ranging from repressed and uncomfortable narratives to overtly political manipulation and control.

In the context of the studio, the *Unheimlich* is understood as a critical method, an architectural design mechanism situating contextual research within a broader critical and historical process. Our investigations focus on events disseminated in academic texts and artworks (for example Jeremy Deller's *The Battle of Orgreave* [27] and Bill Viola's *The Raft*) [28] and filmic responses to those events for example, Ladj Ly's *Les Misérables* [29] and Mathieu Kassovitz's *La Haine* [30] films which explore the collective in urban contexts.

Ly reframes his lived memories as a child growing up in the Banlieue in Paris to structure a narrative around which a political and sociological condition is described. This weaving of a child-centred narrative, of the familiar, innocent, impacted by hegemonic forces, through layers of visual and scripted content enables difficult and complex contexts to be unpacked, digested and made canny.

(top) The Migrant, (re)enactment, Munira Osman, DS3.1

(bottom) The Raft, (re)enactment, Munira Osman, DS3.1

The familiar, the homely, the recognised, is resituated to expose the uncanny within the spectre of oppression and marginalisation. By 'choreographing' the threads of *Heimlich* and *Unheimlich*, Dadaist exquisite corpse drawings (31) or models are formulated, which in turn through processes of coding and indexing become mechanisms to define spatial and material form-making. In this way, architectural discourse, informed by a number of creative media, can be understood not as a static object, but as an active, critical participant in rewriting shared urban stories.

This methodology aligns closely with the reimagined notion of the uncanny in contemporary art and architectural theory. By re-enactment, through filmic analysis and speculative representation, our studio practice deliberately curates and estranges the familiar, revealing hidden structures, suppressed narratives and overlooked spaces in the city. Opposing the notion of hegemonic tabula rasa in favour of the palimpsest, layering, addition and memory are used as tools for establishing temporalities whilst dislocating normative spatial hierarchies and sequence as a means of describing the experience of estrangement. In this sense, our speculative projects treat the uncanny not as Freud's symptom in need of analysis, but as Vidler's and Foster's generative condition, a critical mode through which architecture can confront the politics of memory, the complexity of collective identity and the possibilities of a more inclusive urban future.

(right) Poll Tax Riots (re)enactment, Jose Navarro-Garcia, DS3.1

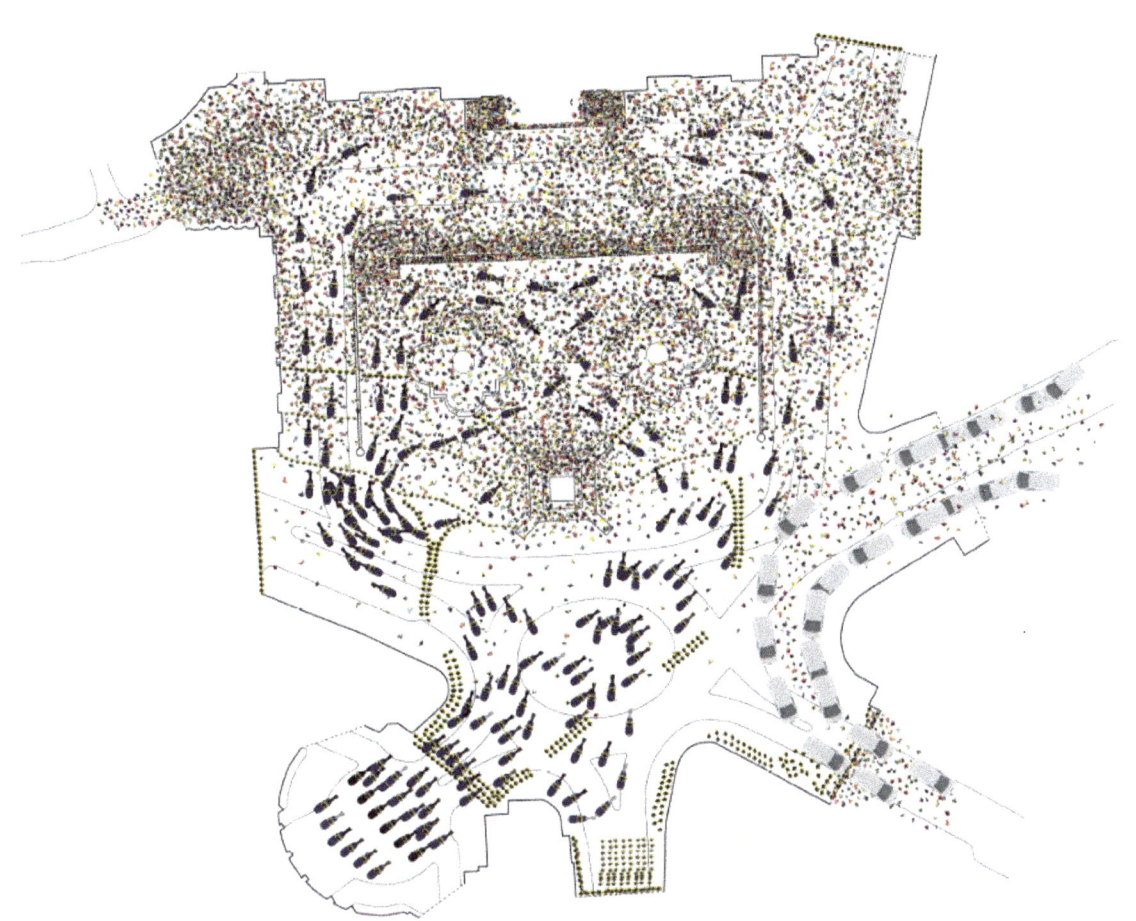

NOTES

(01) Kenneth Frampton, *Modern Architecture: A Critical History*, 2nd ed. (London: Thames and Hudson, 1990).
(02) Victoria Watson, "Past/Future Temporality," in *Exploring the Unheimlich*, ed. Jane Tankard and Jake Parkin (London: University of Westminster School of Architecture + Cities, forthcoming 2025).
(03) Ibid.
(04) Situationist International, "Recuperation," *Internationale Situationniste*, no. 2 (1961).
(05) Raymond Williams, *Culture and Politics: Class, Writing, Socialism* (London: Verso, 1983).
(06) Sigmund Freud, "The Uncanny" (1919), in *The Standard Edition of the Complete Psychological Works of Sigmund Freud, Volume XVII (1917–1919): An Infantile Neurosis and Other Works*, ed. and trans. James Strachey (London: Hogarth Press).
(07) Maria Faraone, *Studio Juggernaut*.
(08) Nicholas Royle, *The Uncanny* (Manchester: Manchester University Press, 2003).
(09) Hélène Cixous, "Fiction and Its Phantoms: A Reading of Freud's Das Unheimliche," *New Literary History* 7, no. 3 (1976).
(10) Royle, *The Uncanny*.
(11) Anthony Vidler, *The Architectural Uncanny: Essays in the Modern Unhomely* (Cambridge, MA: MIT Press, 1992).
(12) Ibid.
(13) Hal Foster, *The Return of the Real: The Avant-Garde at the End of the Century* (Cambridge, MA: MIT Press, 1996).
(14) Brian Eno, "Gossip Is Philosophy," *Wired*, May 1995, https://www.wired.com/1995/05/eno-2.
(15) Situationist International, "Recuperation."
(16) Foster, *The Return of the Real*.
(17) Cornelia Parker, *Cold Dark Matter: An Exploded View* (Exhibition, London: Tate Britain, 1991).
(18) Rachel Whiteread, *House* (Exhibition, London: Artangel, 1993).
(19) Rachel Whiteread, *Cabin* (Sculpture, Governor's Island, New York, 2016).
(20) Foster, *The Return of the Real*.
(21) Gordon Matta-Clark, *Splitting* (Installation/Film, New Jersey, 1974).
(22) Jane Rendell, *Art and Architecture: A Place Between* (London: I.B. Tauris, 2006).
(23) Viktor Shklovsky, "Art as Technique" (1917), in *Russian Formalist Criticism: Four Essays*, ed. and trans. Lee T. Lemon and Marion J. Reis (Lincoln: University of Nebraska Press, 1965).
(24) David Byrne, *True Stories* (USA: Warner Bros., 1986).
(25) Juhani Pallasmaa, *The Eyes of the Skin: Architecture and the Senses* (Chichester: Wiley, 2005).
(26) Eyal Weizman, *Forensic Architecture: Violence at the Threshold of Detectability* (New York: Zone Books, 2017).
(27) Jeremy Deller, *The Battle of Orgreave* (Reenactment, film, installation, 2001).
(28) Bill Viola, *The Raft* (Film, 2004).
(29) Ladj Ly, *Les Misérables* (France: Le Pacte, 2019).
(30) Mathieu Kassovitz, *La Haine* (France: Canal+, 1995).
(31) Michael Sorkin, *Exquisite Corpse: Writing on Buildings* (London: Verso, 1991).

BRIAN ENO: BETWEEN PORTRAIT AND LANDSCAPE

GHOSTS, BELLS, AND THE SONIC CARTOGRAPHY OF SUFFOLK

STEVE BOWKETT

BRIAN ENO: BETWEEN PORTRAIT AND LANDSCAPE
GHOSTS, BELLS, AND THE SONIC CARTOGRAPHY OF SUFFOLK

'...and at last we are part of the machinery'

During my years studying at the Polytechnic of Central London (now Westminster University) between 1979 and 1982, the influence of Brian Eno's sonic landscapes and conceptual frameworks quietly permeated my intellectual and creative development. I had followed Eno's work since his early involvement with Roxy Music in the early 1970s, yet it was during this formative period that his ambient sensibility, marked by a profound shift in how sound, space, and time might be perceived, began to subtly shape my own evolving world-view. Though not always overtly present within my design projects as a student, there emerged a distinct feeling of the uncanny: a sense that I was entering a different mode of awareness, one that challenged conventional aesthetic and perceptual boundaries.

Visits in recent years to close friends, Paul Monaghan and Alicia Pivaro, in the Suffolk countryside near Woodbridge, Eno's birthplace, offered a parallel kind of discovery and a reassessment of my earlier impressions, ones formed during my own university years when Eno's work was quietly shaping my sensibilities. These visits provided a portal not only into the physical landscape that had shaped Eno's early life but also into the deeper resonances between memory, place and creative imagination that underpin much of his work.

(right) Orford Ness Photo Series, photograph by Steve Bowkett

Brian Eno's ambient oeuvre occupies a distinctive position within contemporary sonic culture. Emerging from a background in experimental, electronic and art rock music, his compositions resist conventional musical form, cultivating instead what he describes as 'imaginary landscapes,' immersive, atmospheric environments that operate more like auditory paintings than traditional song structures. These works often function spatially rather than temporally, eschewing melody and rhythm in favour of tone, resonance, and timbre. Within this body of work, a quieter yet enduring influence emerges: the haunting presence of the Suffolk landscape where Eno was born and raised. This terrain, marked by its gentle topography, historic ruination, strategic military location and subtle eeriness, forms the atmospheric backdrop to many of his most enduring pieces.

"I'd gone from making very loud, intricate, witty sorts of things, with anagrams and funny references to other pop records and little pop versions of Duchampian tricks and so on, into this music that had people in general saying, 'Oh well, he's gone soft'. I was really moving into a kind of landscape sensibility of music, the idea being that one is listening to a body of sound presented as being in a particular type of space, a location of some sort. One of the characteristics of recorded music is that the composer is in a position to design not only new instruments, but new locations for them [...] An aspect of this landscape concern is to do with the removal of personality from the picture. You know how different a landscape painting is when there is a figure in it. Even if the figure is small, it automatically becomes the focus - all questions of scale and depth are related to it. When I stopped writing songs, I took the figure out of the landscape [...]

Lately I've felt it beginning to return, but not in a familiar form. This is all a funny reversal because in the early 20th century painters were saying that they wanted their work to be like music, to have the freedom to be as abstract as music. Now what's interesting to me is that music can actually be like painting - figurative, landscape." (01)

The Suffolk coast, with its estuarial mists, wind-blown marshes, and spectral ruins, offers an ideal site for an investigation of the uncanny in Eno's work. In *Ocean of Sound: Aether Talk, Ambient Sound and Imaginary Worlds*, David Toop asks:

"What is ambient music? Calm, therapeutic sound for chilling out or music which taps into the disturbing, chaotic undertow of the environment?" (02)

Sigmund Freud's concept of the *Unheimlich*, translated as the uncanny, describes a psychological state in which the familiar becomes subtly alienated, often eliciting feelings of unease or estrangement. (03) Eno's ambient compositions, particularly those on *Ambient 4: On Land (1982)*, evoke such sensations. Tracks like '*Dunwich Beach, Autumn, 1960,*' '*Lantern Marsh*', and '*Unfamiliar Wind (Leeks Hill)*', reference specific Suffolk locations, yet they are rendered in a mode that abstracts them from geographic realism. As he reflected in a BBC interview, his teenage walks toward Kyson Point, overlooking the River Deben estuary, prompted him to imagine music that *"would stay still, so that you were the person that did the moving in relation to them."* Instead of documenting place, these compositions transform location into effect.

They echo with winds that never blow, footsteps that never arrive, and shadows that never clarify.

(bottom left) Leeks Hill, photograph by Steve Bowkett

(top right) Work, Russel Mills, property and photo of Steve Bowkett

The sense of estranged familiarity these early ambient pieces produce aligns closely with what cultural theorist Mark Fisher terms 'hauntology', a temporal disjunction in which cultural expressions are haunted by lost futures or spectral pasts. (04) The East Anglian coast, long subject to erosion, economic decline, and depopulation, becomes an ideal hauntological setting. Dunwich, once a thriving medieval port, now lies mostly submerged beneath the North Sea, a potent symbol of historical loss and environmental change. Eno's rendering of 'Dunwich Beach' is not one of nostalgia or pastoral romanticism but of ambiguity and spectral presence. As Fisher might argue, Eno's sonic treatment makes the past persist without resolution, invoking memory without delivering closure.

In various interviews, Eno has openly acknowledged the influence of Suffolk on his imagination. Recalling the region's churches 'sitting in the middle of fields completely deserted by any community', he describes a landscape imbued with melancholy, suggesting that:

"everything happened a long time ago." (05)

This formulation frames the Suffolk landscape not simply as formative to his childhood but as a spatial and temporal palimpsest, a geography where historical residue accumulates and contemporary presence recedes. Critics and writers have situated Eno's work alongside other Suffolk-based cultural responses. John Coulthart, for instance, draws parallels between Eno's sonic landscapes and the prose of W.G. Sebald in *The Rings of Saturn*, a book whose walking tour of East Anglia unfolds through digressions, memories, and spectral reflections. (06)

Sebald's Suffolk is a place of drift and dissolution, marked by absent populations and haunted buildings. Grant Gee's beautifully observed documentary *Patience* (after Sebald) further reinforces Sebald's notions of 'Echo Space', where 'the words stop, and the pictures take over.' Like Sebald, Eno uses the region not simply as a location but as a generator of mood and psychological state. His track titles serve as points of entry, but the works themselves dissolve specific referents, instead producing something akin to what landscape theorist Kenneth Olwig calls 'landscape as scenography', a stage for the performance of memory, trauma, and identity. (07) Landscape theory offers further tools for understanding the affective force of Eno's ambient compositions. James Corner, in discussing landscape as an active process rather than a static entity, proposes that landscape is something one does, not merely sees. (08) In this light, Eno's sonic works can be understood as acts of landscape-making, crafting new perceptual terrains from the emotional and sensory residue of lived experience. Similarly, Nigel Thrift's non-representational theory foregrounds atmosphere, affect, and pre-cognitive sensation as central to understanding space. (09) Eno's ambient music does not represent Suffolk; it generates the feeling of being suspended within it, at once present and ghostlike.

'THE BELLDOG': SONIC MEMORY AND THE RETURN OF THE FIGURE

One striking instance of Eno's landscape sensibility merging with more figurative, human elements occurs in his collaboration with Dieter Moebius and Hans-Joachim Roedelius of Cluster, particularly on the track, 'The Belldog' from *After the Heat (1978)*.

(bottom left) Orford Ness Photo Series, photograph by Steve Bowkett

(top right) Orford Ness Photo Series, photograph by Steve Bowkett

Eno recalls that the song was inspired by a dream in which he encountered:

"a huge dog with bells around its neck, wandering through an empty city." (10)

The dream's imagery is at once surreal, playful, and unsettling and connects directly to Freud's notion of the uncanny and the anticipatory undercurrents that run through much of Eno's work.

In this track, unlike his purely ambient compositions, Eno's voice returns, carrying a fragmentary narrative that seems to hover between song and spoken word: "In the dark sheds we were at the machinery." The lyrics are sparse, yet their delivery, floating over a bed of sustained synthesizer tones and gentle rhythmic pulses, reinforces the sense of a presence that is neither wholly here nor entirely absent. The sensation is as if one were on the edge of something, a something about to happen. The belldog itself is less a character than a sonic apparition, an aural metaphor for something sought yet always receding. The closing line on the track suggests a merging of these worlds: '…and at last we are part of the machinery' a reference to 'Organic Machinery' the enigmatic message supplied by one of the Oblique Strategy oracle cards, created by Eno and artist Peter Schmidt in 1975 as a means of sidestepping rational thinking whilst engaged in the creative process. Mark Prendergast interprets this shift as part of Eno's ongoing experimentation with the balance between abstraction and figuration. The belldog becomes a motif for the reintroduction of 'the figure in the landscape' that Eno had earlier removed. (11)

Whilst not an isolated example, the song stands at a threshold, bridging his early song-based output and his later, more immersive soundscapes. Its dreamlike quality is not a departure from his ambient ethos but an expansion, suggesting that the boundaries between portrait and landscape, between human presence and environmental atmosphere, are permeable and subject to continual redefinition.

PORTRAIT, LANDSCAPE, AND URBAN VERTICALITY: MISTAKEN MEMORIES OF MEDIAEVAL MANHATTAN

The relationship between portrait and landscape is not only conceptual but at times also literal. *Mistaken Memories of Mediaeval Manhattan*, a video created whilst living in a New York apartment (1980–81), was filmed from his window with the camera lying on its side, creating a portrait orientation rather than the usual landscape format. The consequence was that, in replaying the footage, the TV monitor, normally set up for landscape viewing, had to be turned on its side, a literal twist on the notion of landscape back to portrait. This orientation aligns conceptually with the verticality of Manhattan itself.

Ambient 4: On Land (1982) supplied the soundtrack for the video, which was displayed in galleries, creating a layered interplay between sound, cinematic form, and the spatial sensibilities of portrait versus landscape. (12)

Eno's video turns the urban panorama into a vertical meditation, echoing the same attentive, atmospheric sensibility found in his aural Suffolk landscapes.

(top) Orford Ness Photo Series, photograph by Steve Bowkett

(bottom) Suffolk Topography Map, OS Opendata Maps, layered with photograph by Steve Bowkett

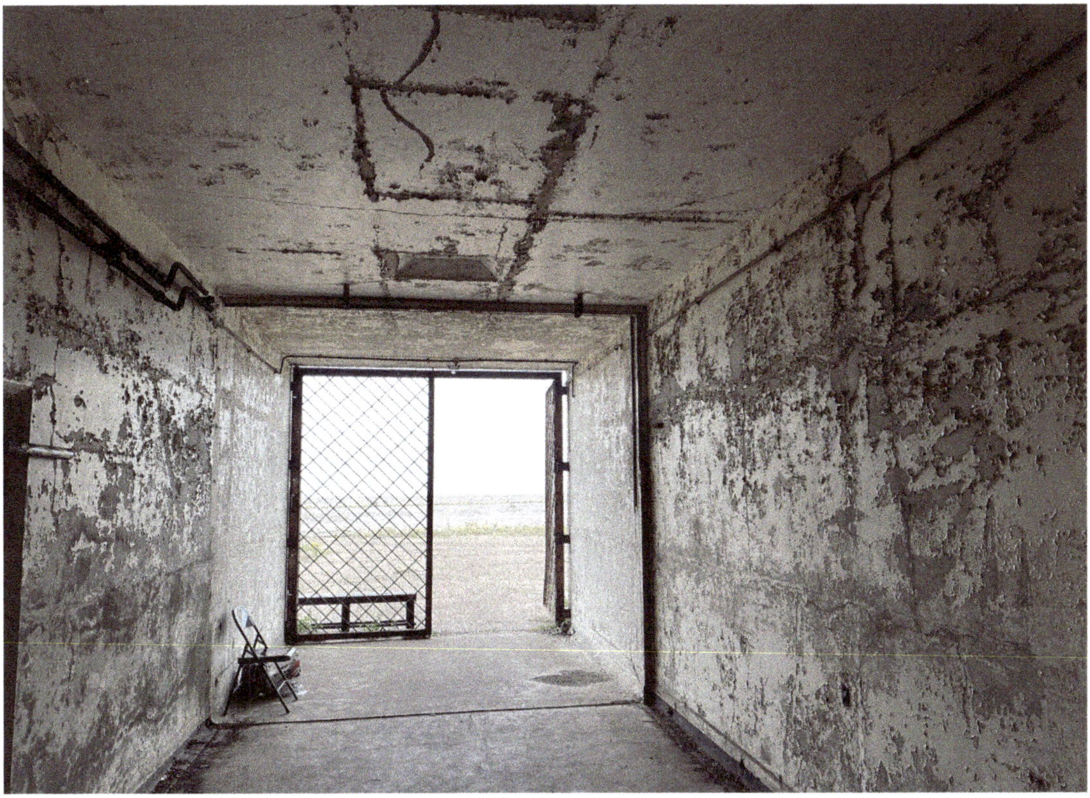

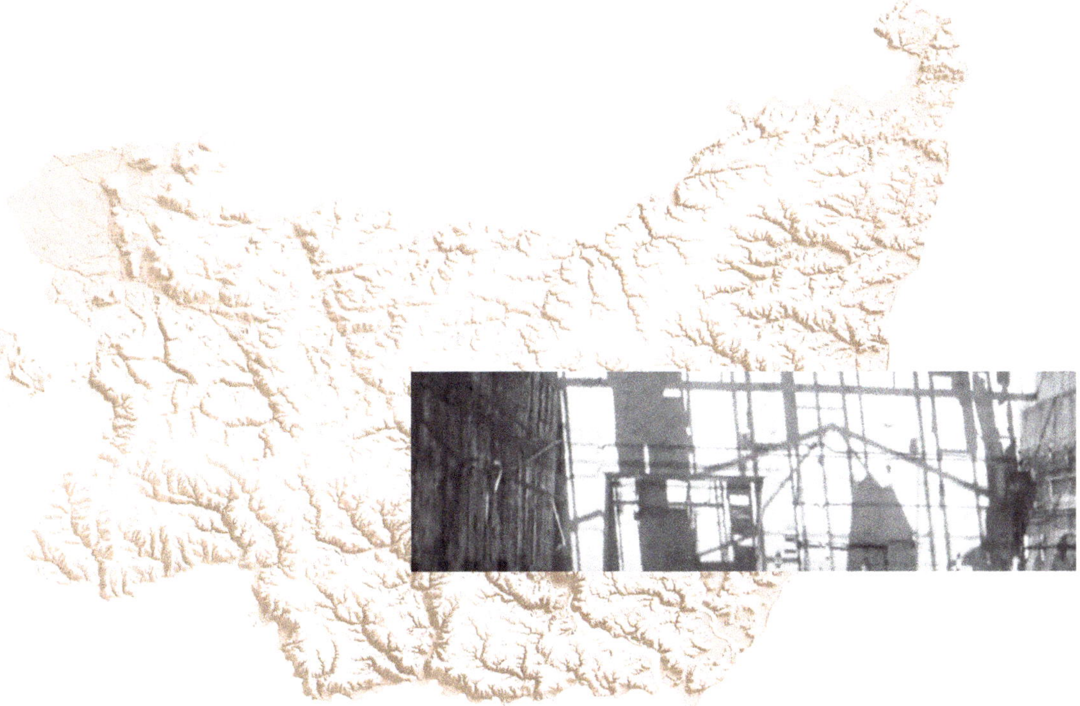

Sound and image coalesce to generate a liminal perceptual space, one that resonates with both memory and imagination, uniting distant rural pasts and immediate urban experiences. The viewer is invited to inhabit Manhattan differently, not as a flattened, conventional skyline, but as a vertical labyrinth, a scaffold of human ambition and aspiration punctuated by shadows and echoes. This verticality mirrors the psychological layering found in Eno's Suffolk compositions, in which each sonic element exists in dialogue with space and memory. By juxtaposing urban portraiture with rural landscapes, Eno engages with a continuity of spatial perception. Both settings, be they the marshes of Suffolk or the skyscrapers of Manhattan, are treated as loci of affect, memory, and imagination. The camera's rotation, forcing viewers to physically realign their gaze, underscores how perception is mutable, contingent upon both bodily and cognitive orientation. The urban, like the rural, becomes a canvas upon which time, memory, and sound converge. In this sense, Eno's work anticipates contemporary notions of psychogeography, where the sensory experience of a city or a rural landscape is navigated as much through imagination and memory as through physical movement.

BELLS: RITUAL, MEMORY, AND ACOUSTIC SPACE

Bells occupy a particularly resonant position in Eno's conceptual and sonic imagination. In a 1995 conversation, he reflected on how the sound of church bells from his Suffolk childhood became embedded in his sensory memory, shaping his sensitivity to timbre, resonance, and the way sound articulates space. (13)

These bells, often drifting across fields from unseen towers, were less about marking time in a functional sense and more about defining an acoustic geography, a kind of invisible architecture binding community and place. Anthropologist Steven Feld has described such sonic phenomena as 'acoustemology', in which hearing and listening form a way of knowing the world. (14)

For Eno, bells are not simply instruments but spatial events. Their decay and reverberation extend beyond the moment of striking, producing an envelope of sound that can anchor memory and identity. The connection between bell sounds and ritual, whether ecclesiastical, civic or personal, underscores their power to bind the present to both past and future, much in the way Eno's compositions weave temporal and spatial layers into single immersive experiences. The resonance of bells also recalls Michel Chion's concept of the acousmêtre: a sound source that is heard but not seen, which acquires an almost supernatural presence. (15)

In Suffolk's open landscapes, bells often function in precisely this way, arriving disembodied through the air, their origin hidden by terrain or distance. This disjunction between source and perception intensifies their affective power, reinforcing the interplay of presence and absence that characterises much of Eno's ambient work.

In more recent projects, Eno has extended this engagement with bells into collaborative and site-specific works. His 2003 installation *77 Million Paintings*, though primarily visual, incorporated sound layers that echoed the slow, decaying tones of bells, further blurring distinctions between temporal and spatial media.

(top left) Orford Ness Photo Series, photograph by Jane Tankard
(lower left) Orford Ness Photo Series, photograph by Jane Tankard

(bottom right) Orford Ness Photo Series, photograph by Jane Tankard

These works suggest that bells for Eno are more than a sonic motif; they are an ongoing inquiry into how sound mediates between physical environment, cultural ritual, and personal memory. Among the many textures and tonal qualities that weave through Brian Eno's oeuvre, few are as quietly persistent as the sound of bells. Resonant, metallic, spatially evocative, bells appear repeatedly across his recordings, both as direct samples and as metaphoric presences. They act as sonic signposts, guiding listeners through emotional and temporal landscapes that are as much internal as external. Sonic Palimpsests and the Architecture of Memory
Brian Eno's ambient compositions and conceptual art invite us to reconsider the relationship between sound, place, and memory. His work challenges a representational mode that seeks to capture landscape visually or descriptively, instead generating environments that are at once atmospheric and haunted. The Suffolk coast, with its layered histories, vanished communities, and persistent ghosts, offers a fitting locus for this exploration. The uncanny atmospheres of *Ambient 4: On Land* reflect a poetics of absence and presence, where memory and environment interpenetrate.

The reintroduction of figurative elements in tracks like '*The Belldog*' complicates this further, suggesting a liminal space between portrait and landscape, between subjectivity and environment. The persistent echo of bells punctuates this sonic geography, articulating the temporal folds through which Eno's work moves.

Through his attentive listening and creative re-imagining, Eno composes not only sound but a form of sonic architecture: a layered, shifting palimpsest of place and memory. His music becomes an invitation to inhabit a world where past and present intertwine, where absence is as meaningful as presence, and where the familiar is continuously rendered strange and new.

LIMINAL

Whilst in the process of writing this essay an uncanny confluence of the 'portrait to landscape' narrative appeared on Eno's Facebook page; the announcement of a new collaborative album with artist Beatie Wolfe.

Following their recently released albums '*Luminal*' described as dream music and '*Lateral*' space music, '*Liminal*' is described as standing at 'the point of convergence between Lateral and Luminal'. In the words of Wolfe and Eno:

"If Lateral is a kind of landscape painting, a sonic place, Luminal is a dream-like awakening, a feeling space. Liminal, the newest addition, is a hybrid of the two, a strange new land with a human living and feeling its way through its mysterious spaces. Liminal is set in the borderlands between song and non-song (or "nong" as we call it), where the listener is exploring an intimate and unfamiliar new sonic world, as yet unclaimed, and still ambiguous." [16]

(bottom) Orford Ness Photo Series, photograph by Steve Bowkett

(top right) Image created by Jake Parkin

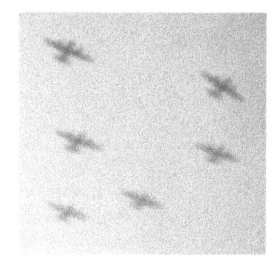

NOTES

(01) Brian Eno, interview by Anthony Korner, *Artforum*, 1996.

(02) David Toop, *Ocean of Sound: Aether Talk, Ambient Sound and Imaginary Worlds* (London: Serpent's Tail, 1995), 276.

(03) Sigmund Freud, "The Uncanny" (1919), in *The Standard Edition of the Complete Psychological Works of Sigmund Freud*, vol. 17, trans. James Strachey (London: Hogarth Press, 1955), 217–256.

(04) Mark Fisher, *Ghosts of My Life: Writings on Depression, Hauntology and Lost Futures* (London: Zero Books, 2013).

(05) Brian Eno, quoted in Eric Tamm, *Brian Eno: His Music and the Vertical Color of Sound* (Boston: Da Capo Press, 1995), 139.

(06) John Coulthart, "The Suffolk Ghosts of Brian Eno," *Feuilleton* (blog), June 6, 2020, https://www.johncoulthart.com/feuilleton.

(07) Kenneth R. Olwig, "Recovering the Substantive Nature of Landscape," *Annals of the Association of American Geographers* 86, no. 4 (1996): 630–653.

(08) James Corner, "Recovering Landscape as a Critical Cultural Practice," in *Recovering Landscape: Essays in Contemporary Landscape Architecture*, ed. James Corner (New York: Princeton Architectural Press, 1999), 1–26.

(09) Nigel Thrift, *Non-Representational Theory: Space, Politics, Affect* (London: Routledge, 2007).

(10) Brian Eno, quoted in Tamm, *Brian Eno: His Music and the Vertical Color of Sound*, 154.

(11) Mark Prendergast, *The Ambient Century: From Mahler to Moby – The Evolution of Sound in the Electronic Age* (London: Bloomsbury, 2003), 205–207.

(12) Tamm, *Brian Eno: His Music and the Vertical Color of Sound*, 165–166.

(13) Ibid., 139.

(14) Steven Feld, "Waterfalls of Song: An Acoustemology of Place Resounding in Bosavi, Papua New Guinea," in *Senses of Place*, ed. Steven Feld and Keith H. Basso (Santa Fe: School of American Research Press, 1996), 91–135.

(15) Michel Chion, *Audio-Vision: Sound on Screen*, trans. Claudia Gorbman (New York: Columbia University Press, 1994).

(16) Brian Eno and Beatie Wolfe, "Liminal," Facebook, 2025, https://www.facebook.com/brianeno.

SAME, SAME BUT DIFFERENT
JAKE PARKIN

SAME, SAME BUT DIFFERENT BY JAKE PARKIN

'Projects are versions [...] same, same but different, each iteration testing what a space could become rather than what it must be'

A shift in material, scale, or setting can transport architectural representation to alternate realities and invite a different form of attention. The central theme of this text is exploring the uncanny, understood as the moment when the familiar becomes strange, and using it as a design method. If we treat material transformation, scalar play and changes of setting as deliberate tools, then architecture moves from static singularity toward a dynamic practice of editing and narration. It becomes a methodology to propose civic futures grounded in use, perception and collective life rather than in a single perfect object. This claim aligns with David Graeber's reminder that:

"the ultimate, hidden truth of the world is that it is something that we make, and could just as easily make differently." (01)

In the studio this is a daily practice of rereading space, altering variables, and measuring how those changes reshape experience. The goal is a careful way to question what seems fixed. DS3.1 has remained an ongoing amalgamation of multiple voices, perspectives and identities since its conception. By continuously exploring the uncanny and rereading space in ways that reveal hidden potential, the studio is set up as a collaboration of experimentation, exploration, and chance.

Educational spaces become the means by which students are invited to look beneath surfaces and test ideas through accountable changes in material, scale, and / or setting. A small object and a large series of spaces can both hold this method. Either can be recast in a speculative future as a transformed version of itself.

(top right) Johannesburg Drawing, Jake Parkin

BROOM

"Trigger: I happened to mention to her one day that I have had the same broom for the last 20 years, very impressed she said have a medal, 20 years, it is a long time Dave

Dave: Yeah! Well it is two decades isn't it.

Trigger: Well I wouldn't go that far.

Del Boy: Um Trig, just a sec, if you have had that broom for 20 years, have you actually swept any roads with it?

Trigger: Well of course! But I look after it well, we have an old saying that has been handed down by generations of road sweepers, 'look after your broom...'

Dave: And your broom looks after you?

Trigger: No Dave, it's just 'look after your broom.'

Dave: Ah that old saying...

Trigger: Yeah and that is what I have done, I have maintained it for 20 years. This old broom has had 17 new heads and 14 new handles in its time.

Sid: How the hell can it be the same bloody broom then?

Trigger: Well here is a picture of it. What more proof do you need?" (02)

The humour lies in the paradox: how can something persist through so much change? Yet the joke clarifies how identity can, sometimes controversially, endure through transformation.

With DS3.1, Jane Tankard has led the unit with Alicia Pivaro, then with Thomas Grove, and now with me. Together we have worked with the relationship between film and architecture as an analytical process.

In New York, Diana Agrest and Mario Gandelsonas treated the metropolis as a text to be cut and resequenced, mixing mapping, semiotics, urban writing and psychoanalysis. (03)

Between the known and the unknown, speculation provokes discomfort and wonder. In that sense the manipulation of spatial variables is not stylistic, it is civic, it is a tool for remaking how the city is lived. The work of Agrest and Gandelsonas suggested film as a way of reading space before digital montage became common in pedagogy. At the AA, In Diploma 10, Bernard Tschumi talked of event and movement, Nigel Coates discussed narrative and the vernacular city and Carlos Villanueva Brandt extends that lineage into the contemporary moment with 'constructs', interactive space and a transformative focus on London. As his former student, I find the opportunity to explore these 'same, same but different' worlds in parallel, creating cross-crits between Westminster and the AA, testing how far narrative and event can be explored through the revisited uncanny.

(top) Timbre Fibre Factory, Carlos Villanueva Brandt, AA Diploma 10

(bottom right) Inflatable Building, Frieze Art fair, unknown artist, photograph by Jake Parkin

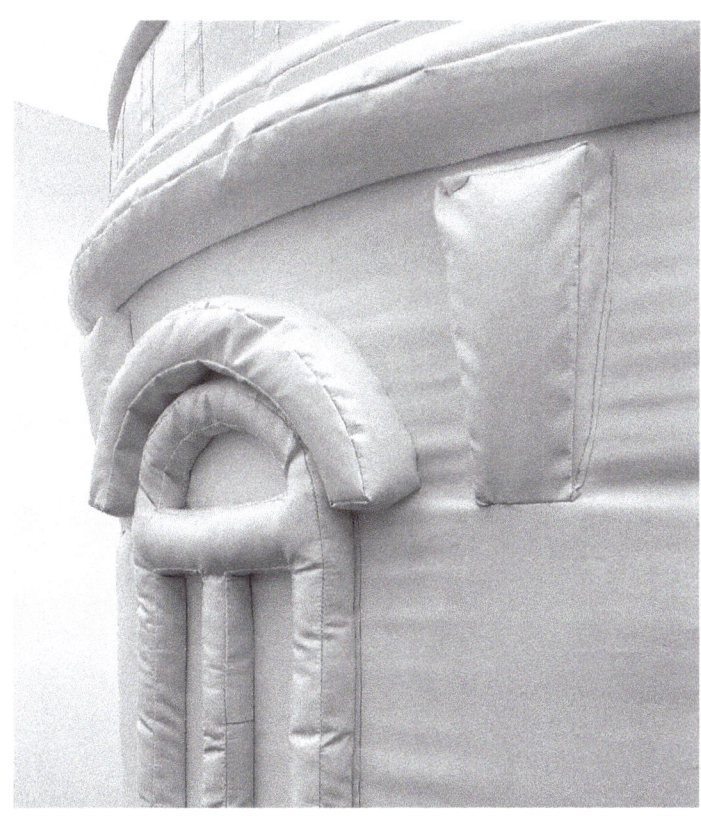

"The piece was daft, sure, but it was not stupid: it was smart, fun and genuinely engaging [...] A lot of my work looks at history, sometimes in a very serious intense way, otherwise in a very playful way, and this is obviously about as playful as you can get. [...] In a way Sacrilege was meant to counteract what I felt was the pomposity of sport and the Olympics [...] as it happened, it was not so pompous in the UK, but the whole Olympics movement seems to be really full of itself, so I just thought, let us do something about Britain that shows we have a sense of humour about our history and we are willing to satirise ourselves almost and have fun with our history and identity." (04)

Jeremy Deller's Sacrilege makes this visible in public. The inflatable replica of Stonehenge, installed during the London 2012 Olympics, recast a national monument as a field of play. The project prompted the reaction that Deller anticipated, with the Daily Mail decrying it as 'Sacrilege'.

The response is as important as the object, showing how a shift in material can reframe touch, access and belonging. The one-to-one cast of Michelangelo's David at the V&A complicates this further. It is identical in appearance to the original and equally untouchable, yet our experience is shaped by collective understanding and institutional framing as much as by matter. The question is not whether the replica equals the original, but what forms of experience different materials and contextual framing make possible and how those differences can transform the way that space is understood. In the last decade, huge advancements in architectural software, digital technology and AI have each transformed the way that we represent and imagine material in space.

BONGO

We create virtual environments where spaces stretch, collapse, vaporise and transform in ways that were once difficult to imagine. Reality itself becomes less important as the boundaries of material shift, allowing us to both dream of and experience speculative 'other' worlds.

Scale continues the argument, whereby our bodies calibrate space: grand doorways signal assembly, compressed ceilings signal control. The office floors in *Being John Malkovich* satirise this with precision, shrinking the worker to fit a machine age of administration rather than a civic age of assembly. (05) Claes Oldenburg and Coosje van Bruggen's enlarged familiar objects estrange the everyday and insist, as Oldenburg argued, on resisting consensus. (06) Similarly, in *Learning from Las Vegas*, Denise Scott Brown, Robert Venturi, and Steven Izenour distinguished the duck and the decorated shed to show how scale and signage shifted when the driver replaced the pedestrian as primary reader of the city. (07) The point is concerned with how scale produces and can reproduce meaning. Frank Lloyd Wright's Hollyhock House rewards the closer look through the scale of the detail, while simultaneously entering our collective cinematic memory in *Blade Runner* at the scale of a speculative future city. 'Googie' architecture at LAX declared itself from the sky, legible from the aircraft. Nigel Coates' Café Bongo in Tokyo placed a plane wing inside a café, a juxtaposition that referenced Fellini's *La Dolce Vita* while speaking to the energy of the city. These examples show how scalar shifts can generate the uncanny through estrangement, towards new forms of understanding.

(left middle) Bird House in New Zealand, Unknown, photograph by Jake Parkin
(bottom) Alexanderplatz, photograph by Jake Parkin

(top right) National Gallery Extension, Denise Scott Brown and Robert Venturi, photograph by Jake Parkin

"In this Allegory, the symbol of the hammer and sickle is broken into 44 pieces, each of which displayed on a plinth and accompanied by a poem by Francesco Leonetti, also composed of 44 lines representing the titles of the corresponding shapes, indicating their market value. The work is not limited to this hint of sarcasm regarding the arbitrary nature of markets but also evokes the themes of fragmentation and ideological reconstruction, of form, and also of the proletariat. The broken symbol is that of work, the allegory of the ideology in which he believes and to whose poetics he remains true. Allegorical fragments of a single project to which he had devoted his whole life, as he said: I have devoted my life, and will continue doing so, to a single project in the hope of transforming the world." (08)

Francesca Giacomelli's account of Enzo Mari describes his allegorical hammer and sickle fragmented into forty-four pieces, each accompanied by a poem. The symbol persists but its frame changes. The deconstruction of the political in this example reminds me of the conversations that we have in the studio: encouraging spatial transformation and questioning the radical implications that follow. Bernard Tschumi's projects can be read in a similar way, design and montage, assembling sequences like an edited film rather than a single shot. (09) A singular moment or design can sometimes feel disconnected, rigid and self-centred in its focus, but by working in multiples, through scenes, sequences, or series, a design can gain depth, continuity, complexity, and a sense of the collective. As an insight it is simple yet incredibly generative. Resist the dream of the single masterwork, and the city can open itself to careful change across time and scene. When considering Mies, the question of 'context' remains divisive. These ideas are continuously explored in the studio, as well as in other spaces such as in the AA Summer School Unit 4 'Assemblages', taught alongside Tanil Raif, Mario Serrano Puche and Aoi Phillips, where Jane Tankard joined us as guest critic.

As a response to Mari's hammer and sickle project, 'contexts' were found, transformed, reconstructed, placed both together and entirely apart.

"Rather than dreaming of the standalone masterpiece, my attention was shifting towards how to nudge what already existed. Developers were already on it. Warehouses were being carved up into lofts and banks were becoming pizzerias. These were the first signs of radical repurposing of existing urban fabric, which squared with my own taste for the warts and all city. Instead of being bulldozed, I knew buildings could be converted and would be all the better for it." (10)

Coates turns us instead to interventions that tease out new meanings from existing conditions. He anticipated the reuse economy that has since defined cities. Sociologist Anthony Giddens names the reciprocity:

"structures are both the conditions that enable social practice and the products of those practices." (11)

Popular culture captures this with films such as *Everything Everywhere All at Once*, where small edits of setting generate entirey same, same but different worlds. (12) This lesson is direct: setting is an active field where small changes unlock new meaning.

"Il semble que la perfection soit atteinte non quand il n'y a plus rien à ajouter, mais quand il n'y a plus rien à retrancher." Translated: "Perfection is finally attained not when there is no longer anything to add, but when there is no longer anything to take away." (13)

Conservative architectural critique is too often obsessed with the sacred singularity, mindlessly repeating the design mantra that adding or removing anything destroys purity. To avoid 'change' altogether ignores the wonderful and complex nature of architecture, people and cities.

(top right) AA Summer School 'Assembled' Exhibition, AA Front Members Room, photograph by James Winata
(left) AA Summer School 'Assemblages' Digital Scans, by Unit 4, led by Jake Parkin, Tanil Raif, Mario Serrano Puche and Aoi Phillips

(bottom right) AA Summer School 'Dis-Assembled' Exhibition, Rear Presentation Space, photograph by Jake Parkin

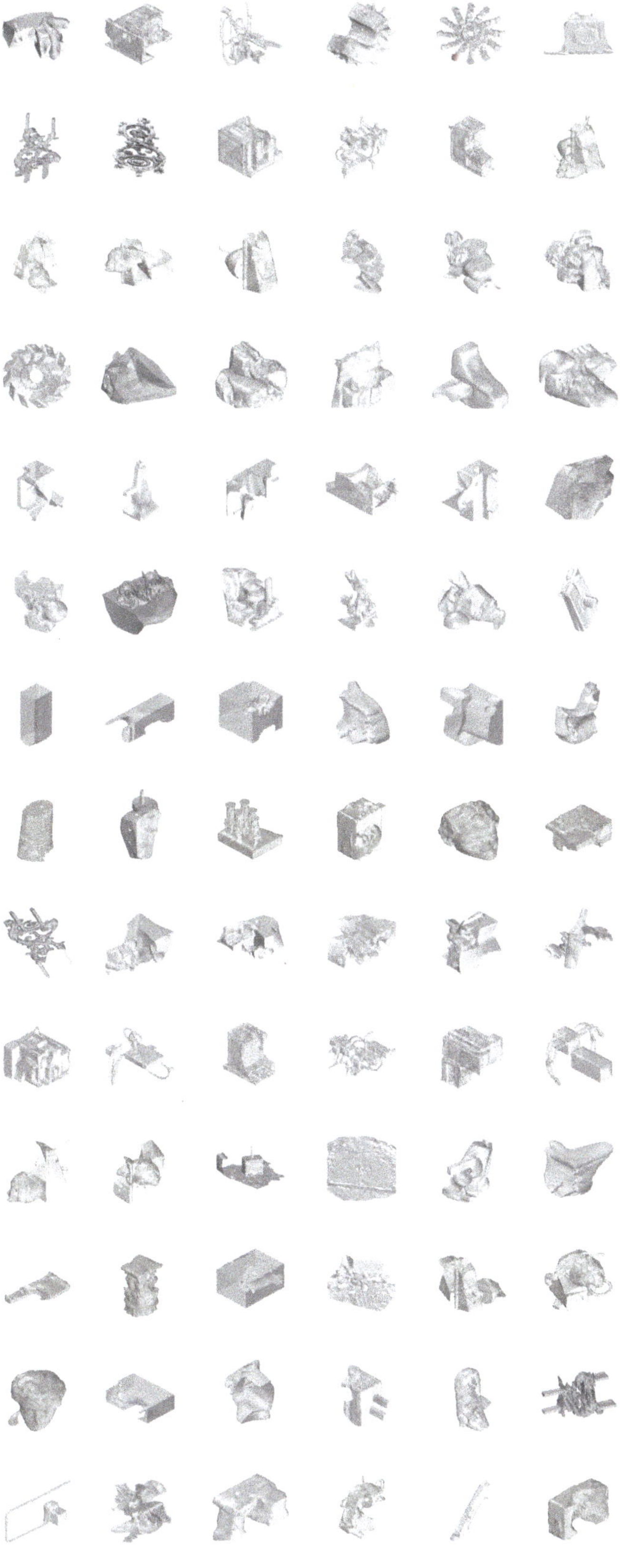

Sigmund Freud helps to name how the uncanny is not the alien but the familiar rendered strange. Doubles, returns, mirrors, the almost same. (14) Sylvia Lavin argues that architecture's most 'kissable' aspect is its surface, where it turns into something else. (15) One of my first students in Leeds, Nicole Oliver, envisioned a project in Los Angeles that gave space to Pipilotti Rist's work in a contested urban setting, deliberatey outdoor, unbiased and accessible. Rist's projections take the notion of kissing space literally, flooding exhibition spaces across floors, walls, ceilings and viewers. (16) Jimenez Lai, before setting up the LA based studio Bureau Spectacular, studied cinematography and his drawings convey notions of series, body, and architecture that each hold incredible relevance in the contemporary setting. (17) His projects have been a great inspiration to me, and they feel uncannily related to our studio work. The convergence of disciplines such as these, film and architecture, has undergone a sustained intensification, where the act of drawing from heterogeneous cultural and material contexts operates less as a gesture of influence than as a generative mechanism. We cultivate this as a primary source of energy, propelling our studio's conceptual and spatial production. Looking forward requires a deliberate glance backward, tracing points of intersection and following the threads that draw one toward the people, places, and objects that have quietly shaped a collective sensibility. The images and projects in this book engage inherited narratives without falling into nostalgia, transforming recollection into a form of architectural agency. Even within my relatively short time leading the unit with Jane, I have become aware of a continuity of thought and practice that stretches before and beyond me, a shared rhythm of curiosity and experimentation that lends the studio its quiet coherence.

I experience the studio as part of an ongoing continuum and look forward to seeing how its histories resurface, same, same but different, perhaps uncovering echoes of experiences in the Northern Soul dance halls of Blackburn and Wigan. Attention turns to scenes of collective exhilaration that reconfigured space on their own terms: the raves that ruptured the Hulme Crescents, the warehouse gatherings of Leeds and Glasgow, and the radical glamour of queer nightlife in London or elsewhere. These moments forged provisional social contracts outside official systems. Their spirit extends to the consideration of site itself, particularly those spaces historically cast as other, overlooked, or misrepresented within architectural discourse. To counteract typological conventions such as housing or retail, the studio projects imagine alternative frameworks organised around complexity, pleasure, palimpsest, and assembly.

BITS

Lefebvre reminds us that space is a social product. (18) Foucault points to heterotopias, spaces that hold multiple orders at once. (19) Karen Barad insists on more than human entanglements, the agency of matter and atmosphere. (20) Vidler reframes the uncanny as latency rather than loss. (21) Tschumi argues:

"the ultimate pleasure of architecture lies in the most forbidden parts of the architectural act, where limits are perverted and prohibitions are transgressed." (22)

All of this folds back into the original claim. Architecture is edited, narrated, performed, and felt. Through material change, scalar play, shifts in setting, we rewrite the world carefully, joyfully, with others.

(bottom) Faith Concourse, Jake Parkin

(top right) Kissing Architecture, Nicole Oliver

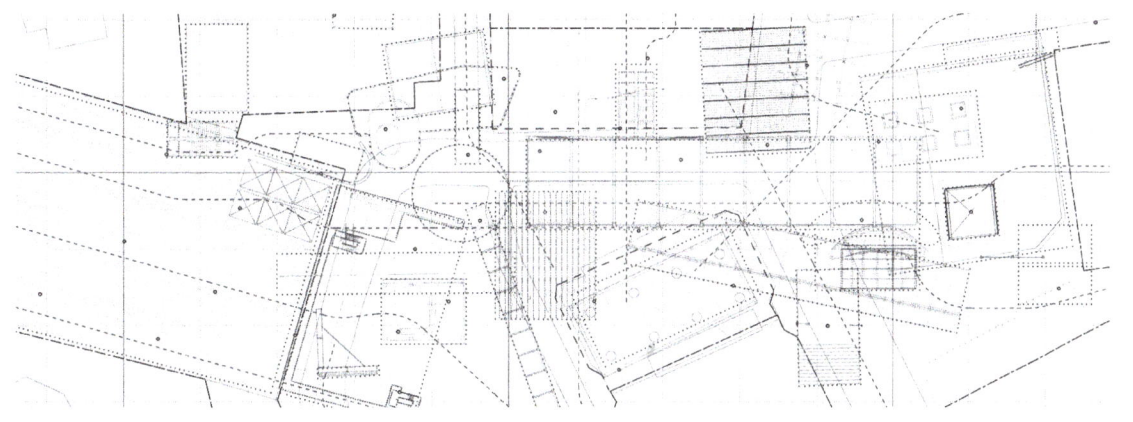

The films we watch, the spaces we occupy, the archives we mine, the music we dance to, are all lenses through which we can see architecture anew. To make differently, we must accept that there is no single view, only fragments, only cuts, each incomplete. Within this field of versions, the uncanny operates as a method rather than a theme, aligning with Vidler's account of the familiar made strange as a condition that can surface through subtle shifts and returns. (21)

Small recalibrations of points, lines and surfaces may create layered readings that exist before they are named, allowing spatial possibilities to register without closure. The studio positions architecture as an ongoing comparative practice. It proceeds by assembling sequences, inviting rereadings, and keeping the relationship between perception and transformation both generative and open. Projects situate themselves among other projects, parts within parts within a larger conversation that remains unfinished by design. These threads suggest an approach that compares filmic editing with architectural sequencing, where frames and cuts sit alongside thresholds and sections. Read this way, projects can be versions within a series: same, same but different, each time testing what a space could become rather than what it must be.

(top) Diploma 10 Long Drawing Series, Jake Parkin   *(bottom right) Assemblage Drawing, Jake Parkin*

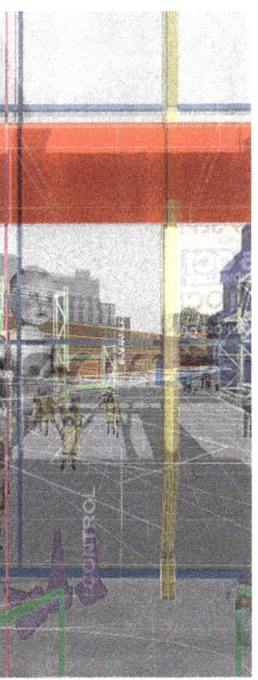

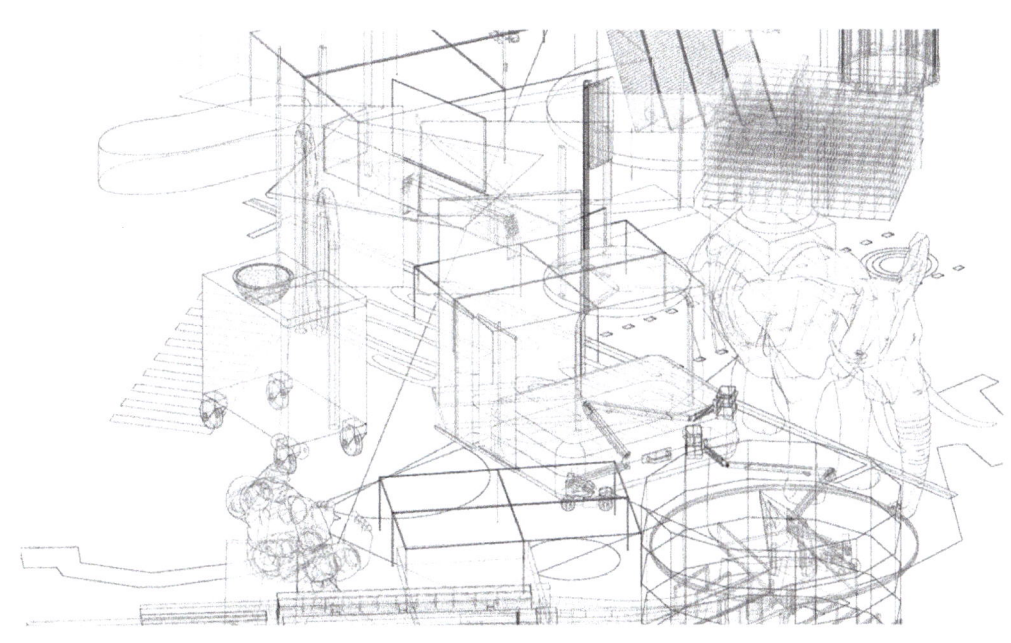

NOTES

(01) David Graeber, *Fragments of an Anarchist Anthropology* (Chicago: Prickly Paradigm Press, 2004).
(02) John Sullivan, writer, *Only Fools and Horses*, season 6, episode 7, "Heroes and Villains," aired December 25, 1996, BBC One.
(03) Diana Agrest and Mario Gandelsonas, *The Sex of Architecture* (New York: Harry N. Abrams, 1996).
(04) Jeremy Deller, *Sacrilege*, inflatable installation, Glasgow International Festival of Visual Art, 2012.
(05) Spike Jonze, *Being John Malkovich* (Los Angeles: USA Films, 1999).
(06) Claes Oldenburg and Coosje van Bruggen, *Claes Oldenburg: Coosje van Bruggen: Sculpture by the Way* (Milan: Fondazione Prada, 2006).
(07) Robert Venturi, Denise Scott Brown, and Steven Izenour, *Learning from Las Vegas: The Forgotten Symbolism of Architectural Form*, rev. Ed. (Cambridge, MA: MIT Press, 1977).
(08) Francesca Giacomelli, "Enzo Mari: The Hammer and Sickle," in *Enzo Mari*, ed. Hans Ulrich Obrist and Francesca Giacomelli, 144–149 (Milan: Triennale Milano, 2020).
(09) Bernard Tschumi, *Event-Cities* (Cambridge, MA: MIT Press, 1994).
(10) Nigel Coates, *Narrative Architecture* (Chichester: Wiley, 2012).
(11) Anthony Giddens, *The Constitution of Society: Outline of the Theory of Structuration* (Cambridge: Polity Press, 1984).
(12) Daniel Kwan and Daniel Scheinert, directors, *Everything Everywhere All at Once* (Los Angeles: A24, 2022).
(13) Antoine de Saint-Exupéry, *Terre des Hommes* (Paris: Éditions Gallimard, 1939).
(14) Sigmund Freud, "The Uncanny," in *The Standard Edition of the Complete Psychological Works of Sigmund Freud, Vol. XVII (1917–1919)*, ed. and trans. James Strachey, 217–256 (London: Hogarth Press, 1955).
(15) Sylvia Lavin, *Kissing Architecture* (Princeton, NJ: Princeton University Press, 2011).
(16) Pipilotti Rist, *Sip My Ocean*, installation, Kunst-Werke Berlin, 1996.
(17) Jimenez Lai, *Citizens of No Place* (New York: Princeton Architectural Press, 2012).
(18) Henri Lefebvre, *The Production of Space*, trans. Donald Nicholson-Smith (Oxford: Blackwell, 1991).
(19) Michel Foucault, "Of Other Spaces," *Diacritics* 16, no. 1 (1986): 22–27.
(20) Karen Barad, *Meeting the Universe Halfway: Quantum Physics and the Entanglement of Matter and Meaning* (Durham, NC: Duke University Press, 2007).
(21) Anthony Vidler, *The Architectural Uncanny: Essays in the Modern Unhomely* (Cambridge, MA: MIT Press, 1992).
(22) Bernard Tschumi, *Architecture and Disjunction* (Cambridge, MA: MIT Press, 1996), 63.

AN ARCHITECTURAL AUTOPSY: 'DISSECTING THE EXQUISITE CORP(U)SE'

PETER J. BALDWIN

AN ARCHITECTURAL AUTOPSY: 'DISSECTING THE EXQUISITE CORP(U)SE' BY PETER J BALDWIN

'...the exquisite corpse shall drink of the young wine'

"Everything tends to make us believe that there exists a certain point of the mind at which life and death, the real and the imagined, past and future, the communicable and the incommunicable, high and low, cease to be perceived as contradictions." (01)

"What strange phenomena we find in a great city, all we need do is stroll about with our eyes open. Life swarms with innocent monsters." (02)

Beguiling and beautiful, confusing, confounding, and seductive, the socio-cultural melange, the tangled tapestry of pluralistic presents, future fragments, and historic hauntings that we so reductively refer to as the city has long held a privileged position within the artistic and architectural imagination. (03) Cast as a dream(ing) theatre of fact(s), fiction(s), and fantasy(s), it has served as a manifold metaphor and macrocosm of the interactions and encounters of human life. (04) Owing to its inherent complexity the city defies traditional representational practices, forms of knowing, documenting, and understanding.

(right) Reparation Drawing, Sneha Sachin Shenoy, DS3.1

Whilst a plan may record the general arrangement of streets, blocks or zonings, revealing a notional orthogonal occupation of the (horizontal) surface, it does little to address the histories, temporalities, and politics of a space, similarly montages and sketches may capture a moment, but often offers little in the way of an explanation of the histo-topographic drivers that shape the conditions and contexts of these socio-cultural events. Even in the face of more novel attempts, that have employed broadened linguistic dexterities, from Cullen's Serial Visions [05] to the more poetic wanderings of the Baudelairian [06] flâneur the city both as a place and conceptual construct has remained reticently enigmatic, paradoxically contingent, at once familiar and unknowable, a spectral entity that hovers just beyond our (intellectual) grasp.

In his seminal essay, the 'Soluble City'. [07] British artist and art historian Roger Cardinal attempts to negotiate this inherent ambiguity, viewing the city through a hexadic matrix of intersecting metaphysical metaphors. Framed as chimeric constellation, a construct of palmipsestuous conjunctions, interconnections and interstitialities, Cardinal's essay does much to explain the city as a surreal construct, brought into being through the syzygistic swerve of objective chance. Yet even the complex ontological conjunctions of the 'sixfold' city of Cardinal's conjecture is an insufficient tool, reliant on imparted abstract(ed) knowledge and cerebral conceptualisation rather than a more intimate experiential knowledge that might be garnered through a more sensuous form of understanding. Seeking this more carnal form of knowing, we are compelled to advance an alternative conceptualisation, extending our hypothesis through by extrapolation.

Cardinal's parting premise, viewing the contemporary city not just as a post-modern, post-mortem, Barthesian [08] 'System of Signs', but as a post-postmodern accretion; an inherently palimpsestuous and pluralistic, multi-authored evidentiary field of contingent clues, discordant debris and Locardian residues. The scene of an (im) perfect crime. [09]

We will not however, solve the uncanny case of the 'Soluble City' through architectural means alone. Augmenting our established arsenal of investigatory techniques with the probative lens of the famed Surrealist parlour game turned (de)constructivist research methodology; the 'Cadavre Exquis' [10] we are afforded both a forensic foundation and the necessary necroscopic instruments of imaginative deduction with which to (un)ravel the tangle of evidentiary traces, charting free fragmentary associations and (un)intentional choreographies, the trajectories of the flotsam and jetsam of contemporary urban life.

EXAMINING THE CORPUS.

Before we can pursue our post-postmodern enquiries, it is perhaps necessary to begin by establishing the cause of our concern. Drawing is long established throughout the creative disciplines as a communicative practice formed of observational recording based on visual representation and pictorial information. Architecture, in addition to this more broadly established communicative role, has traditionally conceptualised the drawing as a mediating object, [11,12] a synthetic condition that allows simultaneously for observational recording, projective imagining and the testing of intuition against a variety of externalised factors, both physical and immaterial.

(right) Peter Baldwin, Cogitations of the Marine Bishop Mendacious, 'Filigreed Gods – Diaphanous Bodies and Sacred Vessels', 2021. Following the Architect Sir Christopher Wren's studies for the Dome of St Pauls Cathedral in London (constructed 1675-1710), my first experimental 'Architectural Autopsy' extends the investigative dexterity of my earlier collage-based practices, simultaneously synthesizing Wren's various design proposals in an attempt to reconstruct Wren's design process and reveal the underlying 'diagram' of architectural intent.

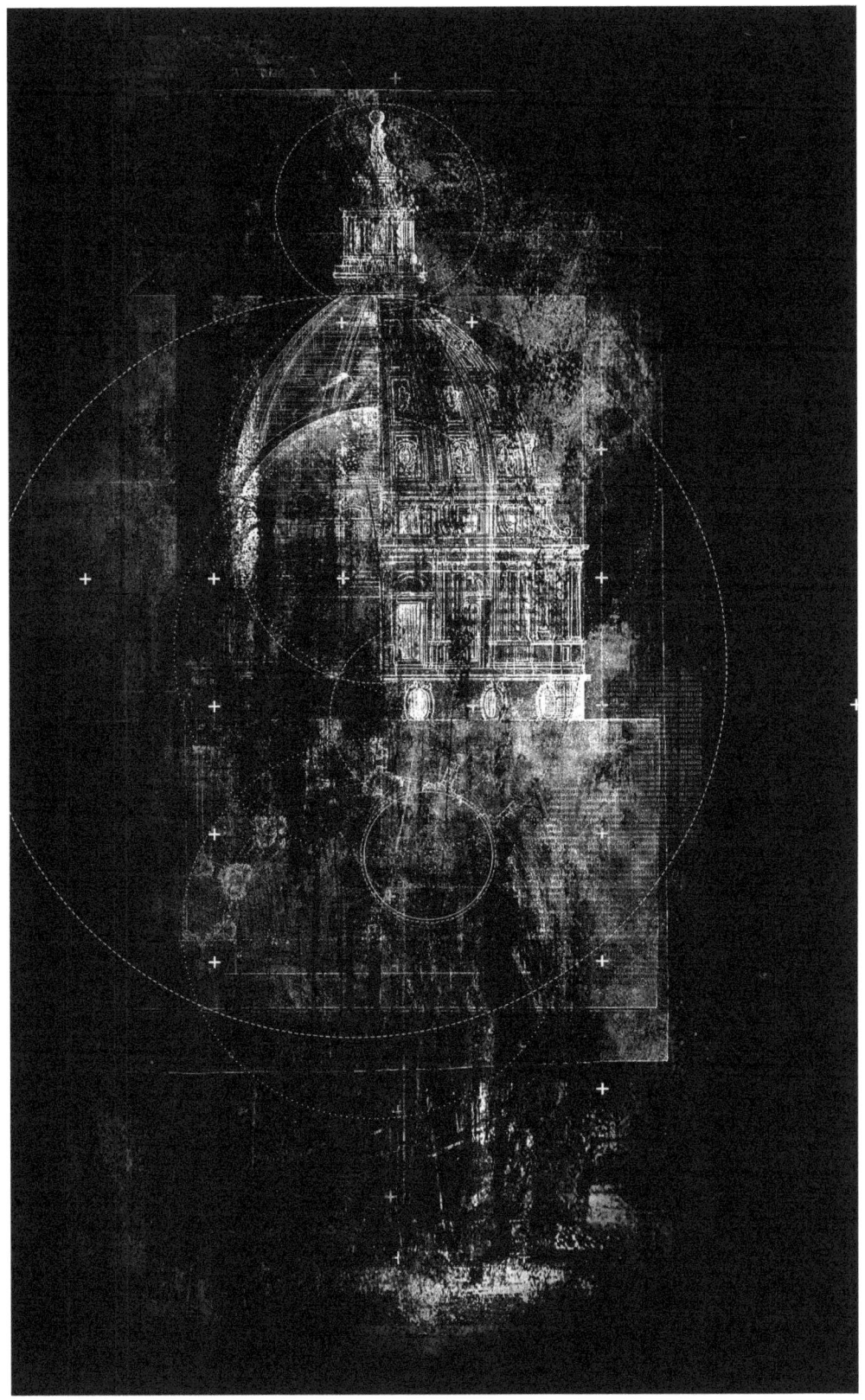

Despite the outward aesthetic similarities, unlike much of the artistic practice of drawing (grounded in classical notions mimesis (13) the replication of themes motifs and forms of the natural world - where such recordings are based on qualitative observations and interpretive reasoning) architectural observation is often partially (at the very least) referenced to a set of absolutes, an empiric abstraction based on the quantifiability of construction data. Yet these self-same quantitative abstractions, whilst undeniably essential for conveying the clarity of construction information essential to environmental and structural stability, limit the drawings capacity to contain the unstable, the atmospheric and the fragmentary.

Even within the architectural Avant Garde with its anti-author-itarian streak and fondness for representational experimentation intended to liberate the subject of architecture from the control of the architecture – making form follow function (or should that be function follows form), has with perhaps one or two notable exceptions shied away from techniques which harness automatism and chance). And yet as the nature of space has shifted, becoming ever move plural, personal, and simultaneous, and our traditional paradigms of description, documentation and discovery have begun to fail, there has been a conspicuous lack of critical conjectural codification of the means and methods with which to confront these emergent territories. Just as the French philosopher Micheal Foucault cautioned, some 50 years ago to survive as a discipline not only must we be conscious of the shifting context of our practice and praxis, we must also make a conscious and conspicuous effort to reevaluate the critical capacity of our tools, the mechanisms and media through which we enact our various agencies. (14)

And so we return to our original observational hypothesises; as our post postmodern condition becomes ever more fragmented, haunted by nostalgic presences of yesteryear and of forgotten futures that will never come to pass, we must cultivate critical and speculative methods that allow us to operate in the pervasive multiplicity we must, as Baudrillard suggests, meet randomness with randomness, (15) we must meet discontinuity with discontinuity, we must meet the swerve of objective chance with our own syzygetic representational strategies.

BODIES OF KNOWLEDGE.

Emerging in the early 1920's as a response to a growing conservatism and a collective cultural rejection of the imaginary, Surrealism, it might be argued, is a cultural (and artistic) movement primarily concerned with the (re)discovery of a transcendent realm of latent creative potential. (16) Existing beyond the limited perceptual range(s) of the waking mind, this sur-reality cannot be directly witnessed, its existence is instead known through the (en)actions of subtle mechanisms and the (inter)play of more esoteric forces and fields. For surrealisms principal theorist and co-founder Andre Breton, this transcendent state was most often encountered unexpectedly, arriving serendipitously, born from the phantasmagorical miasma of hypnagogia; (17) the protean thought-scape of half remembered fragments and imagined figments that awaits the (un)wary traveller, as they cross the threshold of the dream. Such was the suggestive power of these uncanny, (un)conscious conjunctions, that they were seen as revelatory, the diaphanous disclosure(s) of deep(er) meanings and half-hidden truths.

(right) Theatre of the Moon, Olha Petrachkova, DS3.1

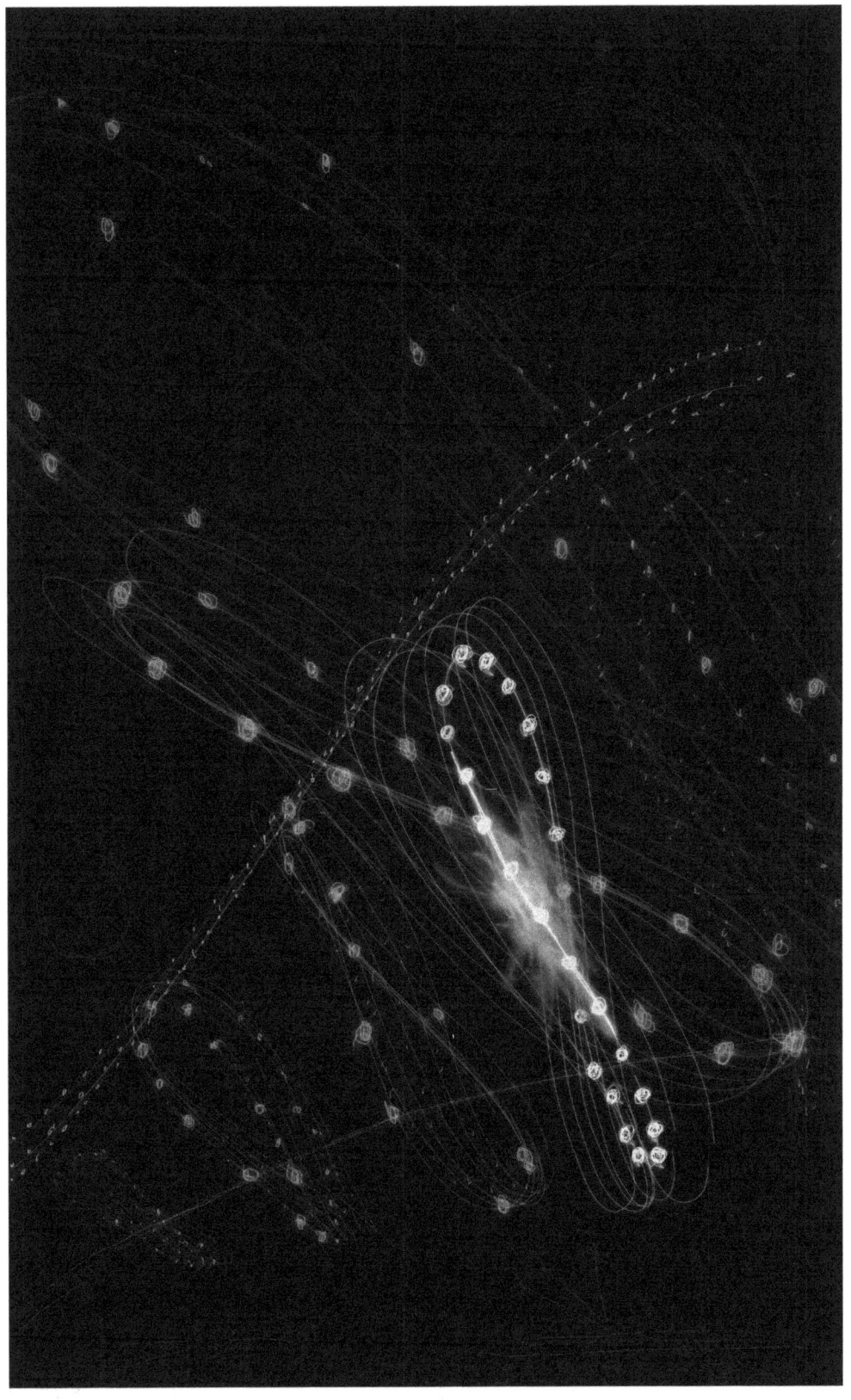

In seeking to evoke these states of (visual) confusion and cognitive dissonance, many surrealist artefacts rely on (mis)understanding, the non sequitur and the double take, the oblique glance and the unexpected object or adjacency, to cultivate confusion and harness it in the pursuit of creativity.

It should, perhaps, come as little wonder then that collage, a creative practice predicated on the (appropriative) arrangement and assembly of (pre)existing fragments would become so beloved by surrealism and its many proponents. From Rauschenberg's 'Combines' [18] to George Hugnet's 'Poèmes Découpés' [19] irrespective of the media of production, the collage constructs meaning through compositional structuring and metaphorical relationships rather than direct representation. As these image objects are manipulated and reconfigured achieving new positions and proximities their meaning as sign-signifiers becomes volatised, rendered as metaphoric, allegoric or connotative exchange values through this free(d) association. Yet even this proximate liberation is limited, owing to the singularity of authorship and the absoluteness of compositional, and therefore creative control. Taking its name from the first sentence so deduced 'Le - cadavre - exquis - boira - le vin - nouveau', (the exquisite corpse shall drink of the young wine) [20] the now famed parlour game turned experimental creative method and artistic research praxis extends the associative logic of the collage through the introduction of a multi author(ed) invective. As each 'player' creates a section or sections of the cadaver they can neither see nor are they told what precedes their fragmentary contribution relying on dead reckoning to inform their contributions.

The resultant chimera combines aspects of both compositional choice and the unpredictable swerve of chance, as each players effort is brought together through at a point of arbitrary meeting. Offering both personal and plural readings, meaning becomes contingent, a Locardian Feedback-loop, [21] a mutable construct open to interpretative (re)reading, reciprocal exchanges and multiple imaginative understandings.

EXQUISITE (EN)TANGLEMENTS.

Yet for the architectural drawing to become an exquisite corpse it requires a curious double dislocation, from not only our architectural training, but from our preconceived notions of authorship and the role of the author in the construction of meaning as we surrender absolute compositional control to the exquisite choreography of chance. Prompted by the provocatively paired probative lenses of Cardinal's Surreal Sixfold and Pataphysical Playwright Alfred Jarry's seminal symbolist novel *The Exploits and Opinions of Dr Faustrol 'Pataphysician'* (1927) [22] - which recounts the eponymous doctor's somnambulistic odyssey through the spectrally mediated streets of sleeping Paris - my own, half-decade long deductive derive [23] 'Filigreed Gods – Diaphanous Bodies and Sacred Vessels' (2019 -) considers, amongst an ever growing list of developmental détour[nement]s, [24] the formation of one such Frankensteinian Forensic framework; an augmentation of the architectural medium, necessitated by the need to document, represent and interrogate the increasingly complex and contradictory web of socio-political cues and techno-cultural clues that constitute the cyberspatiality simultaneity of contemporary (urban) life.

(right) Peter Baldwin, One Thousand Varied Matters, Or at the Professors Table, 'Filigreed Gods – Diaphanous Bodies and Sacred Vessels', 2021 Inspired by Sarah Wigglesworth's 'Rituals of Eating' Series (2002) this drawing describes and documents one instance of the Conclave of Architectural Alchemists. Combining choreographic diagramming, various conversational fragments, and the consumption of various victuals and libations with the Cadavre's clinemenic swerve the drawing serves as an Alembic, an embryonic environment in which emerging ideas and observations discussed during the proceedings can gestate and grow.

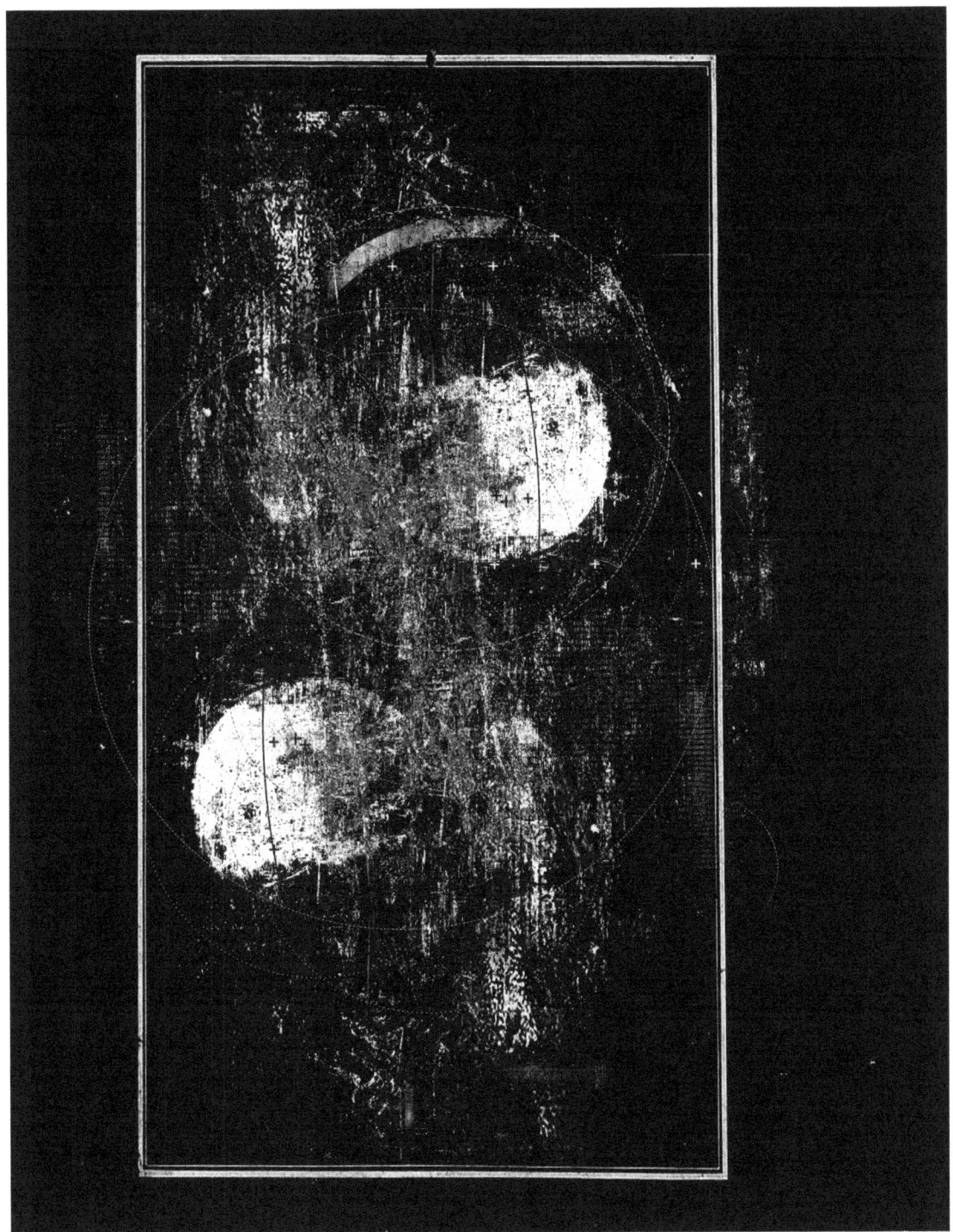

Combining the Prima Materia(ls) of analytical architectural documentation (plans, sections, elevations and other instrumental measures) with more esoteric and unstable forms of evidentiary ephemera (from metaphoric figments and allegoric fragments to atmospheres, ambiances and gut reactions) these drawings are a form of Forensic Reconstruction. Unburdened by the preconceived notions of a necessary wholeness, these drawings instead invoke the protocols of chance as the differing depositions of data; the notable characteristics of the scene, the site, and/or the architectures potential function, are brought together in a simultaneous rendering of spatial and semiotic protocol.

CHIMERIC CADAVERS.

By allowing the drawing to synthesise and sustain these simultaneous, superimposed sets of information and multiple media types we suspend the rules of immediate resolution creating the necessary cognitive elbow room for surprise and serendipitous discovery.

Applied to the city, or indeed any of its individual architectural components, the development of the chimera drawings challenges our preconceptions of site and place, of, restructuring the syntax of programme and place, allowing the architectural lexicon to evolve as a means of exploring, comprehending and ultimately mapping this plastic multiplicity, this synthetic Wunderkammer, the associative, unpredictable, and uncanny qualities of the city.

Yet, what better way could there be to understand the architectural condition that to evoke and enact it?

As we scan the syncopated surface of the cadaver, we become embroiled within its evidentiary field – compelled by intuition, instinct and, perhaps, a morbid curiosity to unravel the tangle web of evidence. As we search for these conclusions and speculate on the nature of the conditions described we become increasingly implicated, co-conspirators in the co-construction of meaning.

Perhaps dear Bernard was right after all; perhaps the only way to truly commit architecture is to co-commit murder… (25)

(right) Peter Baldwin, And Therein it Lay Unspoken, that Most Precious and Precarious of Things, Yet, Always, was the Truth in All Matters, 'Filigreed Gods – Diaphanous Bodies and Sacred Vessels', 2024 Combining both semiotic signifiers and spatial surveys these Frankensteinian Fetishes, forensically reconstruct not only the site or programme, but its socio-cultural, techno-political, and psycho-spatial (pre)dispositions, in an alchemic attempt to distil the quintessent core of the (intended) architectural experience – the (un)scene of the crime.

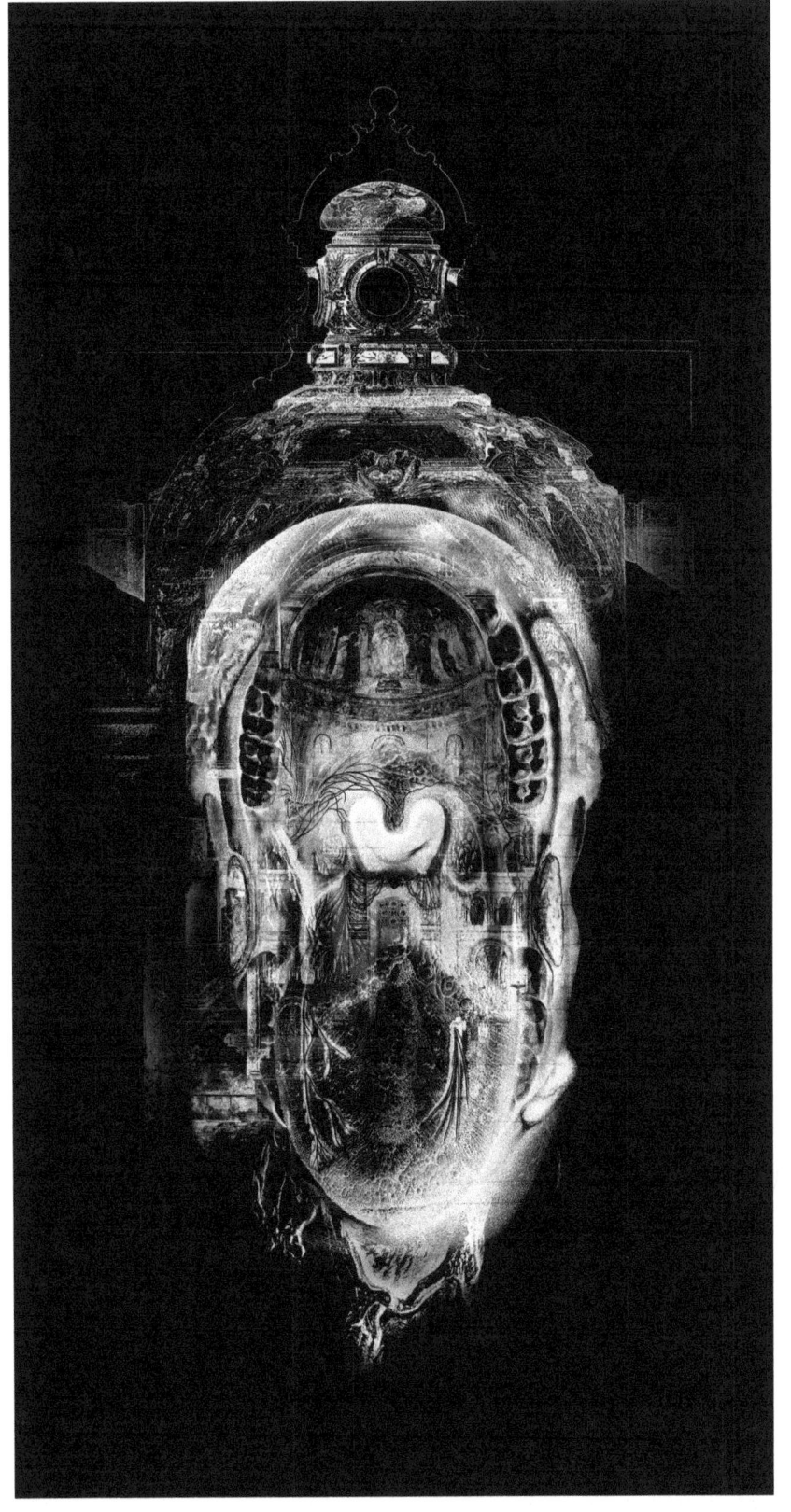

NOTES

(01) André Breton, *Manifestoes of Surrealism* [1972], trans. Richard Seaver and Helen Lane (Ann Arbor: University of Michigan Press, 2010), 123.
(02) Charles Baudelaire, "La Fanfarlo" [*Bulletin de la Société des Gens de Lettres*, 1847], trans. Raymond MacKenzie, in *Baudelaire: Paris Spleen and La Fanfarlo* (Indianapolis: Hackett Publishing Company, 2008).
(03) Roger Cardinal, "The Soluble City: The Surrealist Perception of Paris," in Dalibor Vesely, ed., *AD Surrealism and Architecture* 48, no. 2–3 (1978): 143–149.
(04) Neil Spiller, ed., *AD A Sublime Synthesis: Architecture and Art*, no. 5 (September/October 2023): 128–133.
(05) Gordon Cullen, *The Concise Townscape* (London: The Architectural Press, 1961).
(06) Op. cit., Baudelaire.
(07) Op. cit., Cardinal.
(08) Roland Barthes, "The Death of the Author," trans. Stephen Heath, in *Image Music Text* (London: Fontana Press, 1977), 142–148.
(09) Jean Baudrillard, *The Perfect Crime* (Radical Thinkers), trans. Chris Turner (London: Verso).
(10) André Breton and Paul Eluard, *Dictionnaire Abrégé du Surréalisme of 1938* (Paris: Corti, 1989).
(11) Alberto Pérez-Gómez, "Questions of Representation: The Poetic Origins of Architecture," in *From Models to Drawings*, ed. Marco Frascari, Jonathan Hale, and Bradley Starkey (London, 2007), 11–22.
(12) Dalibor Vesely, *Architecture in the Age of Divided Representation* (Cambridge, MA: MIT Press, 2006), 13.
(13) "Mimesis," *Merriam-Webster.com Dictionary*, Merriam-Webster, https://www.merriam-webster.com/dictionary/mimesis, accessed 24 June 2024.
(14) Michel Foucault, *The Archaeology of Knowledge* (New York: Pantheon, 1972).
(15) Jean Baudrillard, *Passwords*, trans. Chris Turner (London: Verso, 2000), 50.
(16) Op. cit., Breton, 2010, 161.
(17) André Breton, *Poems of André Breton: A Bilingual Anthology*, trans. Jean Pierre Cauvin and Mary Ann Caws (Austin: University of Texas Press, 1982), xxi.
(18) Robert Rauschenberg, *Combines*, ed. Pontus Hultén (Los Angeles: Museum of Contemporary Art, 2006).
(19) Georges Hugnet, *La Septième Face du Dé: Poèmes – Découpages* (Paris: Editions Jeanne Bucher, 1936).
(20) Alastair Brotchie and Mel Gooding, *Surrealist Games* (London: Redstone Press, 1991), 143–144.
(21) Edmund Locard in Reginald Morrish, *Police and Crime-Detection* (London: Oxford University Press, 1940), 72.
(22) Alfred Jarry, *The Exploits and Opinions of Dr. Faustroll, Pataphysician*, trans. Simon Watson Taylor (Cambridge, MA: Exact Change, 1996).
(23) Guy Debord, "Theory of the Dérive" [1958], trans. Kenneth Knabb, in *Situationist International Anthology* (Berkeley, CA: Bureau of Public Secrets, rev. ed., 2006), 62–66.
(24) Guy Debord, "A User's Guide to Détournement," trans. Kenneth Knabb, in *Situationist International Anthology* (Berkeley, CA: Bureau of Public Secrets, rev. ed., 2006), 14.
(25) Bernard Tschumi, *Manifesto 3: Advertisements for Architecture* (London: Architectural Association Press, 1976–77).

SECTIONING THE *UNHEIMLICH*

JANE TANKARD

SECTIONING THE *UNHEIMLICH* BY JANE TANKARD

'*...the uncanny can be understood as a form of memory that is lost, reconfigured and returned in altered form, occupying the space between subjective experience and objective history.*'

The physical spaces of a building's 'other', can be revealed through a number of informal and formal means of representation, but in the frame of the uncanny, the section is particularly compelling. At undergraduate Part 1 the section has become the critical signifier of student ability and skill: the separation between the digitally generated rhino-model and the completed autonomous section is, for good or otherwise, critical to proving competence. But through critical engagement with the section as site of revelatory intersectionality, other possibilities spring to life. In DS3.1 this process begins with filmic splicing and montage, smudging, blurring and slippage and the constructing of the exquisite corpse. (01) As Gordon Matta-Clark's full-scale chain-saw dissections of redundant, disused and discarded buildings demonstrates, the architectural cross-section is a tool that can reveal the hidden, concealed or obfuscated. The section splits and slices surface and material / flesh to expose voids, layers of making, evolution and construction, helping us to become acquainted with and confront the unknown, the unacquainted, familiar yet not, like La Passante: when you see her, you acknowledge she exists, if only in a fleeting moment of *Unheimlich*. (02)

(right) Camden Locus, Yi Shen, DS3.1

BASEMENT

"The cellar dreamer knows that the walls of the cellar are buried in the earth. He experiences the earth as a force of resistance. The rationality of the roof is opposed by the irrationality of the cellar." (03)

This separation and symbolic opposition is so central to notions of the domestic and the unconscious mind, that Carl Jung, in his Psychology and Alchemy, notably states:

"The conscious mind behaves like a man who, hearing a suspicious noise in the cellar, hurries up to the attic." (04)

Whether the underground spaces of a mansion secretly housing a starving family in Parasite (05) or the archive located beneath Mies van de Rohe's Barcelona Pavilion, in which broken or replaced remnants of the building's inhabited life are laid to rest, the basement is a space where the 'other' can reside. From archive to service infrastructure and the people (and the other hidden people) who maintain it. Robin Evans's *The Projective Cast: Architecture and Its Three Geometries* offers a framework for understanding the section not as a neutral, objective representation, but as a projective, paradoxical agential device, capable of generating architectural thought, form and memory. Evans states that:

"geometry […] may be an active agent in the links between thinking and imagination, imagination and drawing, drawing and building." (06)

In Freud's terms, the *Unheimlich* is that which transforms the homely or familiar into the unsettling and in the context of our studio, the architectural section functions as an uncanny tool, disclosing the latent, the infrastructural, the temporal, the disremembered. Drawing, as Evans reminds us, is not a transparent transmission but a selective projection, revealing through omission, distorting through convention and creating through its very act of representation. Robin Evans's longstanding preoccupation with architectural drawing as an agent of formation, not just representation, is a central point of reference when making drawings within the context of the studio. Evans argues that drawing is not a conduit for architecture but a generator; the potential building obeys the drawing as much as the drawing attempts to describe the building.

"The subject matter […] will exist after the drawing, not before it." (07)

Inspired by Evans notion, that the architectural drawing is propositional, DS3.1 considers the architectural drawing, and specifically the section, as a 'psycho-spatial' cut, one that exposes the interstitial condition of architectural 'otherness', whether real, conceptual or relational, that operates as a critical gesture of the uncanny, exposing concealed infrastructures, absence, hidden containment and paradoxical or synergistic relationships. In terms of methodology, the dynamic sectional drawing can be understood as a site for addition, adaptation, accretion, layering, cutting.

(top) Where the Body Turned Sunward, Malak Huseynova, DS3.1

(right) Sectional Models, Ozlem Incedal, DS3.1

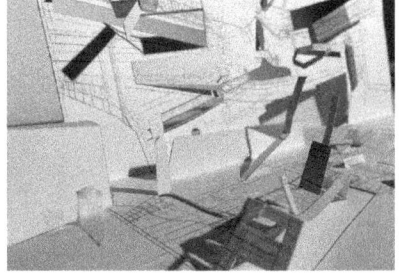

Evans disrupts the notion of orthographic projection as a purely objective abstract construction. Drawing techniques define the field of visibility, suppressing some elements and exaggerating others. Delving into the paradox of distortion serving revelation, he cites de l'Orme's parallel projection techniques, which produce forms that are:

"more unsettling, less predictable," expanding beyond *"the conventional inventory of forms."* (08)

In the section, form is fractured, continuity is disrupted, and hidden volumes become visible in the plane of representation. Yet, this visibility is partial; the immersive, layered, infrastructural spaces still resist full transparency.

The section acts as a critical device: a cut through our field of visibility that reveals overlooked spaces: cavities, holes, in-between spaces, deposits of use and memory, operating within Vidler's notions of the architectural uncanny revealing the hidden within the familiar constructional conditions. (09) The Barcelona Pavilion occupies a unique place in the mythology of modern architecture. Celebrated for its seamless planes, exquisite materials and apparent weightlessness, it has often been presented as a pure, autonomous object: an emblem of a modernism that aspired to dematerialise both structure and history. Its photographic canon, most notably the images that circulated after its reconstruction in 1986, reinforces this reading: a floating travertine plinth, a hovering roof, and a sequence of polished surfaces untroubled by depth or labour.

Yet beneath this celebrated surface lies an underworld rarely acknowledged: a basement that functions as both a technical repository and an archive of the Pavilion's own discontinuous history. This hidden layer, accessible only to maintenance staff and rarely represented in drawings, contains fragments from the Pavilion's dismantling in 1930, materials associated with its reconstruction and the residual detritus of its afterlife. It is, in effect, a material unconscious: a place where the Pavilion stores the evidence of its own erasure and return. The section, if drawn to include this earth-bound void, would transform the familiar image of the Pavilion. Instead of a weightless icon, it would become a stratified palimpsest, anchored by a murky archive beneath the plane of display. Robin Evans reminds us that architectural drawings are never neutral documents. They:

"make it possible to see some things more clearly by suppressing other things: something gained, something lost." (10)

The sections and plans that constitute the Pavilion's official image enact precisely this kind of selective vision: they frame a story of lightness and openness by omitting the infrastructural mechanisms and service spaces below. In doing so, they do more than misrepresent, they project a certain architectural ideal into being. Evans's observation that the subject matter will exist after the drawing, resonates here. (11) The Pavilion's revered section creates an object that never fully existed in such purity, erasing the contingency of its foundations in order to maintain the fiction of a hovering plane.

(right) Falling Parliament, Ozlem Incedal, DS3.1

The uncanny emerges at this moment. Freud's notion of the *Unheimlich* describes that which should have remained hidden but is brought to light. The Pavilion's basement is precisely such a site: familiar yet estranged, part of the same architectural body yet disavowed in its public life. To descend into that space, or even to imagine it, is to destabilise the polished image above. The celebrated surface becomes in fact the lid of a container, the exhibitionary frame becomes the threshold of an archive. What is most uncanny is not the mere existence of this basement but the fact that its concealment has been so thorough, its erasure so effective that for decades the Pavilion was remembered as if it floated free of any such weight. If the section were to be drawn with full disclosure, it would puncture the myth of autonomy that surrounds the Pavilion. It would force an acknowledgment that modernist architecture, far from immaterial, relies upon storage, labour and matter that rarely enter its iconography.

The section is therefore not simply a technical cut: it is an ethical and historiographic instrument. To reveal the basement is to reveal the Pavilion's own repressed temporality the fact that it was dismantled, stored, reconstructed and is still maintained through an invisible system of cleaning, maintenance and protective activity. In this light, the Barcelona Pavilion becomes less a timeless object and more a temporal palimpsest: a building with a double body, one above ground, one below. The architectural drawing, in its canonical form, has conspired to produce the former by suppressing the latter. A counter-section, one that traces the subterranean archive, could function as a form of historical psychoanalysis, bringing the Pavilion's unconscious to the surface.

DISAPPEARING ACT

The Tugendhat House in Brno (1930), also designed by Mies van der Rohe, is widely celebrated for its sliding glass wall: a vast panel that lowers mechanically to dissolve the boundary between salon and garden. In canonical photographs, this moment is presented as the epitome of modernist openness: the house appears to merge seamlessly with the garden landscape, the boundary between interior and exterior fully erased.

Yet this image of dematerialisation depends on an act of concealment. The glass does not vanish into thin air; it descends into a deep mechanical pocket housed within the basement wall; a void rarely depicted and almost never discussed in the celebratory narratives of the house. The section becomes here a device of revelation and mystification. In most published representations, the wall is drawn as an elegant line, its thickness reduced, its cavity omitted. To include the pocket would be to acknowledge the machinery behind transparency: the motors, counterweights and guides that make the vanishing act possible. Robin Evans argues that the architectural drawing is not a passive record but a projection of intention:

"It carries intention; it is propositional." [12]

The Tugendhat drawings, in their edited form, project an ideal of seamless continuity by overlooking the infrastructural void that enables it. From the perspective of the uncanny, this pocket is a minor yet potent site. Freud described the uncanny as the moment when the familiar becomes estranged by the return of what was repressed.

(top) Section, Wizana Ahmed, DS3.1

(bottom left) Camden Room, Yi Shen, DS3.1

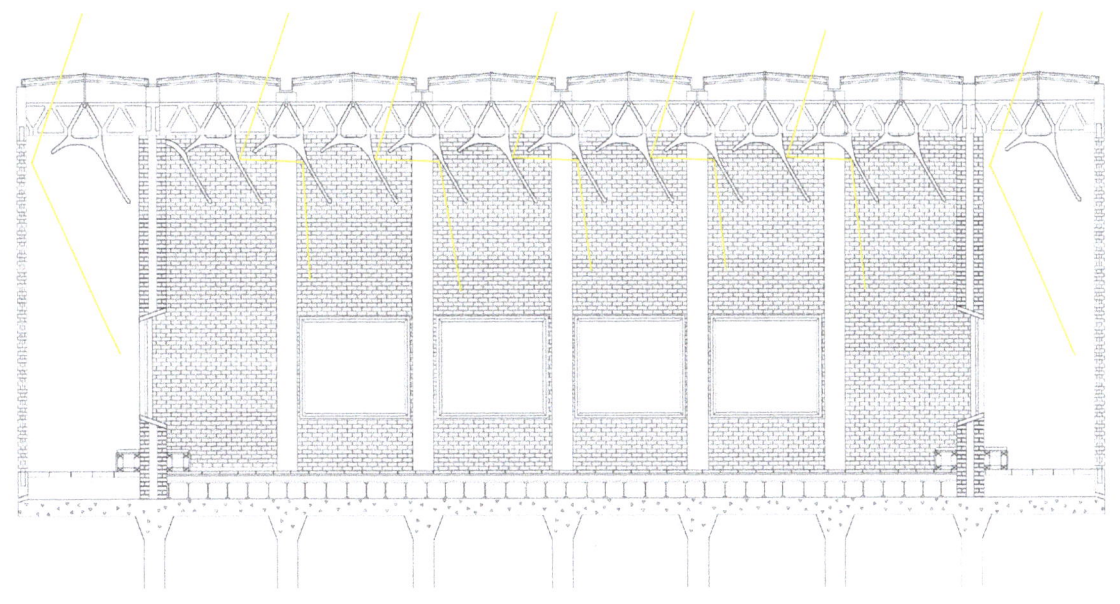

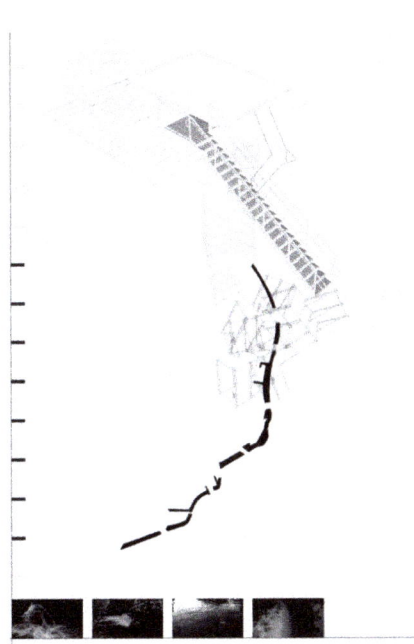

The sliding glass, celebrated for its absence, leaves behind a concealed volume that is both integral and excluded. It is the tomb of transparency: a hidden cavity that sustains the illusion of openness while remaining itself invisible. One might say that the house is haunted by this void, which lurks at its very threshold between inside and outside. Evans's reflections in *The Projective Cast* on doors, passages and thresholds are instructive: (12) he notes how architectural elements that negotiate passage are often the most conceptually loaded yet least represented. The glass pocket is precisely such an element. It is a threshold turned inward, a cavity that allows modernism to stage its dematerialisation while displacing the apparatus elsewhere. To acknowledge this cavity in section is to disrupt the image of the Tugendhat House. It introduces friction into what is usually portrayed as effortless transparency. It shows that openness is not a natural property of the architecture, but a performance achieved through hidden labour.

The uncanny here is not an anomaly but a structural condition: the absence that enables presence, the void that makes the view.

GHOST

The Farmers' and Mechanics' Savings Bank in Minneapolis (1891), designed by Louis Sullivan, holds a different kind of secret. In 1995 Clare Cardinal-Pett, an architectural academic at Iowa State University, discovered a set of full-scale drawings of the building's construction and decoration. These drawings had been forgotten for nearly a century, surviving the building's changing ownerships, its economic cycles and the fading of its original programme.

They were not part of the bank's official value system of currency and contracts passed through the vault, but these drawings endured, dormant and invisible. (13)

Evans's observation that 'the subject matter […] will exist after the drawing, not before it' (14) reminds us that the drawings are not passive remnants of a historical design process, but active 'potentials', carrying Sullivan's intentions forward across time until their rediscovery (re)activated them. Their latency is architectural, shaping the bank's ornament when first produced, then becoming an archive of its making and finally emerging as historical treasure, long after their original function as a contractor's mapped guide, had expired. The vault is an uncanny space, another basement and in this case a chamber of deferred presence, where drawings outlived their original purpose and became something else. If one were to draw a section through this building with that vault in mind, it would no longer read as a neutral service zone. It would become the building's true core: a repository of its aesthetic DNA, its ghostly double. This case foregrounds another aspect of Evans's thinking: that drawings have 'directional agency'. (15) They project futures, but those futures may not unfold on schedule. The Farmers' Bank drawings projected ornament into the early 20th century, but they also projected a latent archive into the late 20th, when they re-emerged as historical documents. The uncanny lies in this temporal fold: a drawing that belongs to two times at once, a line that waited decades to become visible again.

Gordon Matta-Clark's practice makes the section real at 1:1, his interventions expose hidden construction, structure and voids, making new connections and spatial sequences.

(top) Refuge, Wizana Ahmed, DS3.1 *(right) Night Elevation, Isabella Testolin, DS3.1*

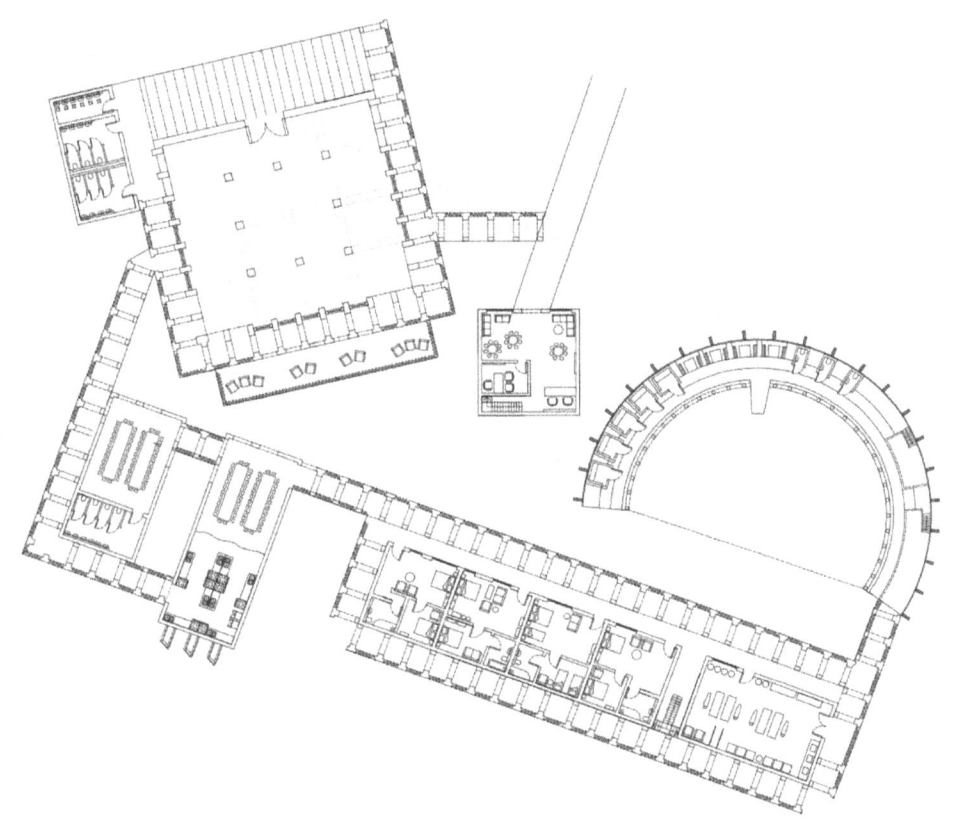

In works including Day's End or Splitting, (16) Matta-Clark 'sections' architecture physically, walls contain voids, floors are fissures. The cuts are uncanny intrusions, surgical, abrupt, revelatory, where hidden space and structural paradoxes are made visible through rupture and dismembering. Evans's representational section and Matta-Clark's physical cut share a conceptual lineage: both disclose the repressed in architecture. Their difference lies in matter, drawing versus demolition, but the result in both it could be argued, exposes the architectural unconscious, the infra-visible, the negative spaces that shape our experience. In contrast, Rachel Whiteread's House (17) inverts or reverses the section: instead of cutting into architecture, she casts its voids into solid form.

The casting of the negative space of a house transforms emptiness into monolithic presence, an uncanny reversal. From Evans position, Whiteread's work acknowledges that the most compelling spaces are often those that are absent - the latent voids that drawing rarely represents. The section extracts such voids visually, whilst Whiteread extracts them materially. The uncanny lies in inhabiting absence: the space you cannot enter becomes a formidable structure, monumental and estranged. For DS3.1, Evans's theoretical framing provides a unifying lens: drawing is generative, sections reveal while concealing, geometry is active, nothing is passive. The Barcelona Pavilion's basement, the Tugendhat's hydraulic housing, Sullivan's drawings, Matta-Clark's cuts and Whiteread's House each manifest the section's power to transform the familiar into the *Unheimlich* by exposing the interstitial and overlooked. In each instance, the section is not a scientific document but a psycho-architectural cut.

It is where architecture's unconscious reveals itself as a ghostly presence, its underbelly, its memory. The *Unheimlich* is not an external spectre but an internal one, exposed through the drawing (or cutting) of the section.

THE INTERSTITIAL BODY: INTERSECTIONALITY AND THE UNCANNY.

The *Unheimlich* has traditionally been approached as a psychic and spatial phenomenon, a moment where the familiar becomes estranged, or where the home reveals its latent unfamiliarity. Psychoanalytic and architectural theory have mapped this territory through thresholds, liminal spaces, and haunting residues. Yet, what is often absent from such accounts is the embodied dimension of the uncanny as lived and negotiated by those whose very presence is positioned at the margins: the racialised, the queer, the itinerant, the feminised, the working-class service worker whose labour maintains the domestic and urban spaces that others claim as home. Intersectionality, as theorised by Kimberlé Crenshaw (18) and expanded through the writings of Audre Lorde (19) and bell hooks, (20) insists that identity is not a singular axis but a dynamic constellation of race, gender, sexuality, class, and ability. Within this frame, the uncanny is not only an aesthetic or psychoanalytic effect but a structural condition: it emerges when bodies historically excluded or rendered invisible in the architectural and social order occupy or pass through spaces that were never designed with them in mind. The *Unheimlich*, in this sense, is a byproduct of the refusal to recognise difference as constitutive of the social fabric. The notion of the sectional drawing in architecture, a cross-section that reveals the hidden infrastructures of a building, offers a compelling metaphor for this layered experience.

(top) Sensing the Data Slaughterhouse, Inaaya Amer, DS3.1

(bottom) Mayday Rooms, Rowan St John, DS3.1

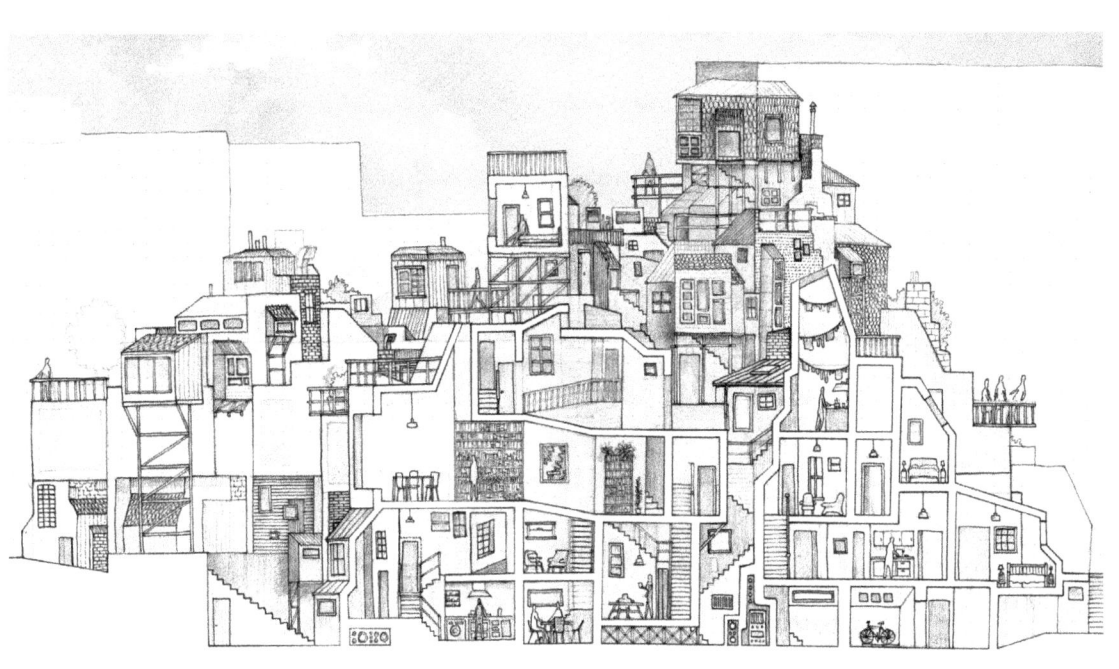

It slices through the apparent wholeness of the home, the street, the institution, to expose its concealed workings: the service corridors, the labouring bodies, the quiet networks of exclusion and maintenance. This cut is itself uncanny, for it discloses that the stable interior is propped upon an interstitial economy, often inhabited by those whose presence is systematically disavowed. Here, the migrant cleaner or the night-shift worker becomes the ghost in the machine, essential and unacknowledged. Audre Lorde warned against the 'mythical norm' that structures belonging, insisting that:

"those of us who stand outside the circle of this society's definition of acceptable women... know that survival is not an academic skill." [21]

In *Teaching to Transgress*, bell hooks framed the classroom as a site where the body and its histories must be present if liberation is to be more than theoretical. They reframed the classroom as a site of embodied possibility:

"The classroom remains the most radical space of possibility in the academy." [22]

To deny the body is to pretend education is objective; instead, she insists on a pedagogy that:

"acknowledges that we are bodies in the classroom"

...And values emotion as epistemic power. This insistence disrupts the mind/body dualism and affirms that liberation is enmeshed with bodily presence. [23]

Paulo Freire called for a pedagogy of the oppressed that does not merely include the marginalised as an afterthought, but begins with their experience as the ground for transformation, a notion that determines how we operate in the studio working hard towards inclusivity, intersectionality and listening [24] and think about how we understand and utilise the section as an extension of our cultural experience and awareness. To read the uncanny through this lens is to ask: whose hauntings are we seeing and whose remain unseen?

The black lesbian poet whose body is both hyper-visible and erased; the traveller whose temporary occupation of space is policed and pathologised; the care worker whose nightly rounds maintain the illusion of seamless domesticity, all inhabit the interstices where architecture, policy and prejudice converge. Their uncanny is not an abstract disturbance of the familiar, but a lived oscillation between hyper-visibility (as threat, as service, as other) and invisibility (as subject, as neighbour, as kin).

The interstitial is both a material and political condition: the corridor, the threshold, the back-of-house, the service entrance, the camp, the shelter. These are the architectures of intersectionality, where the body bears the psychic and structural load of exclusion. To engage with the *Unheimlich* responsibly in architectural discourse demands that we move beyond the fetish of estrangement as aesthetic, toward an ethics of making visible those bodies and labours that have always been there, holding up the walls. But the schism is huge because the driver of the profession is commodity, not society.

(top) Whitechapel Pleasure Garden, Beth Allen, DS3.1

(bottom) Mayday Rooms, Rowan St John, DS3.1

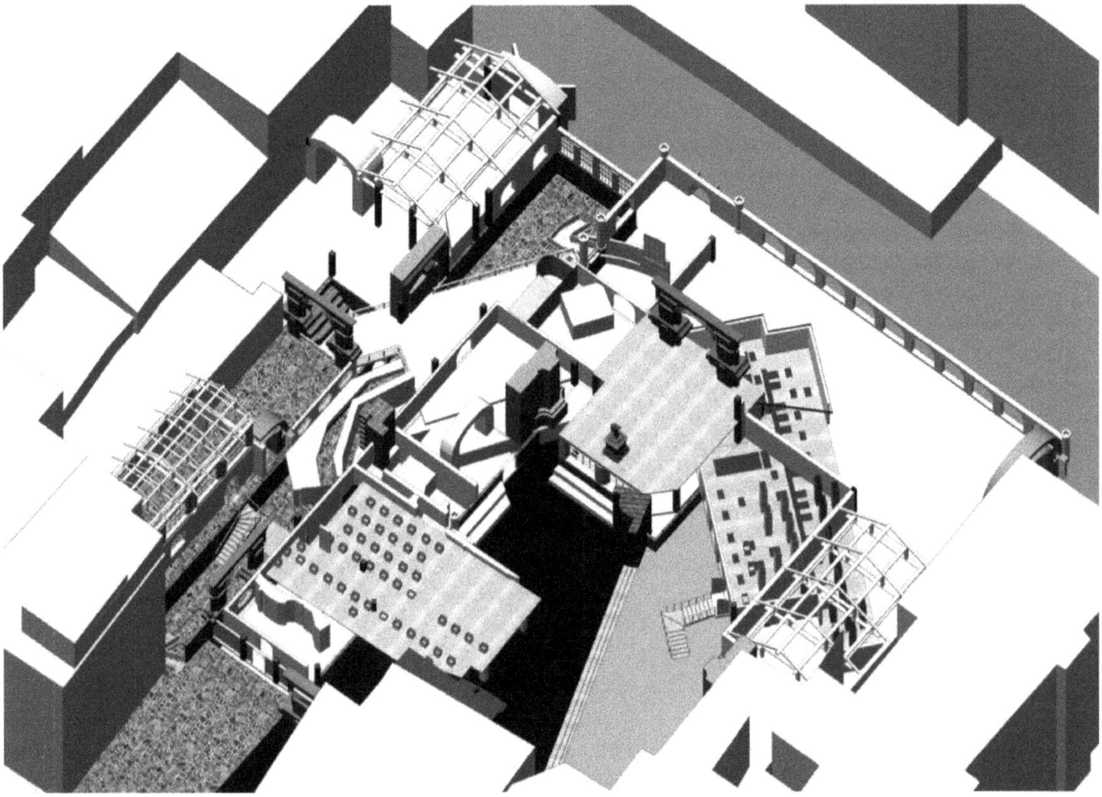

113

MEMORY

If intersectionality exposes the architectures where marginalised bodies are made to carry the hidden structures of everyday life, memory traces how those bodies and labours slip from view, becoming spectral. The interstitial, in this sense, is not only a spatial condition but a temporal one: a threshold between what is remembered and what is made to disappear. The uncanny emerges when these suppressed histories insist on their return, not as intact narratives, but as fragments, distortions, and echoes that unsettle the present. To write of the *Unheimlich* in architecture, then, is to write of memory as a contested terrain, where the violence of erasure meets the persistence of what was meant to be forgotten. In this sense, the uncanny can be understood as a form of memory that is lost, reconfigured, and returned in altered form, occupying the space between subjective experience and objective history. As Svetlana Boym argues:

"memory is not retrieved intact but continually reconstructed, often shaped by nostalgia and loss." [25]

The uncanny, then, is not an absence of memory but its dislocation and repression, resurfacing as a distorted echo that produces estranged familiarity. Sigmund Freud's account of the *Unheimlich* captures this dynamic: the uncanny arises when something once known and intimate, but long repressed, resurfaces in unsettling form. [26] Anthony Vidler extends this logic to architecture, showing how spaces once secure and familiar can become alien through displacement, abandonment, or transformation. [27]

Jacques Derrida's notion of hauntology further underscores this persistence of the past as spectral traces that unsettle the present, neither fully present nor wholly absent. [28] In academic discourse, memory itself is a contested ground. While its value as a construct in architecture is widely acknowledged, the scholar who engages with it often faces accusations of subjectivity or indulgence in so-called 'cosiness'. Yet in the design studio, the very blurring of subjective and objective realms generates a fertile ground for experimentation: superimposition, layering, phenomenology and even intuition open up interstitial sites of creativity. DS3.1 embraces this blurring between the subjective and objective, treating site as a form of metaphorical archaeology, excavated, uncovered, revealed. Threads and narratives drawn from local archives, physical observation and experimental making as already touched on combine with careful research analysis to identify events that will lead to the choreographing of process: an archaeology of the familiar and the unfamiliar, a search for ghosts.

"The Representation on the maps of a road, track or footpath is no evidence of the existence of a right of way." [29]

In 1995, I joined the Desiring Practices curatorial team, founded by Sarah Wigglesworth, Katerina Rüedi, and Duncan McCorquodale. [30] The project, comprising a symposium at the RIBA, a series of installations and exhibitions, and a book of collected papers, brought together artists, theorists, and Architects, many of whom refused fixed professional categories and were known simply as practitioners.

(top) The Imaginary, Nicolas de la Flor Rey, DS3.1

(bottom right) The Bridge, Finola Simpson, DS3.1

The majority of participants were women, and much of the work explored interdisciplinary thinking at the intersections of psychoanalytic theory, film (Laura Mulvey), (31) and cultural theory within art for example the work of Helen Chadwick. (32) As stated in the project's description:

"Such investigations have revealed an immense new territory for architecture, where gender-consciousness and interdisciplinary work stimulate the creation of new practices which are potentially more accessible to a wider audience."

Desiring Practices did much to introduce me to notions of the liminal, the spaces between, as Katerina Ruedi articulated in a design brief - the potential for an architecture against the grain but in particular the contested body and the creative opportunities in the full breadth of representational media, from photography and sculpture, to film-making and 1:1 construction drawings. The principles of crafting and iterative making, of sharing work, of dissolving autonomy over others and the issues of process-production, of the error in not looking hard enough, of glossing over the surface, are principles that became fully embedded during that brief moment in time, principles that remain central to the studio practice. One of the (accepted) proposals for the exhibitions was by Sylvia Lanvin an artist who explores language. The recently uncovered letter she sent to me in physical form having been typed on an analogue typewriter, reads as follows:

LA PASSANTE.

The Flâneur, gentleman stroller, has the city as the site of his pleasure; he 'charges time with power like a battery'. The spectacle is at his disposal. He idles, window shops, stops for a little cognac here, a coffee there, observes at his leisure. The fall of night is no cause for haste. There is no female equivalent except La Passante, the woman who passes by. She cannot stop, cannot partake of the pleasures of the city unless chaperoned or accompanied by another form of protection, unless she is herself a pleasure of the city. She must keep moving or she will become one more of all the commodities on display. In standing still she becomes a worker, of the day or night, a mass article, street sign of the city. Walter Benjamin notes of Baudelaire that the street is always his arena for amorous encounter, never the closed house, the 'maison de passe'. The street walker doesn't walk far, she inscribes her position on a short and wellworn route, easily recognised or remembered. The streets one might say, are named for her:

"Ada, Adela, Adelaide, Adelina, Adeline, Adrienne, Alba, Alexa, Alexandra, Alexis, Alice, Alicia, Alma, Alwyne, Amber, Amelia, Amethyst, Amina, Anatola, Angel, Angelica, Annabel, Anna, Anne, April, Arabella, Arcadia, Ashley, Astra, Atalanta, Augusta..."

(A geographer might start to trace her passing in a reference book that has lost sight of its intended purpose).

(top left) La Passante, Sharon Kivland, Design Practices Exhibition, 1995, photograph by Jane Tankard

(bottom right) La Passante, Sharon Kivland, Design Practices Exhibition, 1995, photograph by Jane Tankard

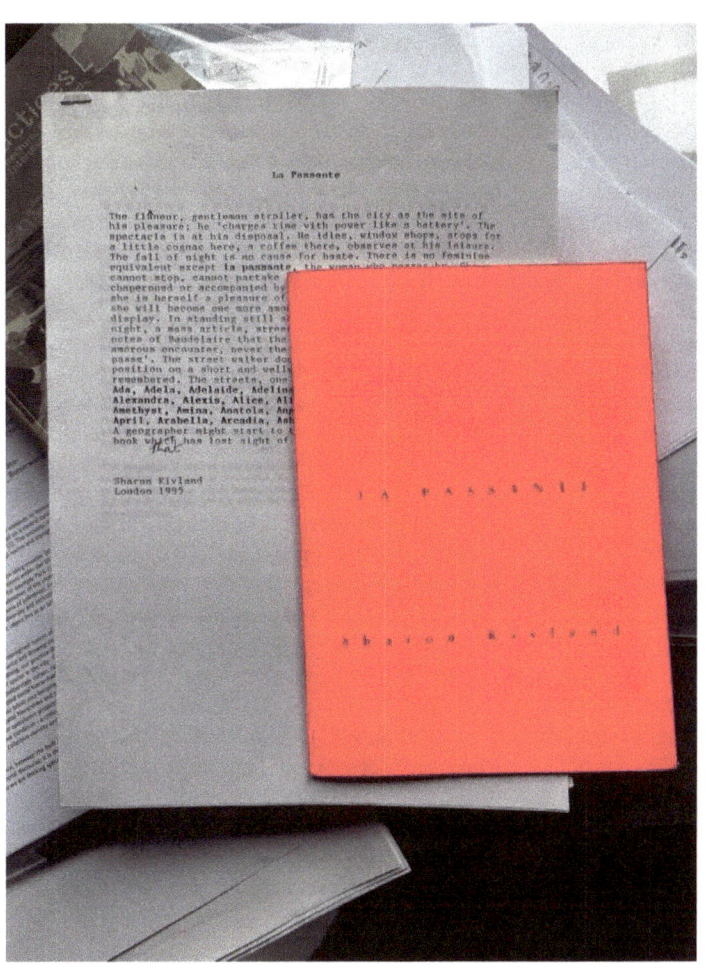

Whilst wandering the streets of Limehouse on a studio dérive, we came across a number of notices posted by someone who named themselves 'Louise Brown, local prostitute', see images opposite. (33, 34) Unlike the usual colourful, image-based, glossy flyers and postcards pinned to telephone box walls in the late 1980s and 90s, these A4 posters were striking in both their simple appearance and their unusual urban locations, always beyond arms reach, high up and requiring a ladder, mostly on lamp posts and the backs of traffic signs very basic with a simple text on photocopy paper.
It was clear that the process of advertising had had some kind of evolutionary process, perhaps because of an initial failure to address the intended audience or in response to customer feedback or, perhaps simply on personal reflection. Either way, the poster had been printed and then amended; large black words (about 48pt) on ordinary white paper that post-printing had been underlined and graphically organised by hand with a thick marker pen to become a message much more akin to a poster with a headline. 'Affordable Prostitute, Louise Brown' is enclosed by a drawn box with shading inside the box around the letters and below some underlined contact information. This woman La Passante is communicating from within the domestic interior, no longer taking up the space of the urban street walker, safe or otherwise from the troubling question of where she is located in the Flaneur' city, she reaches out in analogue form. Perhaps her phone died.

"But tell us, is the poster scantily clad? It will know how to lure the broken and the bored, like a convergence of the lonely alleyways to where there's a bit of sunshine. The poster sitting high up the post, hard stapled in place by a towering pimpy hand. It's all love somehow from free teenage hugs (like touches bursting with hope) on the one hand and on the other a pound's worth of shell love (hard handed and devoid of something). Most of us live somewhere in the middle, one foot either side, hoping, hopping as we feel sure or insecure. Who is your father? That happened in the middle of the spectrum too.

Can we all live together, in this kind of a convergence city of alleyways (where we tolerate), and 15 mins in any direction (where we infect with joy) passing all kinds of important people and places along the way: the reliable trash man in uniform (the deepest lover of the city), ladies in headdress, birds named red breast, ancient watching-us forests, swings, cars and cars, heat islands, water flows, Ascot coats, and cute Asian babies, and the lovely hidden lakes for skinny swims washing our psyche and our belly buttons.

Does the scantily clad have a reserve fund for her spot, or a pension? Does it cover root canals and shaky tongues or just braces for looks? This is a major moment in the institutional fund of society, how we keep our sewers clear, our buildings escapable, and our lake edges crispy. The money comes from the full spectrum of love." (35)

(bottom left) Note from Jane's daughter listening to her reading the text to the Studio Juggernaut group date

(top right) Street Poster, Limehouse, photograph by Jane Tankard

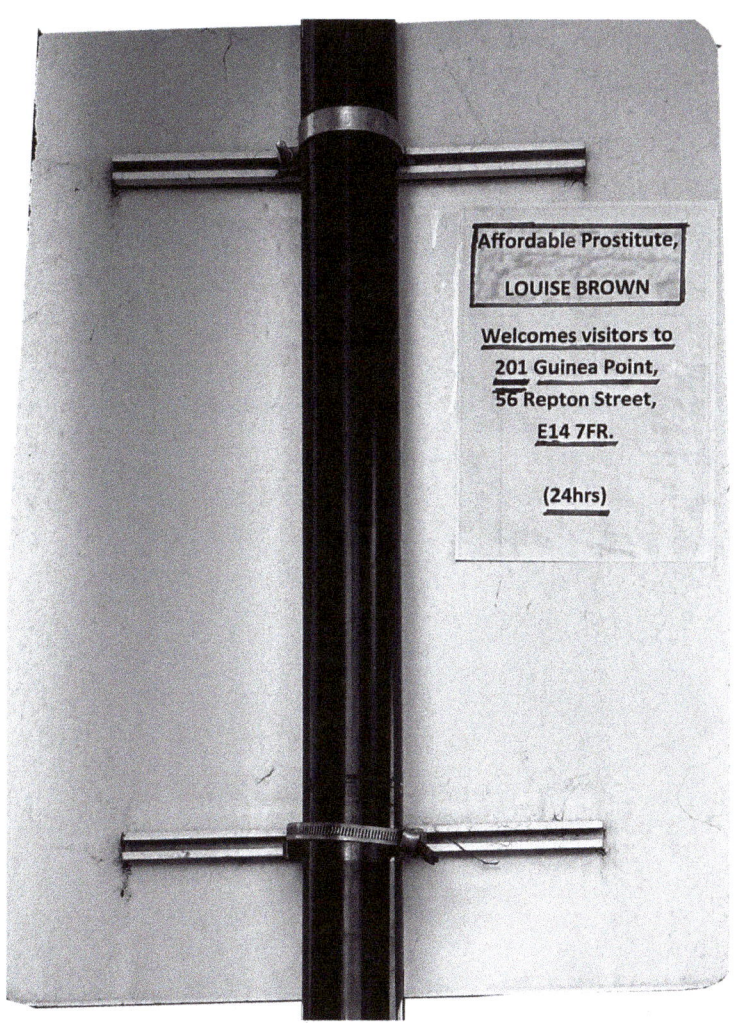

Your not allowed to use the term prostitute anymore by the way its not politically correct

You have to say sex worker

> Ok!!!! Its her text though the sex worker's I mean

Ok hahaha

Someone told me off the other day for using prostitute

The posters become markers of the individuals who make up any local community. Louise evolves our understanding of client and neighbourhood context. A number of intriguing questions emerge, both in relationship to the notion of the city as gendered space and the potential for spaces of transgression to be valued, even celebrated. Spaces where women have agency and autonomy were tabled and configured, with the notion of a sexy, flirtatious and visceral architectural language excavated and reformed, from peep show to pornography.

Drawing inspiration from the pioneering work of Carol-Ann Schneemann, whose kinetic paintings explored the relationship between the human body and its surroundings, seeking to push the boundaries of what is possible in dance and performance art, (36) Isabella Testolin designed a piece of adaptive architecture specifically to stimulate the senses and create environments that inspire transgressionary creativity, while fostering a sense of community and inclusivity. What does this mean for a final degree project, but more importantly, for Louise? We contact a local sex-worker support group and Social Condenser stops being theoretical and becomes a project with La Passante centre-stage. Aligning the streetwalker with the middle-class artist/performer Carole-Anne Shneeman, the project asks what the New York Judson Dance Theatre reconvened in Limehouse could offer Louise and her network; the group suggests a space for performance artists and, one woman clarifies, their 'estranged dysfunctional parents'. This particular journey through the uncanny may be described as a memory lost and reconfigured, a space in which forgetting and remembering fold into one another.

To call a space uncanny is to recognise that memory can be a catalyst for transformation: erasing, rearranging and resurfacing in unfamiliar forms. Freud named this idea of the uncanny as the familiar made strange; Vidler found it in the estrangement of built form; Boym understood it as nostalgia's reconstructive force whilst Derrida thought about it as the spectral persistence of the past. But at the moment of the manifesting of this project, at its core, the uncanny can be understood as a mechanism that reveals how memory itself is creative. Working with the political recuperation of alternative, disruptive lifestyles and behaviours manifesting in adhoc and uncontrolled, unfixed, porous architecture, reworking the past into something at once intimate and alien that can be a transactional is understood as an offering for social exchange.

(top) Sex, Amy Wallace, DS3.1

(bottom right) Viv's Funeral Pyre, Amy Wallace, DS3.1

NOTES

(01) *Cadavre Exquis (Exquisite Corpse)*, Tate, https://www.tate.org.uk/art/art-terms/c/cadavre-exquis-exquisite-corpse.
(02) Susan Buck-Morss, *The Dialectics of Seeing: Walter Benjamin and the Arcades Project* (Cambridge, MA: MIT Press, 1991).
(03) Gaston Bachelard, *The Poetics of Space*, trans. Maria Jolas (Boston: Beacon Press, 1994 [orig. 1958]).
(04) C. G. Jung, *Psychology and Alchemy*, trans. R. F. C. Hull (Princeton, NJ: Princeton University Press, 1968).
(05) Bong Joon Ho, dir., *Parasite* (Seoul: Barunson E&A, 2019; distributed by Neon), film.
(06) Robin Evans, *Translations from Drawing to Building and Other Essays* (Cambridge, MA: MIT Press, 1997).
(07) Ibid.
(08) Ibid.
(09) Anthony Vidler, *The Architectural Uncanny: Essays in the Modern Unhomely* (Cambridge, MA: MIT Press, 1992).
(10) Robin Evans, *Translations from Drawing to Building and Other Essays* (Cambridge, MA: MIT Press, 1997).
(11) Robin Evans, "Figures, Doors and Passages," in *Translations from Drawing to Building and Other Essays*, ed. Robin Evans (Cambridge, MA: MIT Press, 1997).
(12) Ibid.
(13) Clare Cardinal-Pett, "Detailing," in *Desiring Practices: Architecture, Gender and the Interdisciplinary*, ed. Katerina Rüedi, Sarah Wigglesworth, and Duncan McCorquodale (London: Black Dog Publishing, 1996).
(14) Robin Evans, *Translations from Drawing to Building and Other Essays* (Cambridge, MA: MIT Press, 1997).
(15) Ibid.
(16) Mark Wigley, *Cutting Matta-Clark: The Anarchitecture Investigation* (Zurich: Lars Müller Publishers, 2018).
(17) Rachel Whiteread, *House*, ed. James Lingwood (London: Artangel and Phaidon Press, 1995).
(18) Kimberlé Crenshaw, "Demarginalizing the Intersection of Race and Sex: A Black Feminist Critique of Antidiscrimination Doctrine, Feminist Theory, and Antiracist Politics," *University of Chicago Legal Forum* 1989, no. 1 (1989).
(19) Audre Lorde, "Age, Race, Class, and Sex: Women Redefining Difference," in *Sister Outsider: Essays and Speeches* (Trumansburg, NY: Crossing Press, 1984).
(20) bell hooks, *Ain't I a Woman: Black Women and Feminism* (Boston: South End Press, 1981).
(21) Ibid.
(22) Paulo Freire, *Pedagogy of the Oppressed*, trans. Myra Bergman Ramos (New York: Continuum, 1970).
(23) Svetlana Boym, *The Future of Nostalgia* (New York: Basic Books, 2001).
(24) Sigmund Freud, "The Uncanny" (1919), in *The Standard Edition of the Complete Psychological Works of Sigmund Freud, Vol. XVII (1917–1919): An Infantile Neurosis and Other Works*, ed. and trans. James Strachey (London: Hogarth Press, 1955).
(25) Anthony Vidler, *The Architectural Uncanny: Essays in the Modern Unhomely* (Cambridge, MA: MIT Press, 1992).
(26) Jacques Derrida, *Specters of Marx: The State of the Debt, the Work of Mourning, & the New International*, trans. Peggy Kamuf (New York: Routledge, 1994).
(27) Sharon Lanvin, *La Passante*, hand-published document produced to coincide with the *Desiring Practices* exhibitions (1995).
(28) Katerina Rüedi, Sarah Wigglesworth, and Duncan McCorquodale, *Desiring Practices: Architecture, Gender and the Interdisciplinary* (London: Black Dog Publishing, 1996).
(29) Laura Mulvey, "Cinematic Space: Desiring and Deciphering," in *Desiring Practices: Architecture, Gender and the Interdisciplinary*, ed. Duncan McCorquodale, Katerina Rüedi, and Sarah Wigglesworth (London: Black Dog Publishing, 1996).
(30) Laura Smith, *Helen Chadwick: Life Pleasures* (London: Thames & Hudson, 2025).
(31) Laura Mulvey.
(32) Helen Chadwick.
(33) Street Poster, Limehouse, photograph by Jane Tankard
(34) Note from Jane's daughter listening to her reading the text to the Studio Juggernaut group date
(35) Maria Faraone and Studio Juggernaut research group, unpublished writing.
(36) Sabine Breitwieser, ed., *Carolee Schneemann: Kinetic Painting* (Munich: Prestel Publishing, 2015).

SPECULATIVE CITY: TWO ISTANBUL TYPOLOGIES FOR URBAN COLLECTIVISM

DENIZ ÇETIN + ÇAĞDA ÖZBAKI

SPECULATIVE CITY: TWO ISTANBUL TYPOLOGIES FOR URBAN COLLECTIVISM BY DENIZ ÇETIN + ÇAĞDA ÖZBAKI ALTINBAŞ UNIVERSITY, ISTANBUL

'This [...] appears as a kind of control mechanism for the society's strangers, bachelors, namely, others'

This paper examines Istanbul's urban Hans and neighborhood/community orchards (Bostans) as spatial manifestations of collective living and production, urban practices that date back to the Byzantine and Ottoman periods. These spaces, hybrid sites of work, lodging, trade, and cultivation, created distinctive social and economic identities in Istanbul, identities that continue to shape the city's urban fabric, daily life, and community practices. Hans and Bostans operate as material and symbolic forms of sustainability, ecology, and self-sufficiency, and they also embody resistance to contemporary neo-capitalist urban politics.

URBAN HANS

Hans are mixed use buildings that enable commercial transaction, storage, and temporary accommodation for travellers and traders in urban and rural contexts. [01] Originating in Central Asia, they developed in Iran and, under the influence of the Anatolian Seljuks, were incorporated into Ottoman social, economic, and commercial life. [02] The plan of a Han generally consists of a central courtyard surrounded by porticos that act as a deep threshold to rooms beyond that serve as workshops, domestic accommodation, sites of exchange and temporary use. Usually two stories high, with storage and commercial activities on the ground floor and accommodation on the upper floor, [03] this hybrid use accommodated both travellers and local specialised trade. [04] Traditionally, Hans were considered 'doors opening to the outside world', where tradesmen and craftsmen from different communities met and exchanged not only goods but professional culture, ensuring the cosmopolitan merchant class gained a privileged status in Ottoman society. [05]

(top) Ecological Enclave, Hafsa Syed, DS3.1

(lower right) Kuzguncuk Pervititich Hill, photograph by Deniz Çetin

Provincial Hans also served as physical hubs linking Istanbul and other parts of the empire; the mix of permanent and transient inhabitation enabled the circulation of knowledge, beliefs and experience as part of a socio-cultural network. In terms of accommodation, Hans functioned as temporary houses for strangers, facilitating social and commercial interaction. In addition to traders and travellers, civil servants, soldiers and workers resided in Hans, which were understood as controlled spaces where strangers and their activities were monitored and isolated from city dwellers. Han 'keepers' registered residents and goods, ensuring security, enforcing rules and maintaining the Han as a policed public dwelling for the 'unidentifiable visitors' of Ottoman society. [06] According to Ottoman records of the early 19th century, Istanbul housed 593 Urban Hans. [07] One example is Kurşunlu Han in Galata, a harbour district on the northern side of the Golden Horn dating back to the Byzantine period and the Genoese colony of the 13th century. Built in the 16th century, Kurşunlu Han occupies the site of the Byzantine church Hagia Thekla and the Genoese church of San Michele. [08] During the Genoese period, Galata was a walled trade city, with San Michele Church adjacent to a loggia used for public and commercial activities, accommodation, shops, and storage. Kurşunlu Han inherited this heritage of social assembly and gathering. [09] Kurşunlu Han, likely designed by Architect Sinan in 1550, belonged to a foundation under Grand Vizier Rüstem Pasha. [10]

Its rectangular east-west plan has two entrances along this axis, two floors, a central staircase in a narrow courtyard, and porticos around the courtyard on both levels providing access to rooms. [11] The Han supported Galata's thriving commercial and craft culture, including blacksmithing, sailmaking, rope production, and metalwork, servicing the maritime economy of the port. [12] Between the 16th and 18th centuries, Kurşunlu Han functioned as a storage and distribution hub for goods arriving at the port. By the 19th and 20th centuries, it hosted production and storage of maritime trade materials and flammable substances such as alcohol, wine, cologne, and spirits, alongside publishing activities like bookbinding, printing, and newspapers. [13]

Galata became a cosmopolitan harbour district with a multi-national mosaic of inhabitants, traders, merchants, artisans, and travellers. Urban Hans became places of tolerance, where different religious and ethnic groups could live together in communal arrangements. Multiple types of work occurred simultaneously in the same space: a jewellery designer, a spring manufacturer, and a bookbinder might all operate in one building, with overlapping noise, dust, and visitors, illustrating genuine co-working and collaboration. [14] Architecturally, the portico served as a semi-public space between private rooms and the courtyard, defining circulation while generating an open, climatically rich environment that fostered interaction. Historian Edhem Eldem notes that while Galata was not a fully cosmopolitan community, Hans and loggias created nodes of coexistence where production, communication, and accumulation met. [15] In the second half of the 20th century, rapid urbanisation and homogenisation transformed Galata, eroding its multiplicity, commercial identity, and unique urban fabric. Declining sea trade, relocation of business, and gentrification threatened the legacy of co-existence and co-production in Hans. Today, Hans face touristification, rent speculation, and privatisation, while remaining crucial sites for artisans, makers, and analogue designers navigating contemporary Istanbul. [16] [17]

Istanbul's Hans are currently at the centre of political and cultural debates: they demonstrate how traditional craftsmen and makers - particularly those working in architectural metals, timber, and analogue techniques can coexist with contemporary Architects, designers, and non-conformist makers in the city centre; a cultural intervention that embeds interaction, analogue craft, and collective memory, situating Hans and craft practices within a contemporary urban discourse.

NEIGHBOURHOOD/COMMUNITY ORCHARDS

It can be suggested that we live our daily lives in cities shaped, altered and transformed under the supervision of capitalist governance regardless of community desire or need. Istanbul is not exception. Nevertheless, this was not always the case.

(upper right) Kurşunlu Han (framed by the authors) on Plan d'assurance de Constantinople. Vol. II - Péra & Galata. No: 26. (1905) by Charles Edward Goad (Salt Research, Harika-Kemali Söylemezoğlu Archive).

Throughout its history, there have been significant distinguishing cultural, spatial and institutional specificities that have encouraged and enabled collectivism and co-operation. Bostans urban orchards or vegetable gardens - have been essential to Istanbul's ecological and social landscape for centuries, bringing marginalised communities into the urban fold. These "traditional market gardens" were woven into daily life, supplying fresh produce to the city. [18] Unlike the private gardens of the sultan, called hasbahçe, Bostans were cultivated by diverse social classes, including commoners and officials, often managed by the Bostancılar [19] guilds. By efficiently manipulating space, season, and resources, Istanbul Bostans were intensively, skillfully, and sustainably cultivated over centuries to boost harvests. The master cultivators (gardeners) of the Bostans were regarded as authorities, organised into guilds, and held in great regard. An integral component of Istanbul's identity and memory, production was integrated into urban food systems, sold both wholesale and retail.

Different neighborhoods were known for the speciality crops of their gardens which gave distinct identities to neighbourhoods, for example, fresh string beans of Beykoz, artichokes of Bayrampaşa, lettuce of Yedikule, strawberry of Arnavutköy, cucumber of Çengelköy. [20] Bostans also demonstrate marginalised inclusion, with seasonal workers, migrants, and informal labourers contributing to urban production networks. Typical Istanbul Bostans ranged from 1-1.2 hectares for a small household to 3 hectares for extended families, cultivated intensively to achieve self-sufficiency. [21] Today, approximately 1,000 traditional Bostans remain in Istanbul, vestiges of centuries-old urban agriculture. [22] The archaeological origins of Istanbul date back to the 7th century BC. The first foundation of the settlements was established by Megarians in Chalceodon (Kadıköy) as a colonial city and then radiated in the Byzantine (present-day Sarayburnu) region, where the city walls were founded. [23] Since there were no depicted/drawn maps most information is derived from several written sources from the Byzantine Period (particularly the 10th century).

During this period, there are a vast number of records referring to Bostans as vegetable gardens and orchards. The fortified city of Constantinople was protected by the Land Walls [24] (Walls of Constantinople or Theodosian Walls), which created protected areas ideal for agricultural zones, first noted in the 5th century AD. [25] Monasteries such as *Stoudios* (dated 826) maintained close visual and functional relations with the Land Walls, developing surrounding gardens for cultivation, storage and self-sufficiency. According to Koder's analysis of the Geoponika, orchards developed along the interior of the Land Walls for 2–3 km² and extended another 2 km² externally, feeding the population of the city. [35] Ground floors of towers and peribolos areas were likely used as storage spaces for produce, illustrating how architecture, defence, and food production were intertwined. [26]

Under the Ottomans, Bostans were more formally recorded. In 1735, there were 344 Bostans within the Land Walls, employing 1,301 Bostan-keepers. [38] Guilds of master gardeners controlled cultivation, producing both for palace and market, with legal protections ensuring their continuity. Visual and written records of Ottoman Bostans provide information on names, functions and management. According to Shopov and Han, there were 1301 Bostan-keepers looking after the Bostans within the city walls, many of which held legal protection from intervention of any kind. [27] The Constitution of the Turkish Republic drew heavily upon European archetypes. Since 1923, urban development and industrialization have been pursued in line with this paradigm. Yet, the rapid pace of Westernization was not matched by an equivalent rate of social adaptation. As Bryld observes:

"in Istanbul, Western-style economic institutions, supermarkets, for example, are praised in the media as the modern and efficient urban ideal, in contrast to traditional institutions like neighborhood bazaars, which are often portrayed as dirty, crowded, unpredictable, and backward." [28]

The destruction of Bostans did not begin with the founding of the Republic.

(top) Commune Southwark, Rowan St John, DS3.1

(bottom) Kurşunlu Han, photographs by Jane Tankard

Already in 1854, the Istanbul Municipality had been established to oversee services such as market inspections, street cleaning, road construction, and tax collection. Among its responsibilities was the removal of refuse from the Bostans, a service for which it began to levy taxes in 1909. Archival records from the 1930s to the 1950s document the gradual deterioration of these gardens, driven both by insufficient infrastructure and by policies that enabled their systematic eradication. Research suggests that little change occurred in the rate of Bostan disappearance until the 1970s. (29) However, as Başer and Tunçay argue, *"Istanbul's Bostans became truly endangered in the 1980s, when massive population growth combined with political corruption and speculative investment in housing and development to make real estate the highest-profit sector in Istanbul."* (30) Left unattended and abandoned, many Bostans became prime targets for real estate speculation and were subsequently converted into sites of development. From the 2000s onward particularly after financial capitalism assumed an even more pervasive role in the aftermath of the 2008 global financial crisis the pressure on remaining Bostans intensified further.

CONTEMPORARY BOSTANS: ÜSKÜDAR VILLAGE

One of Istanbul's surviving Bostans is located in Kuzguncuk, a neighborhood on the Asian side of the Bosporus in Üsküdar and visited during the DS3.1 Field trip in 2023. This urban village sits within a topographical valley with the Bostan at the heart of the conurbation, centrally located in the valley cleft. The village's enclosed geography has preserved both its urban pattern and its diverse social structure. Unlike many other Istanbul neighbourhoods, it has resisted conventional gentrification. Its residents, of varied ethnic and cultural backgrounds, have sustained and renewed the neighborhood's heritage in ways that reflect accumulated traditions, shared values and adaptive resilience. Although measures like the 1942 Wealth Tax weakened minority economic influence, Kuzguncuk largely maintained its multicultural fabric, with local solidarity reportedly shielding residents during the 1955 pogroms.

By the 1930s, the neighborhood's population reached around 4,000, with minorities still comprising the majority. The Kuzguncuk Bostan continues to function as a site for agricultural cultivation as well as social and cultural gatherings and it is protected by both the Association of the People of Kuzguncuk and local residents.

CONTEMPORARY ISTANBUL: POLITICAL, SOCIAL, AND SPATIAL PRESSURES

Both Hans and Bostans embody uncanny urbanity: spaces where layers of Byzantine, Genoese, Ottoman, and contemporary Istanbul coexist. The Hans and Bostans act as thresholds between private and public, past and present, producing moments of urban 'uncanniness' where past social practices persist in contemporary life. Both operate as uncanny spaces, historical forms embedded in the modern city, producing analogue knowledge, ecological practice and community interaction. Marginalised populations - seasonal workers, migrants, artisans - find niches within these typologies, sustaining crafts and informal economies. However, contemporary pressures, including gentrification, land speculation and urban renewal, threaten their existence. Today, only fragments of these ecological, social, and historical networks survive.

Urban Hans and Bostans constitute invaluable components of Istanbul's historical and cultural identity, illustrates the ongoing negotiation between tradition and modernity, marginalisation and visibility. They are spaces of coexistence, analogue production, ecological practice and inclusion. Preserving these typologies as active production spaces is essential not only for maintaining social and economic life but also for sustaining the city's traditions of community, craftsmanship, and collective memory. These spaces remind us that cities are not only functional machines but also palimpsests of memory, uncanny presences, and resilient social ecologies capable of integrating the marginalised and preserving historical continuity.

(right) Bostan, photograph by Jane Tankard

NOTES

(01) Ahmet Yaşar, "The Han in Eighteenth-and Early Nineteenth-Century Istanbul: A Spatial, Topographical and Social Analysis" (PhD diss., Boğaziçi University, 2016)
(02) Nazlı Ecem Çınaryılmaz, "Galata Kurşunlu Han (Rüstem Paşa Hanı)" (Master's thesis, Istanbul Technical University, 2019)
(03) Işık Tamdoğan Abel, "Hanlar ya da Osmanlı Kentinde Yabancı [Les Han ou l'étranger dans la ville ottoman]," in *Osmanlı İmparatorluğu'nda Yaşamak: Toplumsallık Biçimleri ve Cemaatlerarası İlişkiler (18.-20. Yüzyıllar) [Vivre dans l'empire Ottoman: Sociabilités et relations intercommunautaires (XVIIIè-XXè siècles)]*, ed. François Georgeon and Paul Dumont (İletişim Publishing, 2018)
(04) Ceyhan Güran, *Türk Hanlarının Gelişimi ve İstanbul Hanları Mimarisi* (Vakıflar Genel Müdürlüğü [General Directorate of Foundations] Publishing, 1976)
(05) Ekrem Işın, *İstanbul'da Gündelik Hayat: İnsan, Kültür ve Mekan İlişkileri Üzerine Toplumsal Tarih Denemeleri* (İletişim Publishing, 1995), 24-25.
(06) Yaşar, "Han,". Tamdoğan Abel, "Hanlar". (07) ibid
(08) Nazlı Ecem Çınaryılmaz and Bilge Ar, "San Michele Church of Genoese Galata (Pera): Historic Records and Material Evidence on its Chronology," *A|Z ITU Journal of Faculty of Architecture* 17, no.2 (2020) https://doi.org/1Q.5505/itujfa.2020.37108. (09) ibid
(10) Güran, *Türk Hanlarının Gelişimi*, 90; Gönül Cantay, "Kurşunlu Han," in *Dünden Bugüne İstanbul Ansiklopedisi 5 [The Encyclopedia of Istanbul from Past to Present 5]* (Türkiye Ekonomik ve Toplumsal Tarih Vakfı [Economic and Social History Foundation of Turkey], 1994).
(11) Çınaryılmaz, "Galata Kurşunlu Han".
(12) Yeşim Desticioğlu, "Otantik Kentsel Mekan Olarak Zanaat Mahalleleri: Galata Örneği [Craft Neighbourhoods as Authentic Urban Place: Galata]" (Master's thesis, Istanbul Technical University, 2021).
(13) Çınaryılmaz, "Galata Kurşunlu Han,".
(14) Catriona McKinnon, *Toleration: A Critical Introduction* (Routledge, 2006), 16; Francesco Chiodelli and Stefano Moroni, "Typology of Spaces and Topology of Toleration: City, Pluralism, Ownership," *Journal of Urban Affairs* 36, no. 2 (2013) https://doi.org/10.1111/juaf.12028; Deniz Çetin and Ayse Şenturer, "Spatialities between Property and the Commons: An Interval of Tolerance," *The Journal of Architecture* 29, no. 4 (2024) https://doi.org/10.1080/13602365.2024.2402372.
(15) Edhem Eldem, "Galata'nın Etnik Yapısı," *Istanbul* 1 (1992) (16) ibid.
(17) Ebru Soytemel and Besime Şen, "Networked Gentrification: Place-Making Strategies and Social Networks of Middle Class Gentrifers in Istanbul," in *Whose City Is That? Culture, Design, Spectacle and Capital in Istanbul*, ed. Dilek Özhan Koçak and Orhan Kemal Koçak (Cambridge Scholars Publishing, 2014).
(18) Türk Ansiklopedisi, "Bostan," in *Türk Ansiklopedisi 7 [Turkish Encyclopedia 7]* (Maarif Basımevi, 1955).
(19) Ayşe Nur Akdal, *Market Gardens and Gardeners of Ottoman Istanbul* (Libra, 2017). (20) ibid.
(19) Ayşe Nur Akdal, *Market Gardens and Gardeners of Ottoman Istanbul* (Libra, 2017).
(20) Bülbül, Ahmet Hamdi. "Şehre Sığmayan Topraklar: İstanbul Bostanları." *Erdem* 87 (2024) https://doi.org/10.32704/erdem.2024.87.001.
(21) Paul J. Kaldjian, "Istanbul's Bostans: A Millennium of Market Gardens," *Geographical Review* 94, no. 3 (2004): https://doi.org/10.1111/j.1931-0846.2004.tb00174.x.
(22) ibid.
(23) Ramazan Özbek, "Modern ve Geleneksel Yerleşimlerde Konut ve Yakın Çevresindeki Kullanıcı Memnuniyetinin Ataşehir ve Kuzguncuk Örnekleminde Değerlendirilmesi [Evaluation of User's Satisfaction from House and It's Close Environment in Modern and Traditional Settlements in the Case of Ataşehir and Kuzguncuk]" (Master's thesis, Istanbul Technical University, 1998).
(24) Henry Maguire, "Gardens and Parks in Constantinople," in *Dumbarton Oaks Papers No. 54* (Dumbarton Oaks Research Library and Collection Washington, D.C., 2000).
(25) Alexander Van Millingen, *Byzantine Constantinople: The Walls of the City and Adjoining Historical Sites* (John Murray, 1899).
(26) Alessandra Ricci, "Intangible Cultural Heritage in Istanbul: The Case of the Land Wall's Byzantine Orchards". *Ulusararası Tarihi Yarımada Sempozyumu, İstanbul* (2008)
(27) Aleksandar Shopov and Ayhan Han, "Osmanlı Istanbul'unda Kent İçi Tarımsal Toprak Kullanımı ve Dönüşümleri: Yedikule Bostanları," *Toplumsal Tarih* 236 (2013)
(28) Erik Bryld, "Potentials, Problems, and Policy Implications for Urban Agriculture in Developing Countries," *Agriculture and Human* 20, no. 1 (2003): 79-86. https://doi.org/10.1023/A:1022464607153
(29) Bahar Başer and Hayriye Eşbah Tunçay, "Understanding the spatial and historical characteristics of agricultural landscapes in Istanbul," *A|Z ITU Journal of Faculty of Architecture* 7, no.2 (2010): 112; Çağlar Keyder, *Istanbul: Between the Global and the Local* (Bloomsbury Academic, 1999); Paul J. Kaldjian, "Istanbul's Bostans: A Millennium of Market Gardens," *Geographical Review* 94, no. 3 (2004): 284–304. http://www.jstor.org/stable/30034275. (30) Ibid

SPECULATIVE CITY: INTERSTITIALITY, PALIMPSEST, AND THE CREATIVE SEAM

JANE TANKARD

SPECULATIVE CITY: INTERSTITIALITY, PALIMPSEST, AND THE CREATIVE SEAM BY JANE TANKARD

'mine the [...] industrial margins as urban terrain where histories, social relations, and material conditions converge'

"....I have tried to piece together the elements of an imaginary that fuelled and outlived the event known as the Paris Commune in 1871 - an imaginary to which the Communards and I have called communal luxury. For seventy-two days in the spring of 1871 a worker-led insurrection transformed the city of Paris into an autonomous Commune and set about improvising the free organisation of its social life according to principles of association and cooperation." (01)

In her book Communal Luxury, Kristin Ross, (02) draws analogies between the lives and intentions of the Paris Communards and contemporary societal movements that challenge the capitalist, techno-utopian visions mapped out by corporate elites in overdeveloped urban contexts. The Communards were artisans and producers, committed to a more democratic, socially integrated urban life and their notion of 'communal luxury', the extension of art into life, has inspired speculative and transformational architecture throughout the 20th century and beyond. Ross frames this vision in relation to Karen Barad's agential realism, (03) suggesting a fluid, evolving world where political creativity and social commonality coexist. It is this space, between Barad's material-semiotic entanglements and the Communards' collective practice, that the studio has used to frame speculative propositions.

(right) City of London Layered Drawing, Jake Parkin

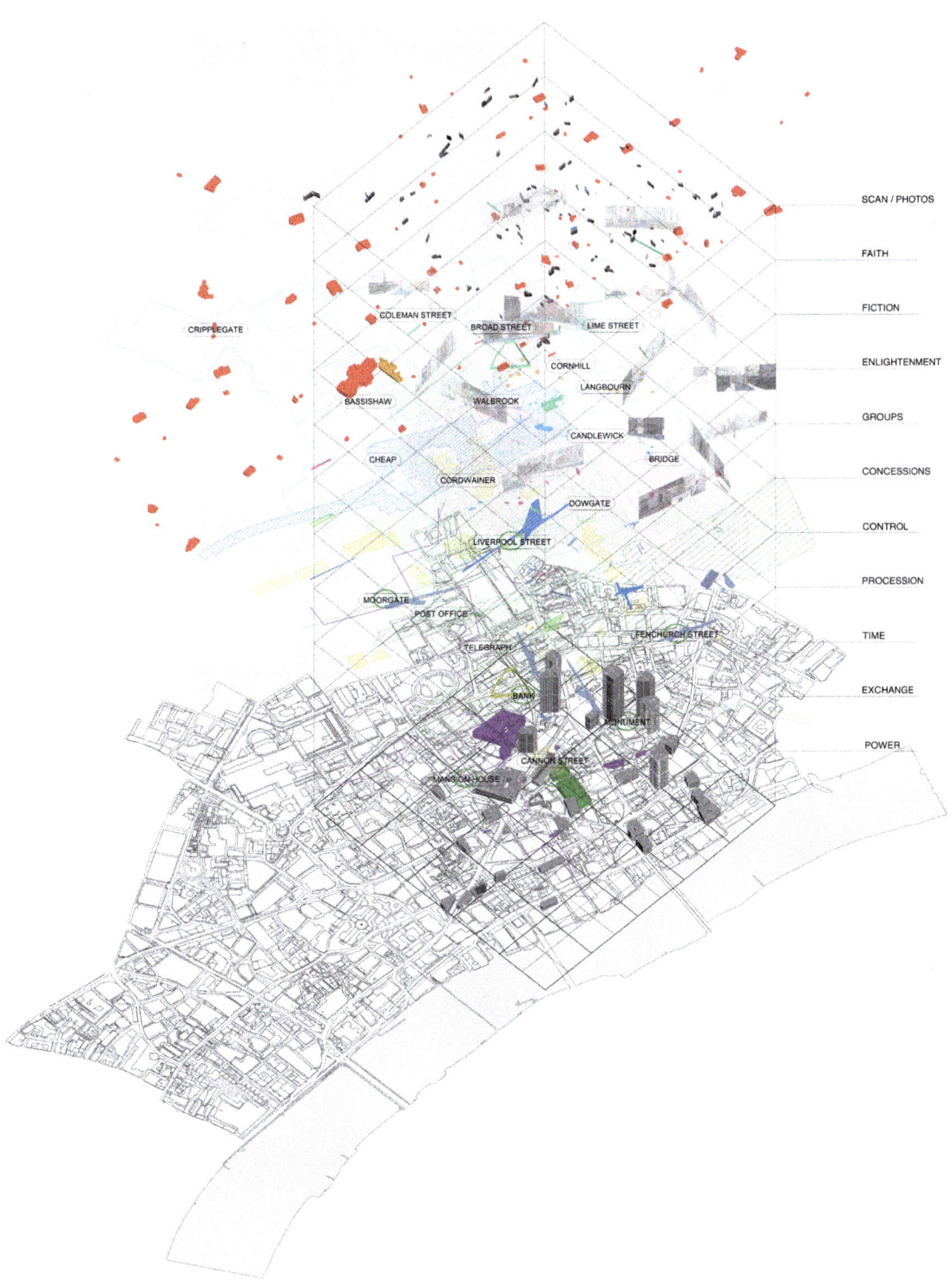

Our briefs have been organised around initiatives that either catalyse transformation or defend communal values eroded by contemporary capitalism, particularly the marginalisation of spaces and practices that integrate art, life and social engagement.

For DS3.1, the notion of the speculative city emerges as a series of frameworks that interrogate, repurpose and activate conditions historically subjugated to capital and profit. While earlier chapters have established engagement with the *Unheimlich* as a method of revealing hidden potential, studio projects increasingly use the concept as a lens through which liminal spaces can be reimagined in three-dimensional form. The gaps, margins and residual layers of urban life constitute both site and propositional terrain; overlaying narratives and observations enables experimentation and translation into radical architectural possibilities for habitation, community and imagination. These marginal, interstitial spaces are not only spatial; they are ethical and political, opening architecture to questions of access, justice, and difference. Intersectionality is central to this approach. Political activist and writer, bell hooks, reminds us that marginality is:

"more than a site of deprivation; it is also a site of resistance"

It is a space from which new modes of being and social relation can be forged. (04) Audre Lorde similarly insists that:

"the master's tools will never dismantle the master's house"

This provocation is especially pertinent when architectural typologies and programmes risk reproducing hierarchies of class, gender, and race. (05) In speculative practice, these insights require Architects to consider not only the physical form of residual spaces but also who inhabits them, who is excluded, and how design can redistribute agency. Margins become sites where the politics of identity, care and social justice are materialised alongside spatial experimentation. Bernard Tschumi's *Event-City* series complements this intersectional perspective by reframing architecture as a staging of actions, events, and conflicts rather than a fixed typology. (06) Margins, in Tschumi's terms, are not inert leftovers but active terrains for unpredictable encounters, temporary occupations and hybrid programming. This lens allows the studio to resist closure, embrace contingency and produce proposals that are radical not through formal novelty alone but through the orchestration of urban life and social possibility.

Interstitiality and intersectionality converge: margins are simultaneously spaces of spatial experimentation and venues for political and social intervention.

Architectural theory supports these explorations. Anthony Vidler, Lebbeus Woods and Stephen Holl emphasize the productive potential of marginal, edge, and interstitial spaces. (07)

(right) Ambika Presentation, Munira Osman, DS3.1

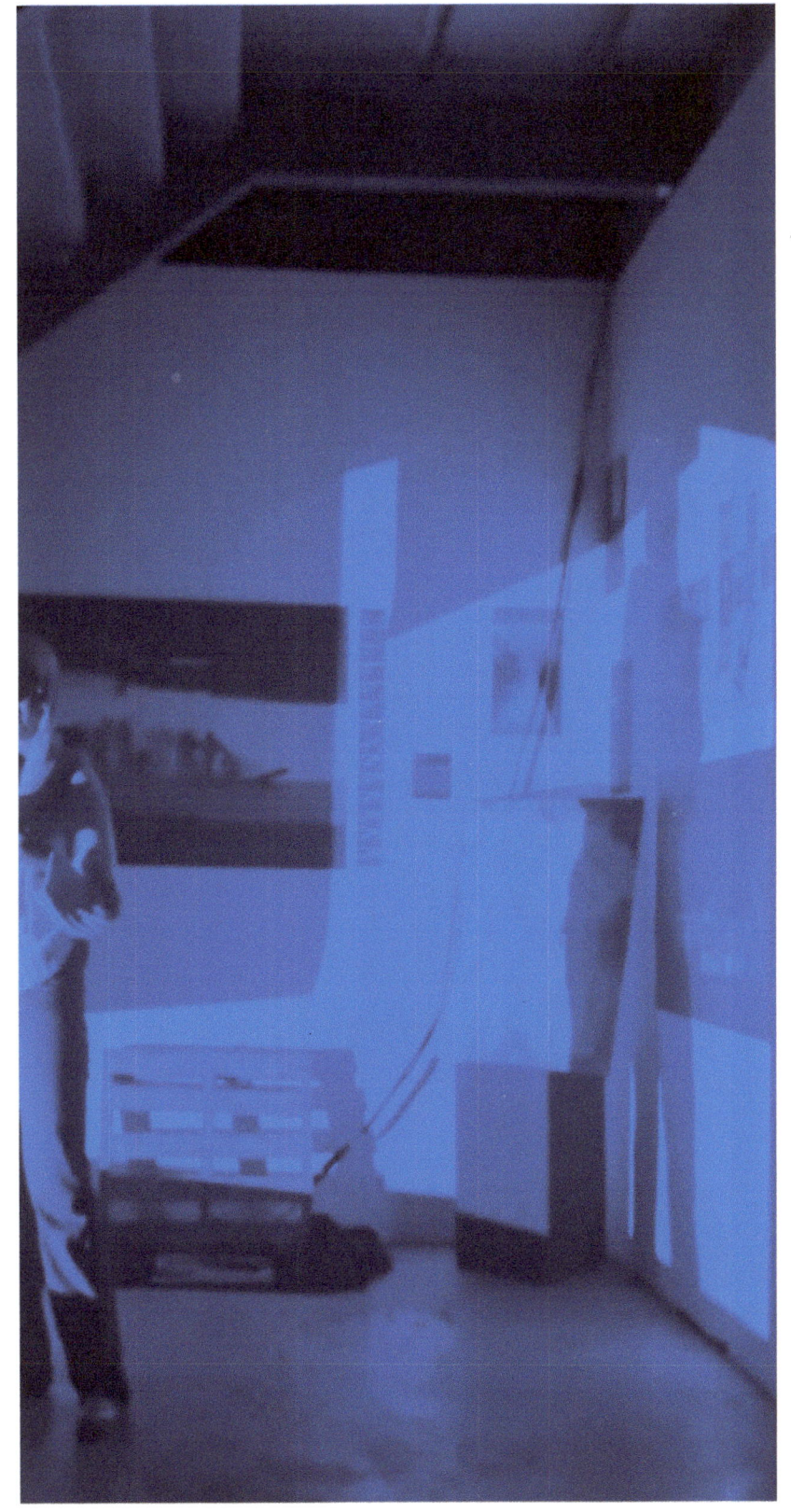

Woods highlights overlooked thresholds and industrial 'leftovers' as sites capable of fostering alternative spatial and social experiences, while Holl describes architecture's capacity to mediate between interior and exterior, perception and atmosphere, emphasizing the 'thickened edge' as a locus of inhabitability and imagination. (08) Katherine Shonfield's concept of smudging demonstrates how abstraction in drawing can reveal overlaps and ambiguities invisible in orthographic representation, enabling designers to mine residual urban margins for histories, social relations, and material potential. (09)

Robin Evans similarly underscores drawing as a medium for exposing hidden spatial and social relations, revealing layers of occupation, movement, and infrastructure. (10) Long, coded drawings and hybrid model-making translate these observations into three-dimensional propositions, identifying structure, materiality, porosity and archaeology as active ingredients of design.

Residual traces, histories, and servicing infrastructure accumulate over time, often obscured or repressed, yet these layers constitute both medium and method for speculative architectural intervention. Urban sites such as Mile End Park, Billingsgate Market and Limehouse demonstrate how palimpsestic analysis can translate into spatial strategies that are simultaneously reflective, performative and anticipatory. Methodologies such as orthographic analysis, choreographic drawing and model iteration enable the studio to navigate these layers, translating observation into strategy while foregrounding temporality, adaptability, and contingency. Through these techniques, margins, seams and residual layers are not simply investigated, they are activated as radical propositions.

In synthesising these approaches, speculative practice emerges as a form of radical architectural thought. Drawing together hooks, Lorde, Tschumi, Vidler, Woods, Holl, Shonfield and Evans, the studio positions marginal and interstitial spaces as sites where formal experimentation, social critique and political action converge. The radical potential unlocked by studying the marginal lies not only in producing innovative spatial typologies but in demonstrating how architecture can resist closure, amplify marginalised voices and catalyse new forms of inhabitation, community and imagination. Building on these principles, the speculative city foregrounds ethical concerns. By privileging the overlooked and non-binary systems of working, architecture becomes a tool for social agency and transformation.

Studio projects illustrate multiple registers of this potential, outlined as case studies in this section. Each proposition engages with utopian thinking not as abstraction but as a mechanism for envisioning social, spatial, and political alternatives. In this sense, architecture functions as a mediator between history and possibility. Mining the creative seam is understood as a means for producing interventions that respond to, reveal and amplify latent urban potential. By working across media and scales, speculative practice generates propositions that are simultaneously grounded, imaginative and socially engaged.

Architecture emerges as a practice capable of reconfiguring the city as a space of contingency, care and creativity, representing a commitment to producing architecture that can transform the social and spatial conditions of contemporary urban life.

(top) United Nations Island, Salaheldeen Elnour, DS3.1

(bottom right) Elevation Abstract, Ozlem Incedal, DS3.1

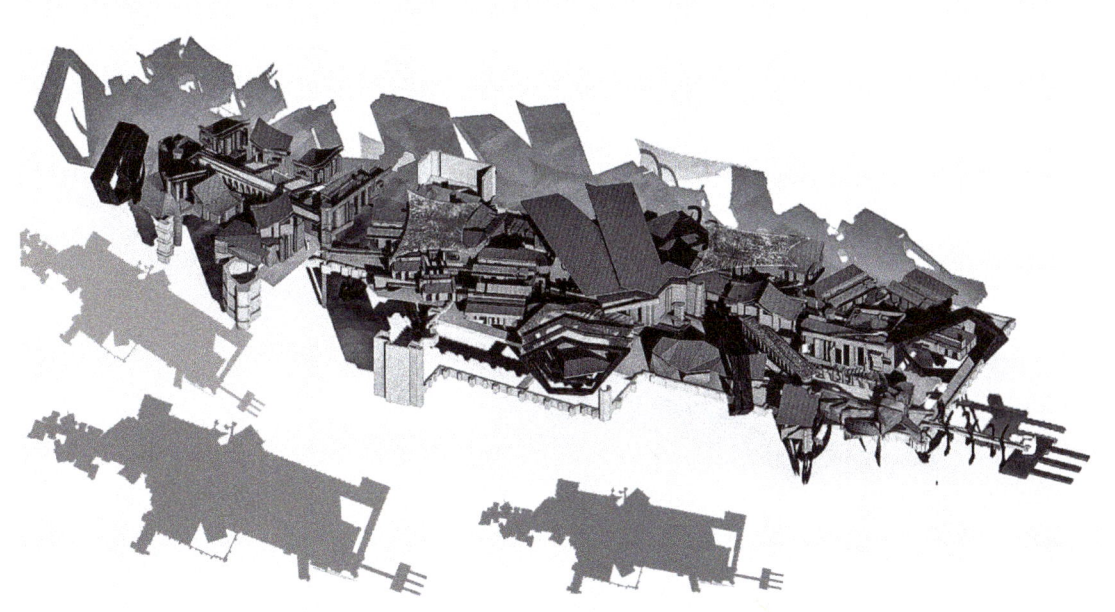
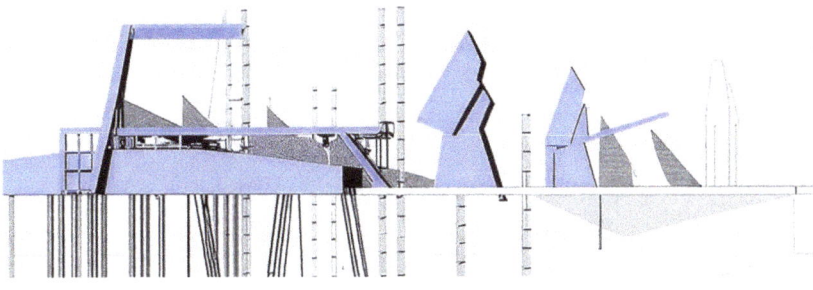

CASE STUDY BY NICOLAS DE LA FLOR REY

'The Mile End Imaginary'

Low tide, grey sky. Two people stand together on wet sand facing the sea. Sky and water merge at the horizon and gazing at this blurring together they dream alone, escaping thoughts of daily concern. The odd bird swoops low, and some shells gain attention; the couple's focus shifts to the beach for a while but then returns to the smudged horizon.

A pink gas canister is ignited in an east London park, early morning. Within seconds we are enveloped in a cloud; disorientated, we see shadows and forms around us, but they have become other-worldly, like us. Softness, suspension and disconnection, diffused light, blurred edges, mental escape, drift.

The Mile End project illustrates the productive capacity of interstitial space and utopian imagination. Conceived as an analogue refuge above the city skyline, the project responds to the pervasive digitalisation of contemporary life. Rather than proposing a monumental architectural gesture, the Mile End Imaginary offers a psychological and anti-performative space: a structure for drifting, observation and dream-like engagement with the 'other'. In a surreal, mist-infused environment, users can communicate with spaces they cannot access in their day-to-day digital worlds: from satellites to bunkers and distant urban margins, the project extends the city beyond its material boundaries and digital representation.

(right) Long Drawing, Nicolas de la Flor Rey, DS3.1

Stephen Graham's reimagining of verticality as a spatial act of liberation (11) becomes the projective pivot for speculation; the project proposes a series of spatial interactions that are both real and imagined. The Mile End Imaginary describes an intersection of analogue communication, early satellite technology and the corporeal. While situated in a heavily codified urban skyline, the intervention activates overlooked vertical spaces, reframing the residual as a locus for agency and imagination whilst connecting the dreamer to 24 hour live footage of satellite imagery and data, transport networks and almost forgotten radio communication.

From above the clouds the visitor can watch a cornfield in Idaho as it is sown, grows, moves, shifts and shimmers in the breeze and its moment of harvest. Like old analogue transmitters, the experience tunes us back into invisible frequencies of human connection from the space station intersecting with a radio antennae on earth to the (re) tuning of long-wave networks.

Methodologically, the project draws on long-section analysis and choreographic model-making to generate spatial sequences that foreground perception, temporality and relationality. In Holl's terms, the space becomes an intermediary, a 'mediated experience' between human perception and the urban landscape. The Mile End Imaginary exemplifies how interstitial space, when read critically and layered with speculative narratives, can serve as architectural mediator.

… Let us now dream, live slowly, and honour the subconscious passing of time, speculation and fantasy.

(top) Smoke tests, Nicolas de la Flor Rey, DS3.1   *(bottom) Model tests, Nicolas de la Flor Rey, DS3.1*

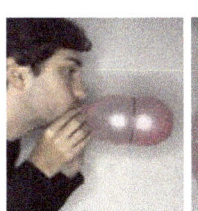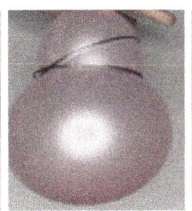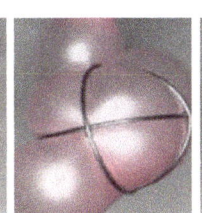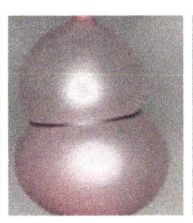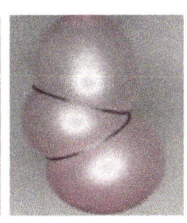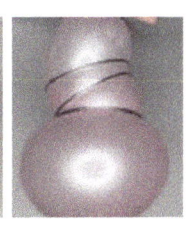

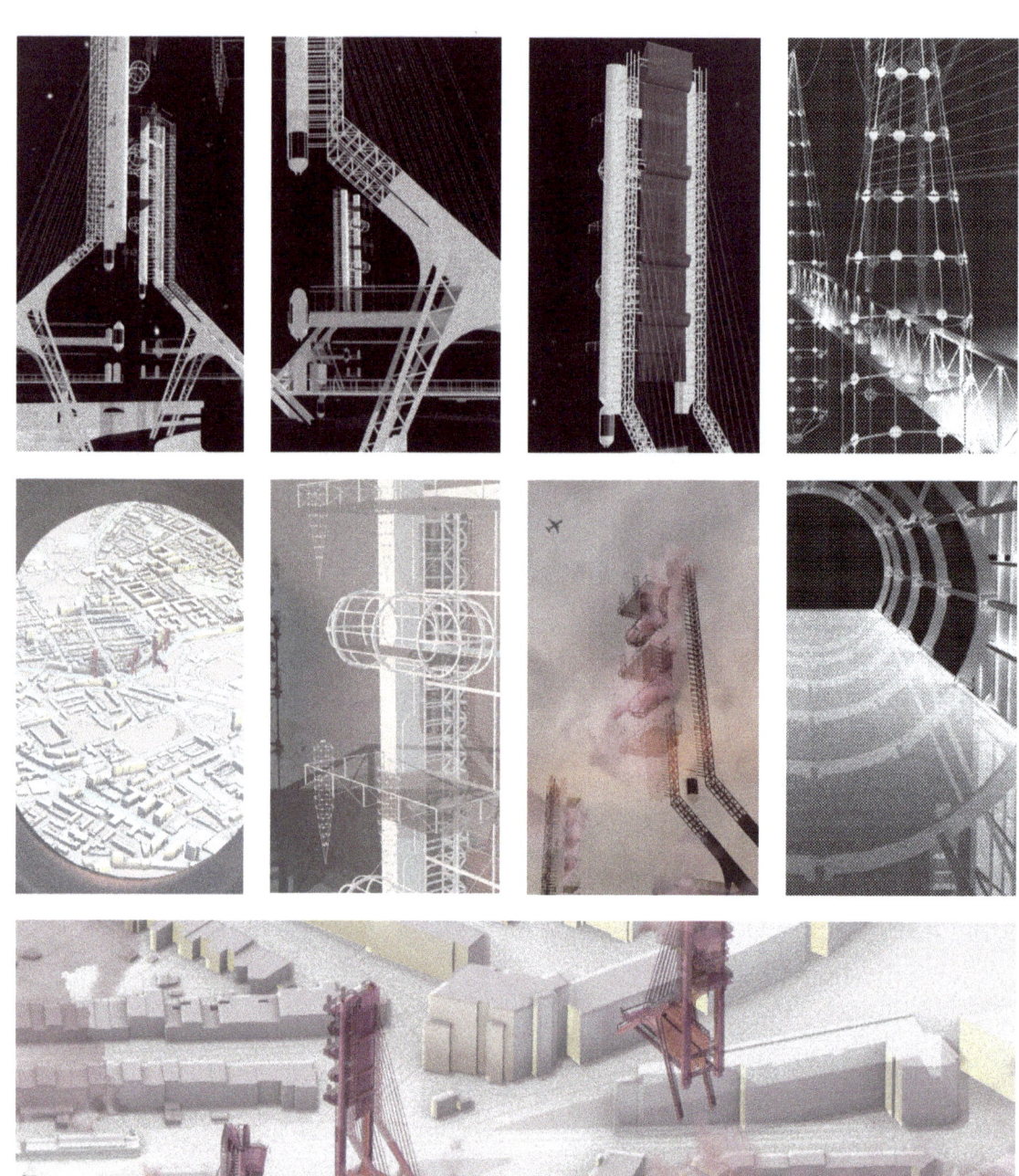

Works by Nicolas de la Flor Rey, DS3.1

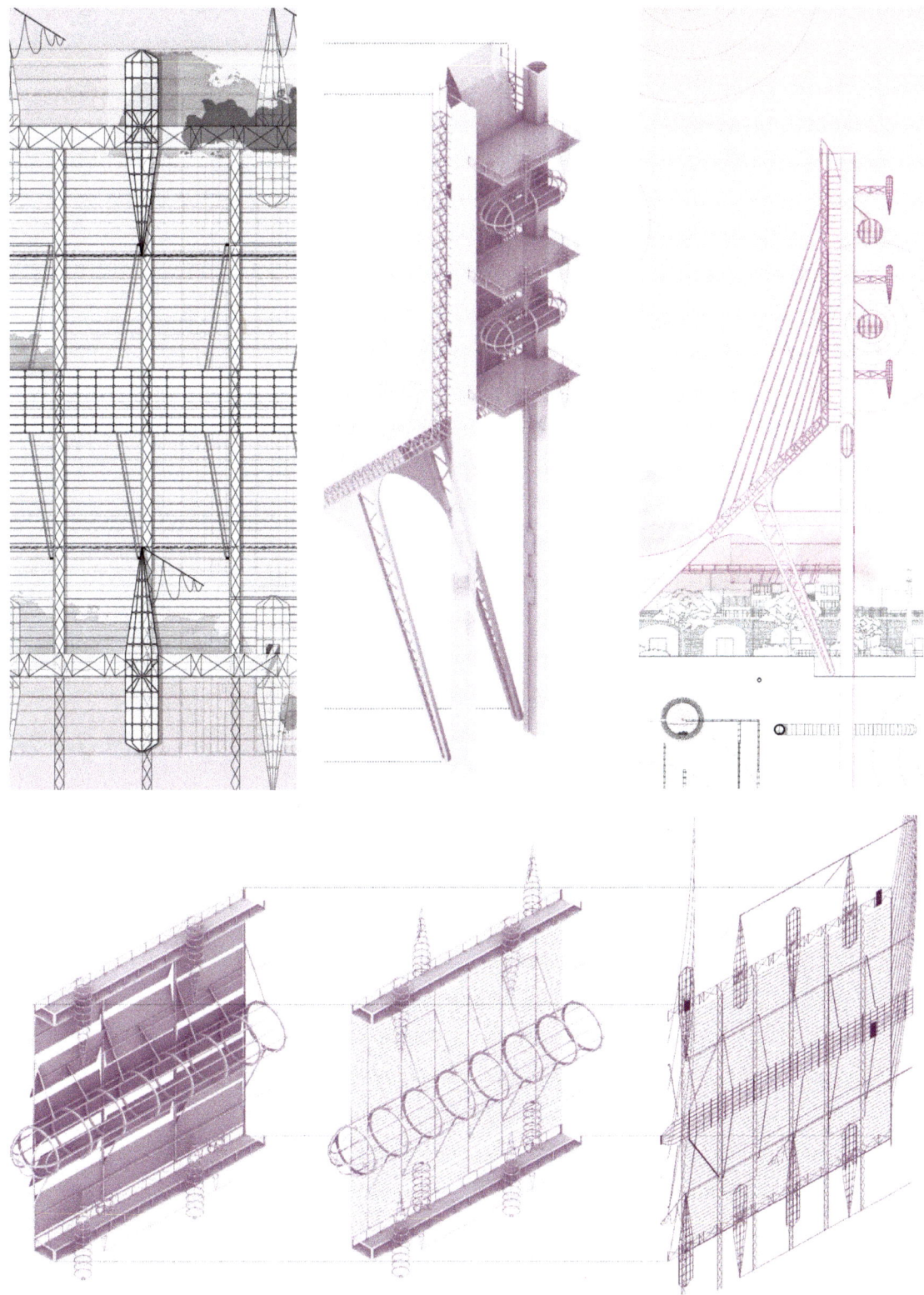

CASE STUDY BY MUNIRA OSMAN

'The Raft at Billingsgate'

The Raft at Billingsgate situates notions of interstitial architecture in overtly political terms. The Raft addresses displacement and exclusion, proposing a floating infrastructure for migrants, refugees and displaced communities within the contested terrain of Billingsgate Market. Interstitiality operates as both material strategy and social critique: the residual industrial margins and dock land edges of the site are reclaimed through performative inundation, asserting spatial rights against processes of privatisation and capital accumulation. The project proposes a new spatial framework for migrants, refugees and displaced communities, reclaiming land, memory and voice within the contested territory of the fish market. It emerges as a protest against global systems of capital accumulation that have weaponised land, wealth and legality to exclude the very people most affected by their consequences. Through the lens of flooding as a mechanism of protection, language and the mechanics of movement, the project explores how architecture might resist displacement and embody a radical form of spatial justice.

Billingsgate is not a neutral site. It is inscribed with layers of colonial trade, social erasure and speculative development. Once a vibrant market at the intersection of community and commerce, it now sits in the shadow of Canary Wharf's corporate skyline, targeted for redevelopment into luxury flats.

(right) Billingsgate Typewriter, Munira Osman, DS3.1

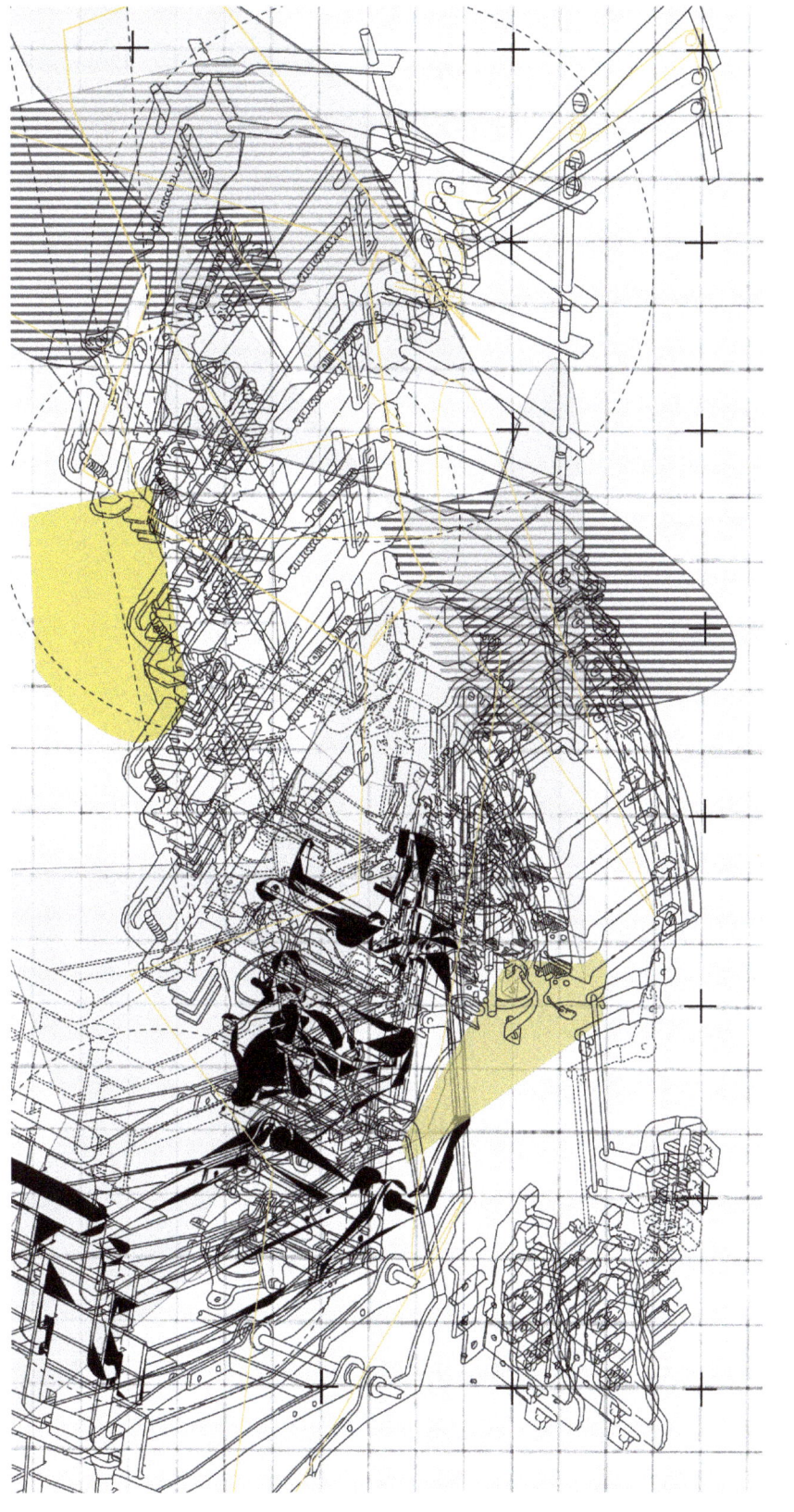

These schemes represent not only the physical erasure of working-class infrastructure but also the ideological dismantling of community itself. In response, the project reclaims the site flooding the ground as a spatial resistance to control and permanence offering a floating infrastructure for communal reassembly. Informed by a series of explorations into displacement, memory and protest, the project began with the design of a responsive inflatable device, a klaxon, that functioned as a warning signal, triggered by rising water levels.

Influenced by *The Raft* by Bill Viola and *The Logic of the Birds,* Artangel, initial investigations reflected on collective trauma, the symbolism of water and the politics of refuge. Water became both material and metaphor, a force of destruction and renewal. The inflatable structure tested how architecture might respond to urgency through impermanence and movement. In Semester Two, the project shifted focus to the mechanics of expression. The typewriter was introduced not as nostalgic technology but as a symbol of liberation.

In contexts where communication is restricted, the typewriter offers autonomy. Its internal mechanisms, particularly its steel levers, were reinterpreted as kinetic components within the architecture. These levers control the inflation and deflation of the structure, allowing it to rise and fall like a sentence being typed.

The building performs through movement, echoing the rhythms of speech and mark-making. Through its adaptive, floating infrastructure, the Raft negotiates the layers of history, context and economised notions of ownership and value, transforming a contested margin into a platform for habitation, communal assembly and resilience. Methodologically, the project deploys filmic analysis, a critique of historical recuperation and layered digital to analogue modelling to generate a spatial proposition that is both contextualised by historical context and proactive in imagining alternative futures. In doing so, the project demonstrates how speculative architecture can transform the interstitial into a terrain of social and spatial justice.

(bottom right) Billingsgate Raft, Munira Osman, DS3.1

Works by Munira Osman, DS3.1

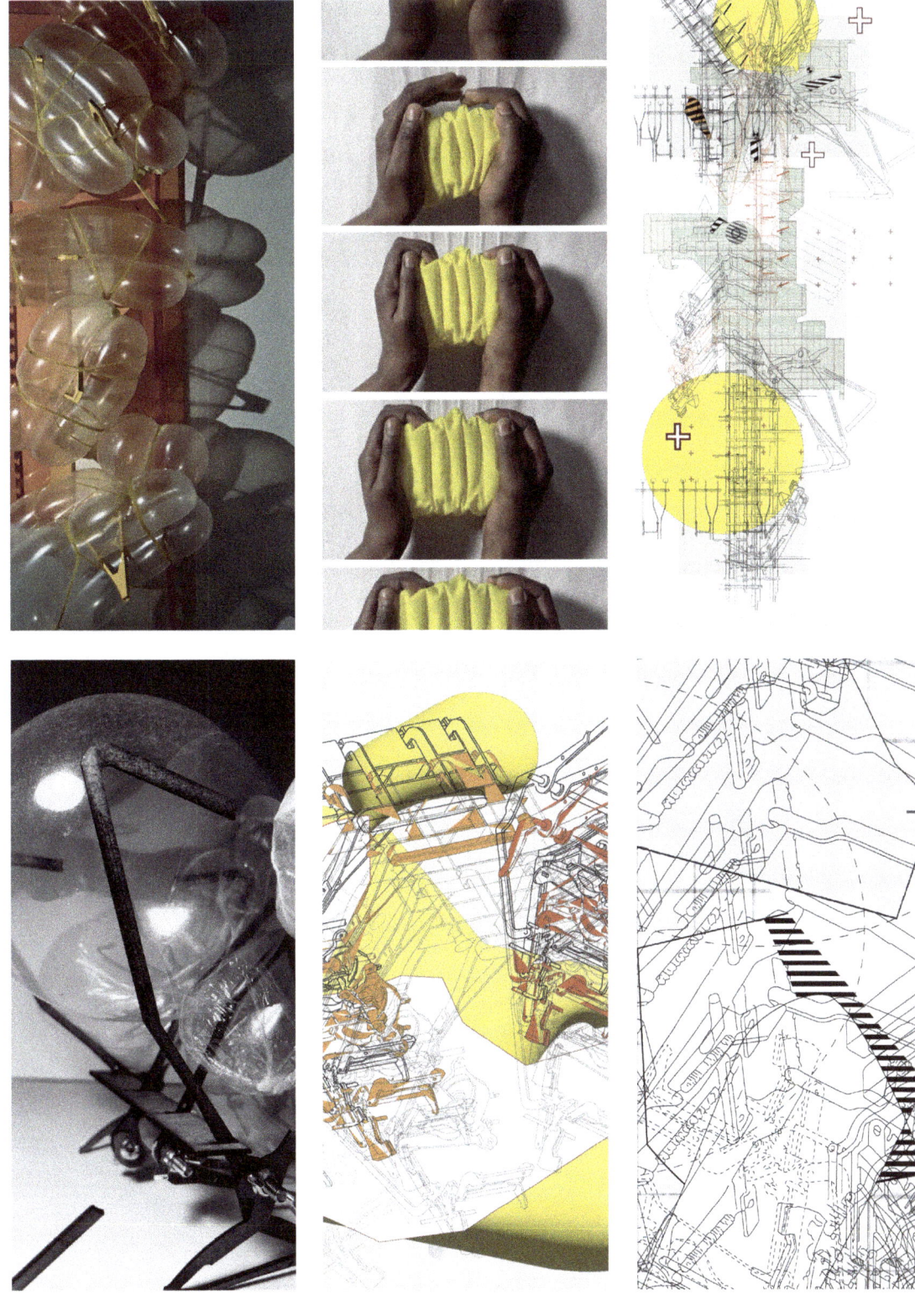

CASE STUDY BY RANIA ELKHARIM

'The Limehouse Archive'

Struggling with his detainment from the city and displacement from the struggle, enforced by walls and water, Blanqui looked to the sky as his revolutionary horizon. He wrote about comets, stars and the expansive (im)materiality of outer space as liberated from borders and bursting with infinite potential.

The Limehouse Archive is an attempt to enable the collection and preservation of stories of adaptation and collective struggles for the recognition and rights of marginalised communities. It is also understood as a library of legal knowledge enabling autonomy and communal agency. Positioned within a fragmented and largely inaccessible site in Limehouse, East London, the project reclaims a disused infrastructural margin along the edge of the DLR. These liminal spaces, isolated by rail lines and private developments, are reimagined as fertile ground for self-government and legal empowerment. Functioning as a repository of knowledge and celebration the archive challenges the systemic exclusion of the GRT community, whose rights are routinely overlooked by legal and governing bodies.

(top) Limehouse Boat Yard, Rania Elkharim, DS3.1   *(bottom) Limehouse Archive, Rania Elkharim, DS3.1*

Through experimental making, the Regent's Canal was understood both as a route and a methodology, revealing interstitial conditions, edge-spaces and disjuncture from East to West London. Experimental filmmaking, forensic drawing and model-making manifested an iterative process that questioned how spatial design might activate agency in urban communities. These methods directly informed the spatial logic of the Limehouse Archive as an assemblage of site-specific, performative and time-based spatial gestures rather than fixed architectural form. The Limehouse Archive draws an explicit lineage to values of autonomy, resistance and spatial reclamation, operating within an ideological framework that embraces the concept of the 'third space', a hybrid zone where cultural identities can be negotiated without erasing difference or demanding assimilation, is central to the project.

Louis Auguste Blanqui's writings on the sky as a revolutionary horizon, [12] informs the architectural proposition; incarcerated and exiled, Blanqui imagined the cosmos as a space liberated from state borders and terrestrial control. This metaphor is instrumental to the Archive's conception: a space that refuses boundaries, that transforms the marginal into the central and that situates creativity as an act of resistance.

The projected constellations on the building's façade, its openness to sound and light and its lack of fixed enclosure all express this ambition: to establish a space ungoverned by conventional laws of ownership or surveilled visibility. The Limehouse Archive examines how interstitial, palimpsestic and utopian strategies converge in practice. Drawing on vernacular methods of story-telling, the Archive translates oral narratives and contested data into architectural form. Its design references Cedric Price's joyful adaptability and Brechtian performance strategies and coded choreographic representation, manifesting as a proposition that mediates individual and collective experience. In terms of notions of the palimpsest, the site's histories of institutionalisation and marginalisation are neither erased nor romanticised; instead, they inform the Archive's programmatic and material strategies for spaces of assembly, recording and reclaiming. The Archive's temporality is underscored by its ritual lifecycle, culminating in ceremonial burning. This act affirms the autonomy of space and memory, transforming the building from static object into a manifestation of collective ritual. In this respect, the project exemplifies a speculative architecture that operates across multiple temporalities, intervening in the present while projecting alternative futures and preserving historical consciousness.

(top) Community Map, Rania Elkharim, DS3.1

(bottom) Limehouse Archive, Rania Elkharim, DS3.1

155

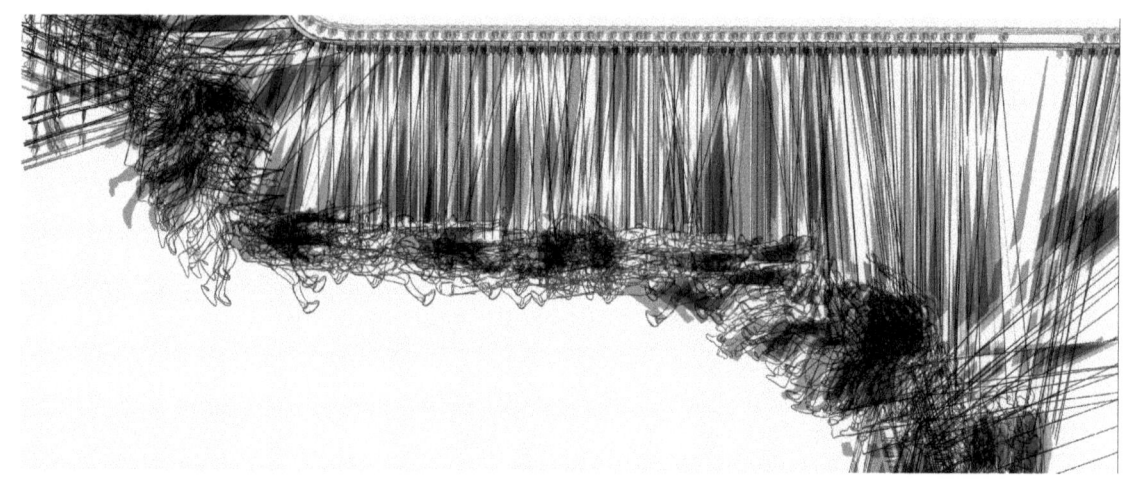

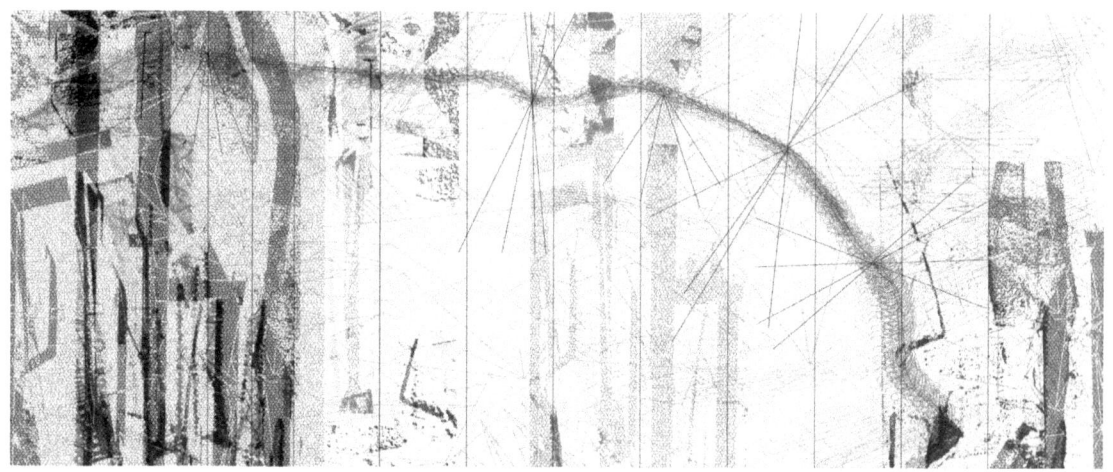

Works by Rania Elkharim, DS3.1

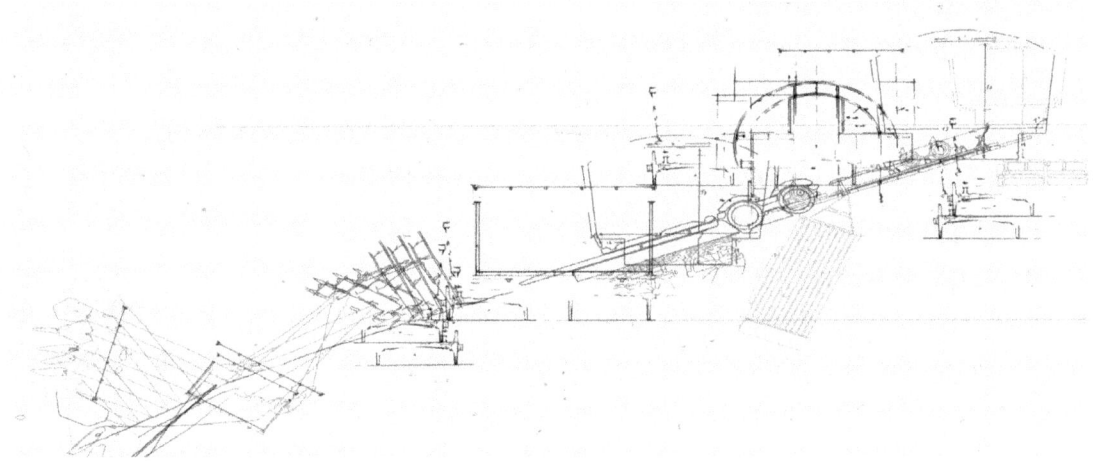

CASE STUDY BY OLHA PETRACHKOVA

'Theatre of the Moon'

"While I hesitated not to acknowledge how familiar was all this, I still wondered to find how unfamiliar were the fancies which ordinary images were stirring up." (13)

How to build an architectural device that could be a home for Edgar Allan Poe? What happens to architecture if its spatial characteristics take the form of 'The House of Usher' familiar and at the same time foreign, cosy and disturbing? How to translate this atmosphere into theatrical logic, where both Poe and the Moon are simultaneously actors and spectators?

This theatre is not an event. It is a dialogue. And the question is not *"What is happening here?"* but *"Who is really watching?"*

Inspired by Poe (14) and Vidler, (15) The Theatre of the Moon exists as a silent monument on twin canal-side sites in Haggerston. Unfolding only when lunar calendar and moment of projection align, the building is hidden in plain sight, visible only through indirect projections from an adjacent kitchen, where a camera obscura casts light and shadow onto a sink, a bathroom cabinet and a windowsill. The Theatre of the Moon's fabric enclosure and steel frame contains seven isolated rooms, each with a single object, evoking traces of life. There's no entrance only a threshold between public and private. It is both architectural and theatrical, where everyday gestures become performances.

(top) Speculative Section, Olha Petrachkova, DS3.1
(bottom left) Stacking Model, Olha Petrachkova, DS3.1
(bottom right) Observatory Test Model Series, Olha Petrachkova, DS3.1

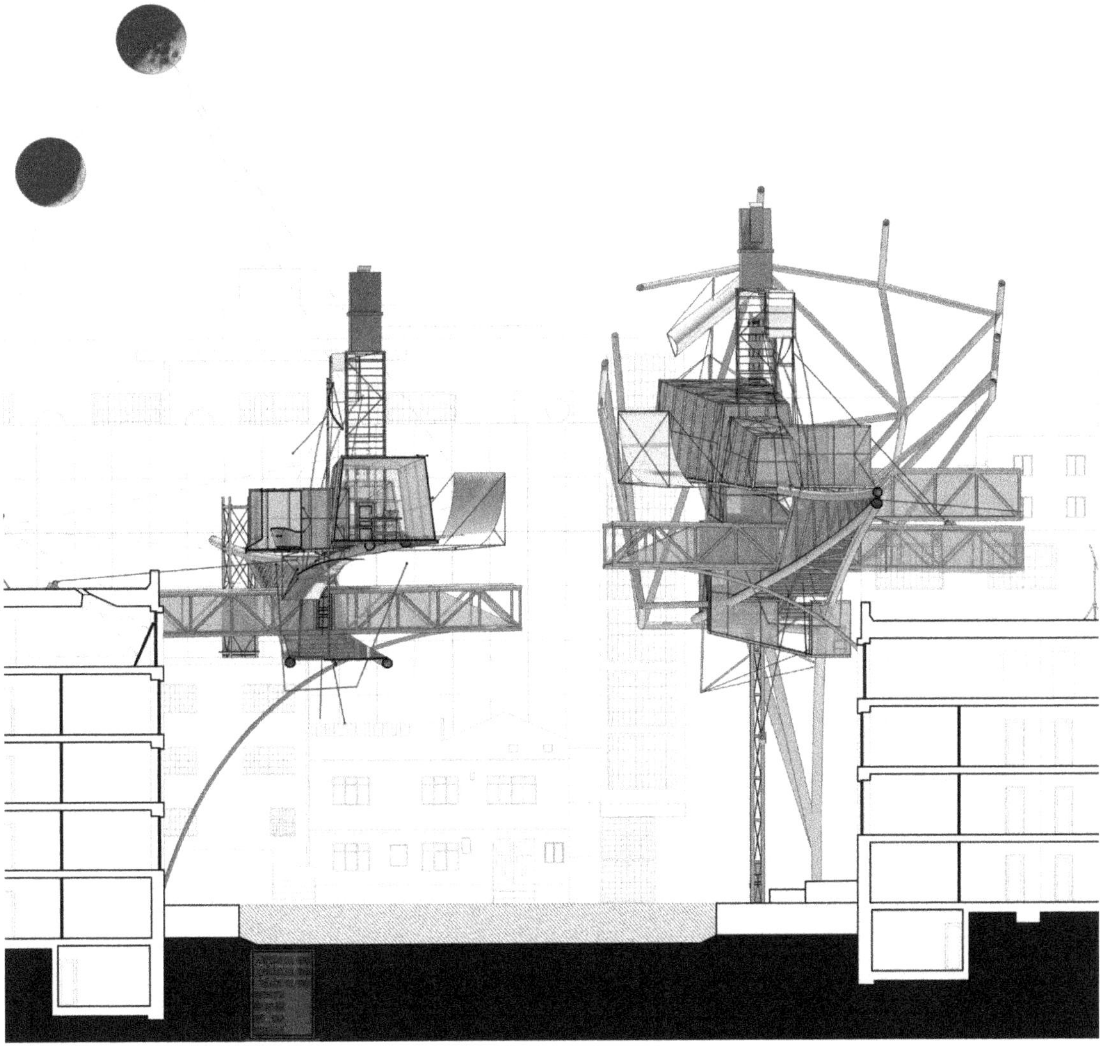

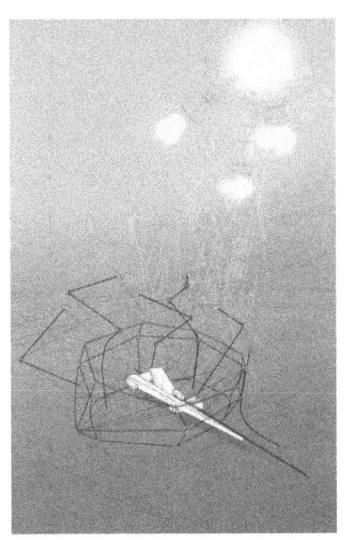

The structure is a space of ritual, merging the domestic and the uncanny, where Poe and the Moon are actors, audiences and mirror images of one another. The dialogue between them is silent, ritualistic, imprecise, like the cycle of light on a night facade. The building does not glow, it reflects. The light is not direct it is refracted through aluminium plates, fabric, the axis of time. The material logic is based on oppositions: hard and soft, geometry and reformation, access and refusal. The domestic is a point of descent, a place of threshold between reality and performance, between the house and the device. Space unfolds only when light, angle and moment coincide. An interior that no one enters but can see in a fragment of projection. Communal Luxury as a Structure of Silence. A theatre that does not need an audience, but does not stop playing. It is financed by the 'Pau Society', a conditional organisation that invests not in the programme, but in the gesture. Architectural action does not lead to event, it leads to presence.

"I am the beginning of everything, because worlds arise in my consciousness." (16)

Closing the curtains.

Opening the door.

Washing the dishes.

Gestures activate space.

The body is the trigger.

Everyday life is the stage. This theatre exists on the border between buildings. It dissolves the wall between private and public. Between reality and image. It allows architecture to look at itself through other architecture. The Theatre exists on the border.

Between light and matter, between everyday life and imagination, between two architectures that mirror each other without touching.

Its space is a system of delay, projection, correspondence.

(right) Obscura, Olha Petrachkova, DS3.1

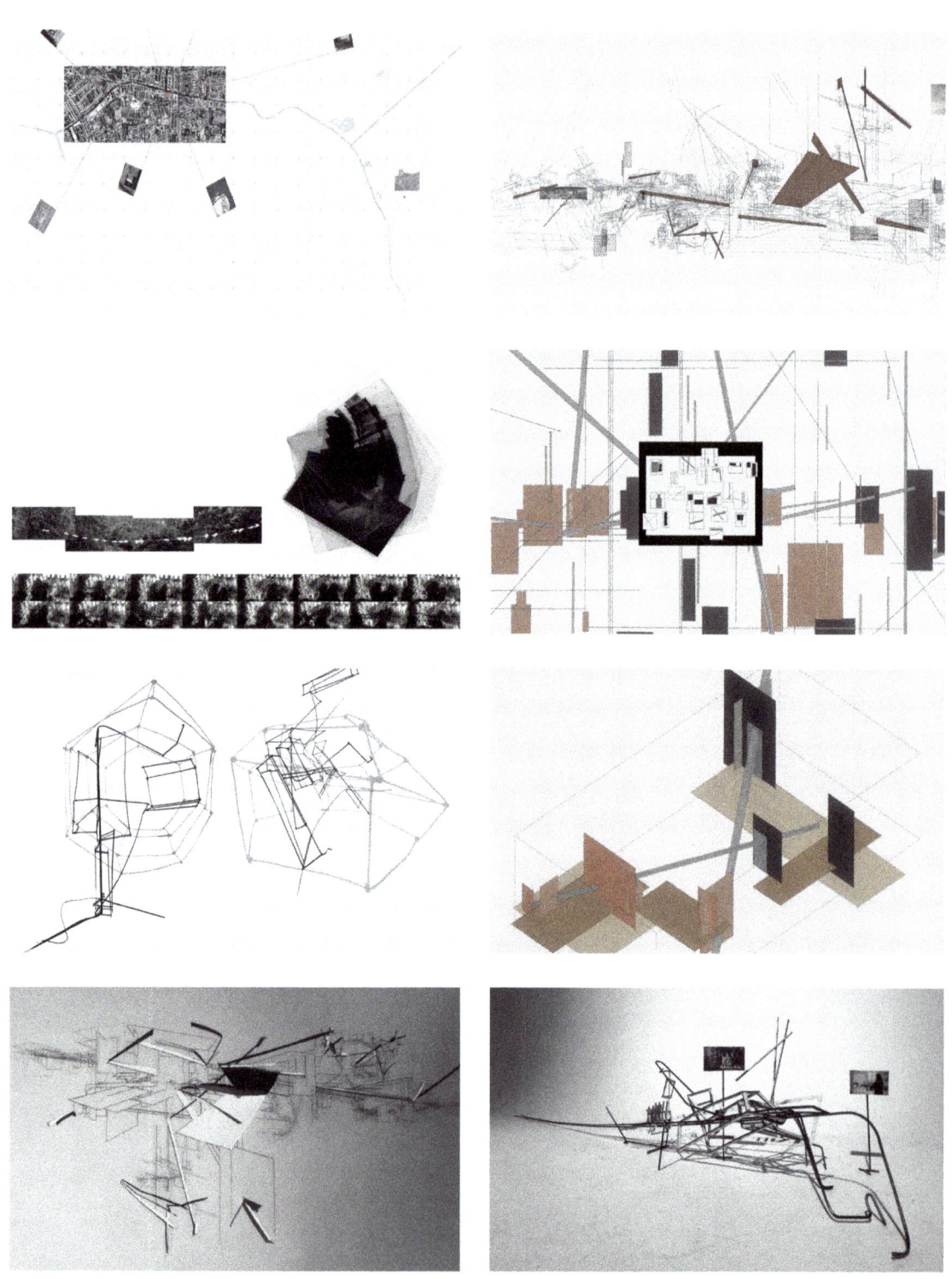

Works by Olha Petrachkova, DS3.1

 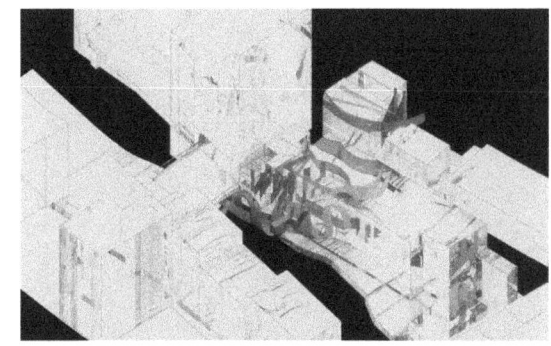
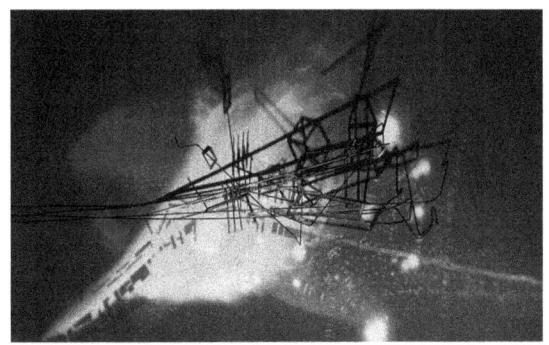 
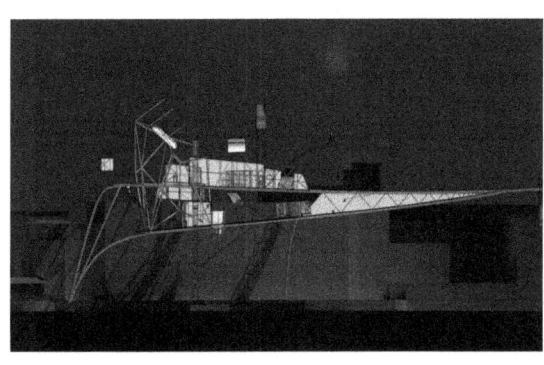 
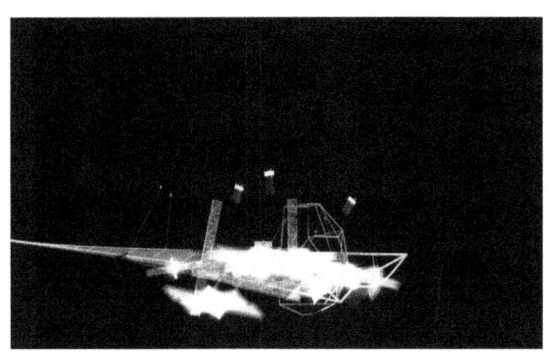 

CASE STUDY BY INAAYA AMER

'The Data Slaughterhouse/Re-inventing the Wetlands'

Emerging from a lineage established in semester one, where parasitic, suspended frameworks loomed above canalside sites of greed, functioning as critical devices for redistribution, framing and exposure of social injustice and deprivation, this early exploration set the groundwork for an architecture of capitalist critique, one that exposes, dissects and metabolises its context. Our interim crit was organised around performative responses to filmic analysis, contextual research and multi-disciplinary installation. 'Reparation Feast' was a theatrical act of consuming architectural proposition, printed on sugar paper, a gesture of both destruction and pleasure. Oranges, peeled and shared, invoked a sensory form of luxury, aligning with the politics of revealing, digesting and transforming architectural space. Set against the capitalist, commodified terrain of contemporary Canary Wharf, the layered memory of the Isle of Dogs histories and the forced displacement of the island's marginalised in the quest for money hangs like a looming entity in London's East End. An obfuscated and forgotten terrain is reconstructed as a living organism. A breathing, fleshy machine emerges, lacerating Canary Wharf's sterile surfaces and revealing the violent tension between digital systems and analogue bodies. Its form expands and contracts as data is farmed and excreted, embodying the metabolic violence of information capitalism. Architectural surfaces are not neutral, they absorb and express affect.

(right) Wrapped Model, Inaaya Amer, DS3.1

The proposed building's ETFE membrane behaves as a reactive surface; registering the heat and trauma of digital violence it expands and contracts in response to the heat produced by internal data slaughter processing. This skin acts as the building's lungs, regulating internal pressure and temperature as the organism digests digital commodities. At the core of this body lies a continuous 200-metre-long central corridor, a spinal column, around which the project is structured. Two primary and one secondary corridor branch from this axis-like nerves forming a connective network that anticipates, directs and stabilises movement. Internally, this structure is inhabited by discrete organs: an anechoic chamber where data is made auditory, a mourning chapel of corrupted files and the grand slaughter hall where heat renders information into form. These spaces perform like organs in a living system, metabolising abstraction into sensation. Externally, tilted load-bearing columns act as limbs, anchoring the building to the ground without disturbing its inner anatomy or the land's biological recovery. These skeletal supports allow the architecture to rise gradually from the terrain, crawling upward until it reaches a stretched posture over 350 metres across the farmed land below. This idea of mobility and parasitism draws from references including Archigram's Walking City and Lebbeus Woods's sketches of fragmented, insurgent structures, [17] informing an architectural proposition that appears to move, resist and assert its autonomy against the urban grid.

The terrain is reshaped into new hills and folds, cultivated to host a pastoral utopia for the alienated working body. Kristin Ross, in *Communal Luxury* [18] describes a future where "the right of everyone to live and work in a pleasing environment" replaces senseless luxury with shared abundance.

The architecture echoes this by transforming waste into a collective terrain, joyous and inclusive. Through the lens of the Situationist critique of recuperation the co-option and neutralisation of radical energies by capitalist systems, the project acknowledges how resistance is constantly threatened with absorption. Yet it also draws from the biological sense of recuperation: a wounded body regrowing, healing, refusing death. This dual reading, recuperation as co-option and as healing, also reflects Wallace Shawn's *The Fever*, [19] where the moral dilemma of beauty and violence is made explicit:

"Your love of beauty could actually kill you." [20]

The Data Slaughterhouse stands as a radical act of reclamation: a metabolic counter-machine, feeding a terrain that is messy, expanding, and defiantly alive. This project is an invitation not to imagine ideal futures, but unfamiliar ones. Instead of seeking (im)material perfection, the work asks how architecture might operate in conditions of uncertainty, transformation and disappearance.

(right) Unwrapped Model, Inaaya Amer, DS3.1

Works by Inaaya Amer, DS3.1

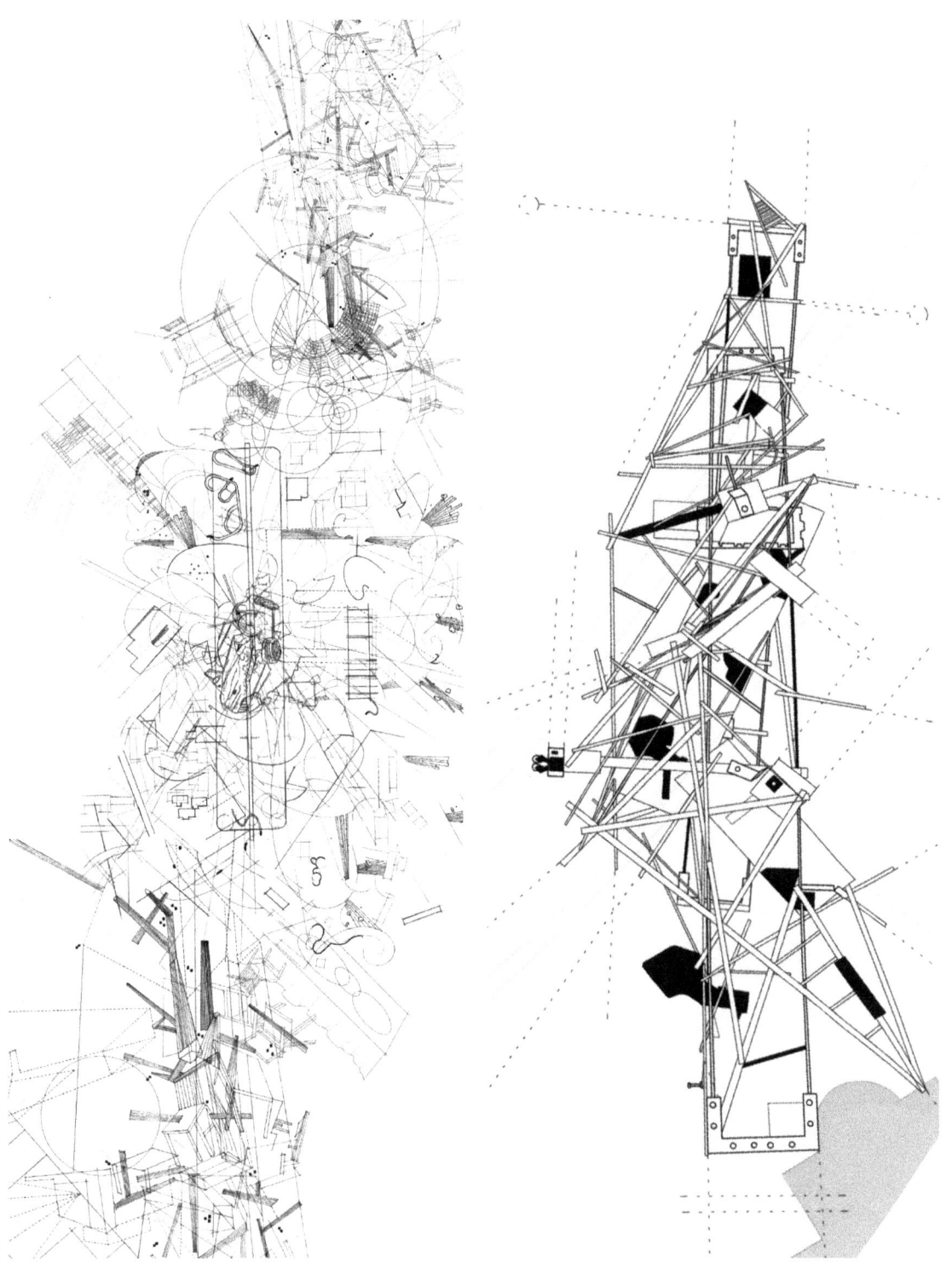

CASE STUDY BY ANGELA DE LA VEGA

'Repository of the Displaced'

Gasholder Park: a speculative machine drifts slowly by the water at the canal's edge, dredging forgotten fragments from the watery depths. Retrieved objects are displayed at the lock gates in a fragmented exhibition, an act of memory and archaeology, giving presence to what had once been erased. Rooted in the uncanny, the installation presents objects without explanation, the rituals of retrieval revealing uncanny thoughts. The Vessel is a network of elevated platforms in Limehouse, a neighbourhood vulnerable to flooding. The drifting machine gave way to anchored structures: excavation transformed into a response to the slow emergency of rising water. As sea levels rise and the ground destabilises, the project addresses not only the environmental threat but also cultural continuity, providing a spatial framework for preserving belongings, stories and rituals. Projections from the *Thames Estuary 2100 Plan* confirm Limehouse's exposure to tidal surges. These are no longer speculations but inevitabilities. In such a reality, the act of *'keeping'* becomes political.

The intervention is conceived as a constellation of raised platforms, each with a retrieval chamber for storing and collecting personal items. More than self-storage, the proposals represent civic structures of care and resilience. A porous grid of frames and passages threads over the site, creating pathways of remembrance. Inspired by Bernard Tschumi's use of the grid as a surface for fragments and events, the platforms become anchor points in a submerged city, offering rhythm and continuity.

(right) Everything Everywhere All At Once Long Drawing, Angela de la Vega, DS3.1

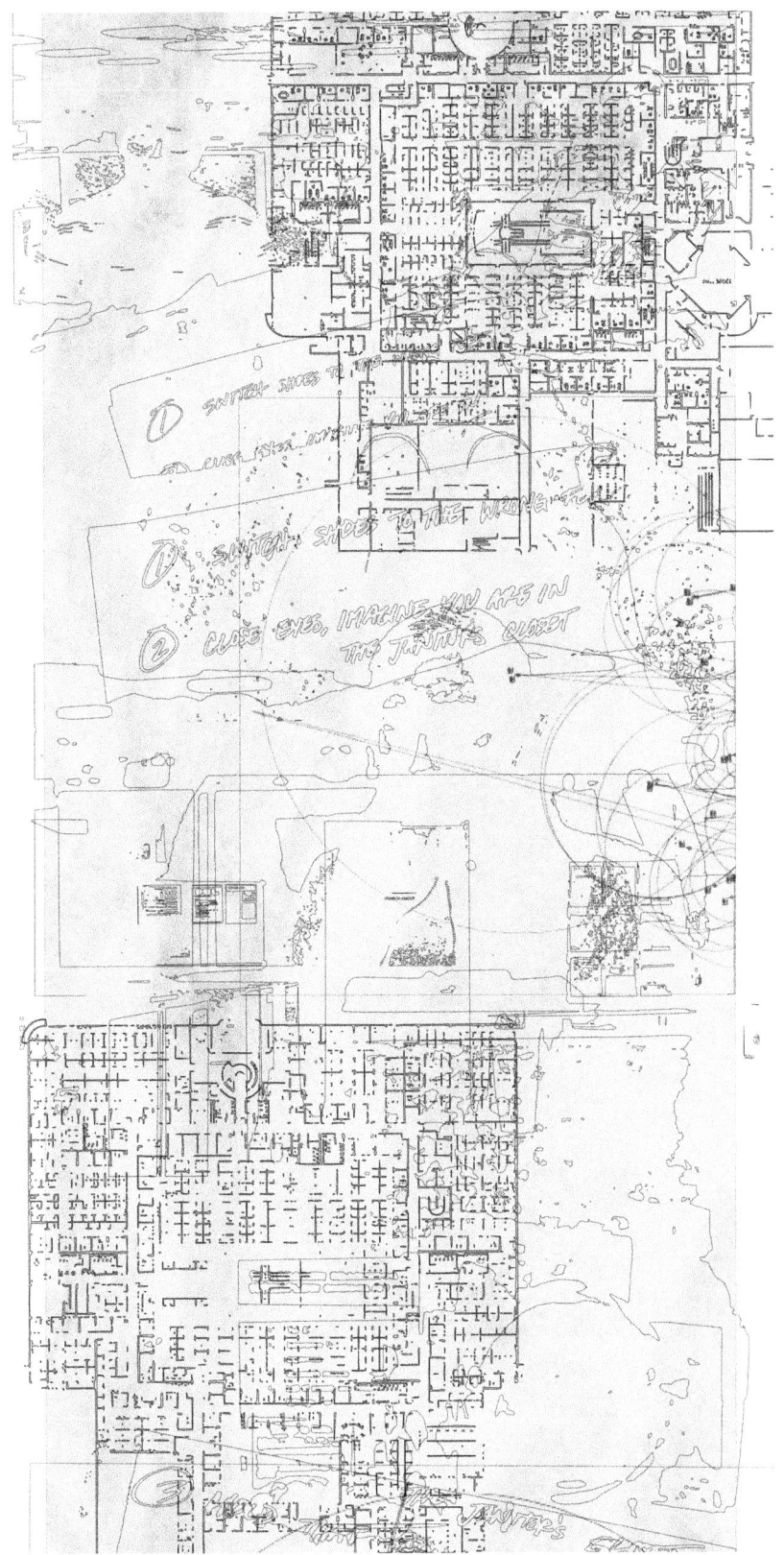

As Walter Benjamin observed, the past and present converge in a constellation; (21) this design embodies that moment between what was, what remains and what is to come.

The project resists the impulse to solve; there is no mechanism to prescribe what is valuable, leaving that choice to communities and individuals. Each platform includes a keeper's house, occupied by stewards who maintain the system and support users. Their presence introduces care into a landscape otherwise shaped by uncertainty. The structure records change rather than resisting it. Tidal lines stain walls, materials rust and age, surfaces absorb time. The site becomes a living document of impermanence rather than a monument to permanence. The project is generous, slow, and open, expanding on the agendas of public bodies including the Environment Agency and Greater London Authority reimagining collective life beyond productivity.

This is not a utopia or vision of stability. It is a quiet infrastructure, a civic project that holds space for care, memory and choice. In a city defined by disappearance, it is a refusal to forget.

(top right) Relief City, Angela de la Vega, DS3.1

(bottom right) Urban Acupuncture, Angela de la Vega, DS3.1

Works by Angela de la Vega

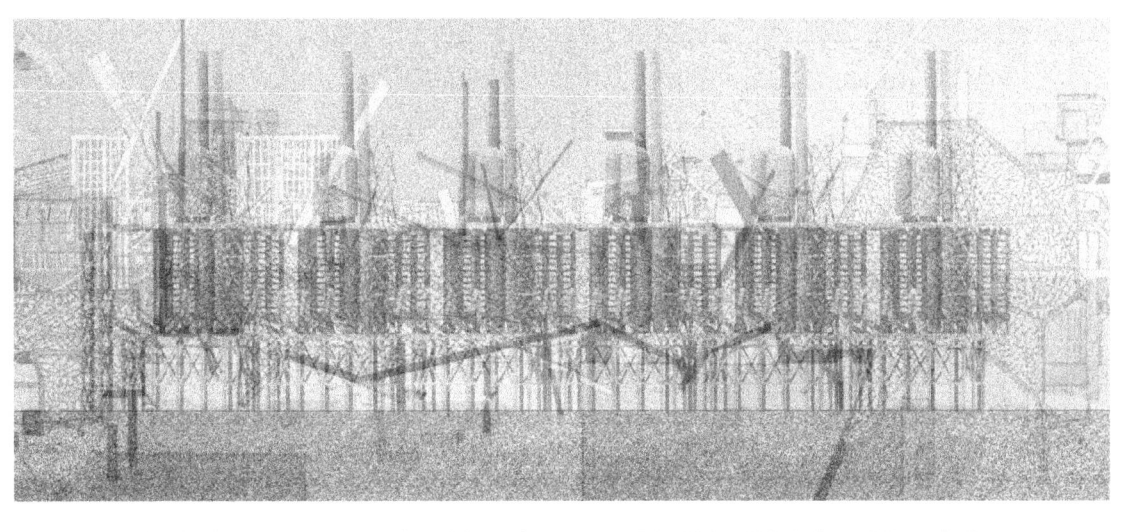

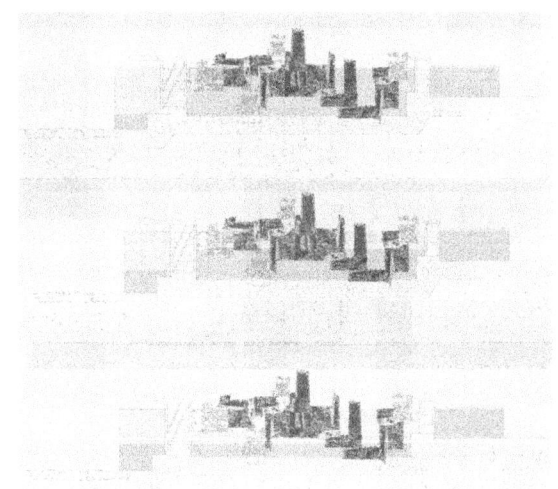

CASE STUDY BY AA'ISHAH BOUTRIG

'After Hours: Micro-Infrastructure for Migrant Workers'

"From this foul drain the greatest stream of human industry flows out to fertilise the whole world. From this filthy sewer gold flows." (22)

The transition from day to night in Canary Wharf alludes to Tocqueville's torrent of humans. (23) The mills and factories, Tocqueville's foul drains, have become the gleaming monuments of capitalism: the bank headquarters that stand as the 'end' result of a tumult that began with the industrial revolution, a revolution that fixed the divide between haves and have-nots, the server and the serviced, on a terrifying, epic, now global scale. Today, a torrent of workers still flows; now bankers, hedge funders and stock-brokers file to or from the tube on their way to or from home. But once almost emptied by night, Canary Wharf becomes inhabited by a new army, unseen and overlooked, the service workers. Unbeknownst to all these workers who come and go, seen and overlooked, there is a pocket of inhabitants completely hidden away: an MI5 surveillance team. We can only assume that their presence is to protect the financial capital of the western world... But in this story the night-workers and surveillance agents work together in a symbiotic and self-supporting relationship of concealment and protection.

(top) Map, Aa'ishah Boutrig, DS3.1
(bottom left) House Photo, Aa'ishah Boutrig, DS3.1
(bottom right) Data Sheets, Aa'ishah Boutrig, DS3.1

The project proposes a network of humble service structures located along London's DLR elevated viaduct, providing essential infrastructure for the city's night service workers. Disregarded and faceless this marginalised, poorly paid but essential urban workforce include cleaners, security guards, carers, hospitality staff and warehouse workers. Often immigrants, working day and night shifts to make ends meet they work to support the rest of society but who is supporting them? The project seeks to celebrate, support and safeguard the night-worker community through a series of light-touch 'service stations' located along the line from Mile End to Bank.

"The night is a space where official maps falter, where zones of control and surveillance flicker and break down, revealing the city in its raw and unvarnished form." (24)

Each unit is modest in scale, proposed as a tower elevated above the tracks, acting as translucent beacons in the dark. The structures represent respite and resistance, offering warmth, light, nourishment and protection in urban spaces often characterised by absence and neglect. Containing facilities such as rest pods, laundrettes, school uniform and lunch pick ups, storage lockers, prayer rooms and communal kitchens, the stations are intended as civic infrastructure on a micro scale.

Running parallel to the visible functions of care and sustenance, a series of MI5 surveillance nodes are embedded in the under crofts of the railway viaducts, where agents are not only intelligence gathering, but also preparing packed lunches, washing school uniforms and maintaining the service facilities above.

The duality of protection and control becomes spatialised. Above ground: community and care. Below ground: observation, surveillance and state presence.

These structures quietly acknowledge the political tensions between visibility and security in the night city. These are not buildings of power or permanence, but temporary sanctuaries that are weathered, mobile and open to adaptation. In opposition to conventional urban infrastructure designed to support capital is the notion of shared time, shared space, an architecture that serves people.

It does not pity night workers, but celebrates their resilience and community. It recognises that for many, the day begins at dusk. A civic proposal of solidarity and care for those who are awake while others sleep.

"To understand the city's soul, we must descend below its surface, into the voids where its deepest conflicts are hidden." (25)

(top) Night Workers, Aa'ishah Boutrig, DS3.1   *(bottom) Night View, Aa'isah Boutrig, DS3.1*

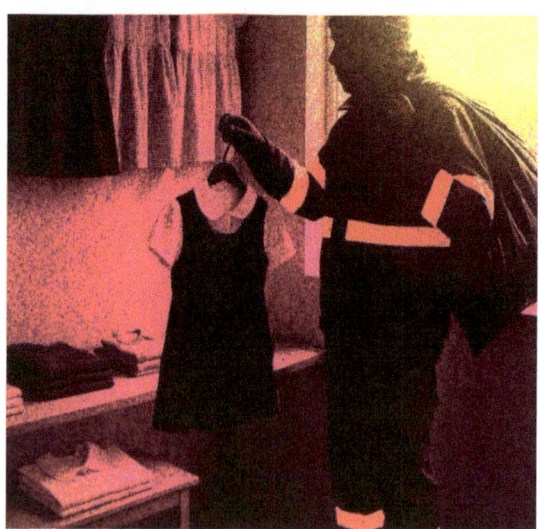

Works by Aa'ishah Boutrig

CASE STUDY BY ALI MONTERO

'Southwark Sexual Health Clinic'

4th June 1913: a woman collides with a race-horse.

The protestor sacrifices her life, but no statue is erected. Instead, memorials to fallen soldiers adorn the streets of London, a posthumous gentleman's club, dripping in national sorrow. Meanwhile, south of the Thames, the bones of 15,000 medieval sex-workers and social outcasts lay underfoot. Their memory is buried deep, unmarked and unnamed in their final resting place.

This injustice is not consigned to the past. In 2020, sex crime, sexually transmitted infections and domestic abuse were at an all-time high in the Borough of Southwark. Rising from the ashes, in direct challenge to the developer led gentrification proposed for the site close to Crossbones and the railway line, a holistic landscape and space of reparation is proposed. Amidst lush and scented vegetation will stand an inner-city women's refuge and sexual health centre. The project will retain the palimpsestic traces of those forgotten and serve to protect vulnerable women in the contemporary community. Emphasising inclusivity and anonymity, the porous architectural language explores physical and phenomenological transparency, safety, support and agency. Visitors can permeate the building as far as they feel comfortable, whilst accessing urgently needed services. Behaviours that include resting, loitering and casual socialising are encouraged through careful detailed design.

(upper right) What Makes a Village, Ali Montero, DS3.1   *(bottom) Horse Drawing, Ali Montero, DS3.1*

183

Feminist methodology rejects institutionalised, hegemonic, capitalist systems of design: working intuitively with post-rationalisation leads to non-linear processes in which precedents, ideas and forms are frequently revisited and laterally reinterpreted.

The image of Emily Davison's collision with the king's horse at the 1913 Epsom Derby, threads throughout the project inspiring processes that challenge conventional means of design and representation.

Early drawings included coded and indexed mappings, reconstructing:

"the relationship between the space of speculation (the drawing) and the space of execution (the building)." [26]

The decision to consider form and programme separately informed ideas of hybrid use and multiple simultaneous programmes. Research into the militant action of the suffragettes revealed how they politicised the domestic realm through action.

This notion, that the domestic interior can be a space of the radical has underpinned this project. The work of Beatriz Colomina, Adolf Loos, bell hooks and Audrey Lorde have been a mainstay in the project's theoretical development.

Colomina defines the domestic interior as feminine: 'the scene of sexuality and of reproduction'. [27] She describes how Loos's architecture uses spatial hierarchy to establish the female occupant as 'in control', with the bedroom overlooking the social spaces below.

The bedroom is positioned 'at the threshold of the private, the secret… At the intersection of the visible and the invisible, women act as the guardians of the unspeakable'. [28] This inspired a consideration of sexuality and sexual health in architecture and led to a programmatic response to the taboo of sex. This proposal is understood as a reparation for gender injustices that took place on the site, attempting to heal the scars of a brutal past by protecting the vulnerable of today.

(top) Site Massing, Ali Montero, DS3.1

(bottom) Site Massing, Ali Montero, DS3.1

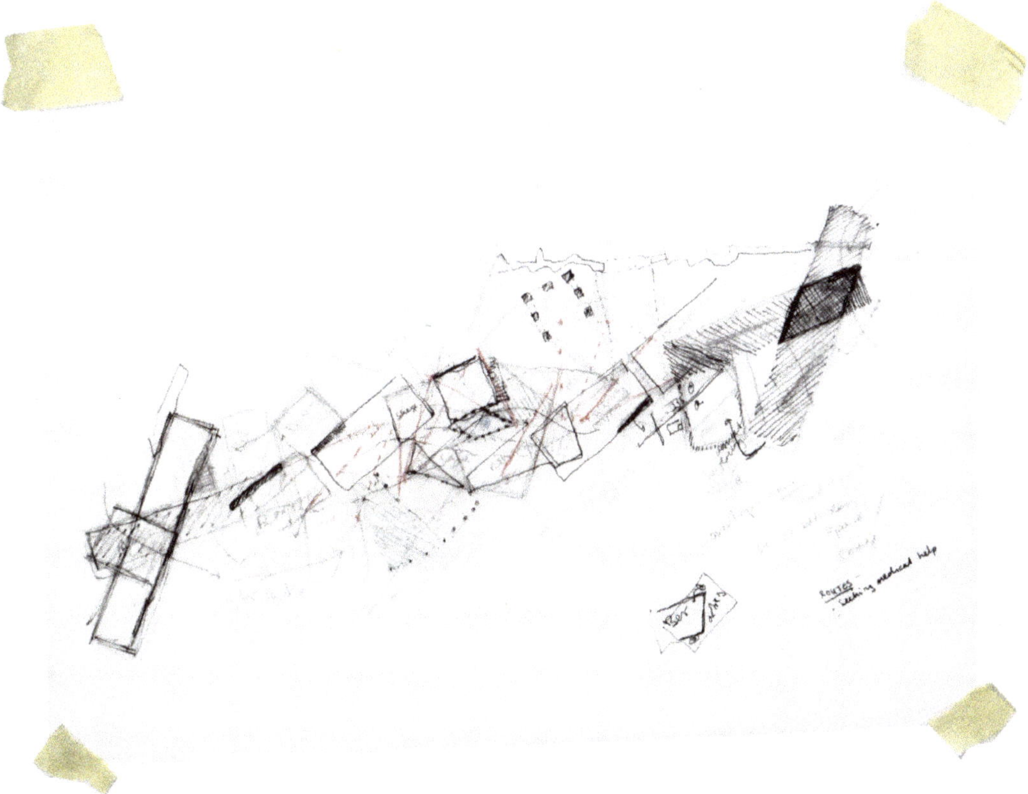

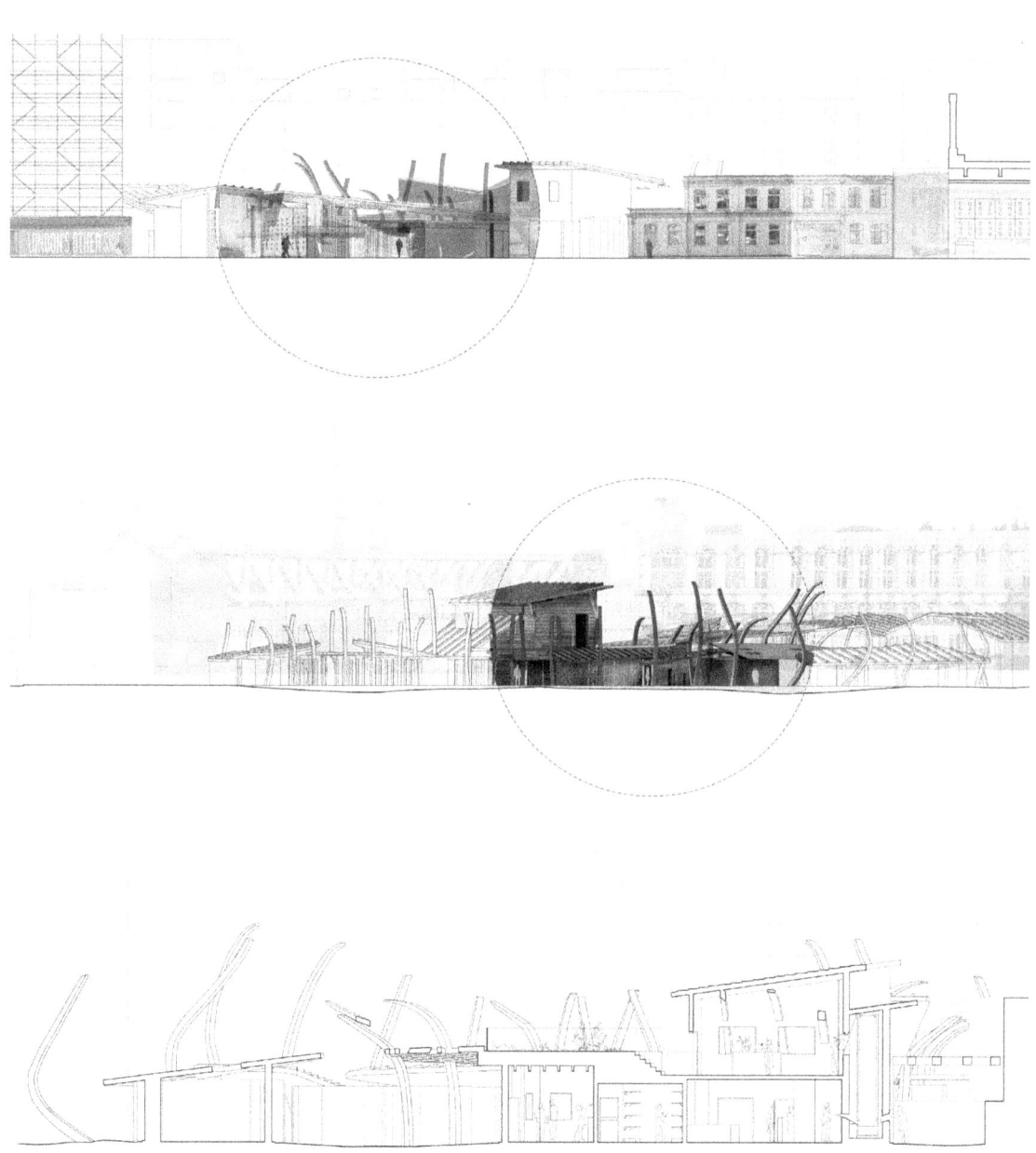

Works by Ali Montero, DS3.1

CASE STUDY BY FINOLA SIMPSON

'Bridge Number 01'

"To figure out someone's power, observe the way they sleep." (29)

The relationship between social deprivation and lack of agency is heightened by environmental crisis. In the documentary film *Cities of Sleep*, (30) control over one's space to sleep in New Delhi separates rich from poor. Nomadism and economic migrancy leave the thousands of homeless adults and children in this sprawling city vulnerable, both physically and mentally to assault and the environment. Apart from the threat of violence and personal theft, the Yamuna River often floods the outdoor communal sleeping areas, saturating any prized possessions and rented bedding. On a good night, the heat of the ground, air and adjacent bodies leave the exhausted little respite from the day's labours. But those who get a prized spot on the cast iron girders of a railway bridge crossing the river have a very different night of rest. Protection from advancing waters and the persistent cooling breeze makes so much difference to the possibility of sleep. Following a detailed exploration of poverty demographics in Tower Hamlets, one of the poorest boroughs in the UK, and flood risk mapping, it seems that Limehouse houses some of the most deprived Londoners in one of the most vulnerable flood-risk areas. The privatisation of the river edges also prevents access to the river on the hottest of summer days. 'Bridge No 1' proposes an inhabited bridge crossing the Thames from Limehouse to Rotherhithe.

(right) Limehouse Flood Map, Finola Simpson, DS3.1

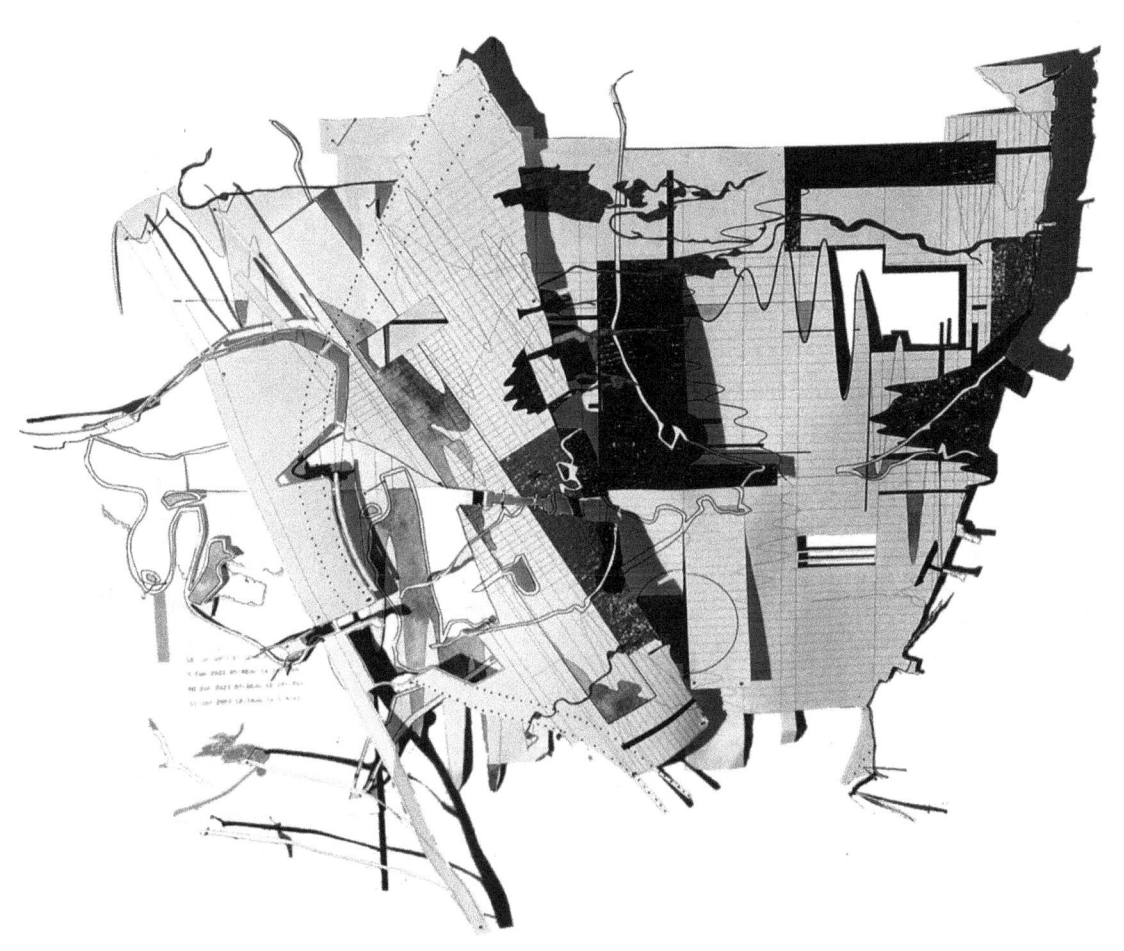

Envisioned as a space of radical settlement and co-habitation, it offers the opportunity for those most vulnerable to climate change to live in one of the most prized locations in London, with self-sufficiency and radical care at its heart. Tidal energy, connection with the water and hybrid functions informed by the S.I. *New Urban Formulary*, (31) has resulted in a programme where traditional typologies are upended.

Sleeping in your artisan workspace (for artists who love their practice), homes in the public library (for those who love to be surrounded by books), a doctor's surgery in a brothel (sex-workers first), a top floor dining space for moon gazing…

The inhabited crossing will provide a non-vehicular connection offering opportunities for endless derive between the north and south banks of the river.

Supported by knowledge sharers and skills teachers inhabiting homes at either end, like the gardener advisors in Cuba, (32) the bridge community will host educational and cultural events to help generate income and sharing.

(top) Digital Bridge Model, Finola Simpson, DS3.1

(bottom) Physical Bridge Model, Finola Simpson, DS3.1

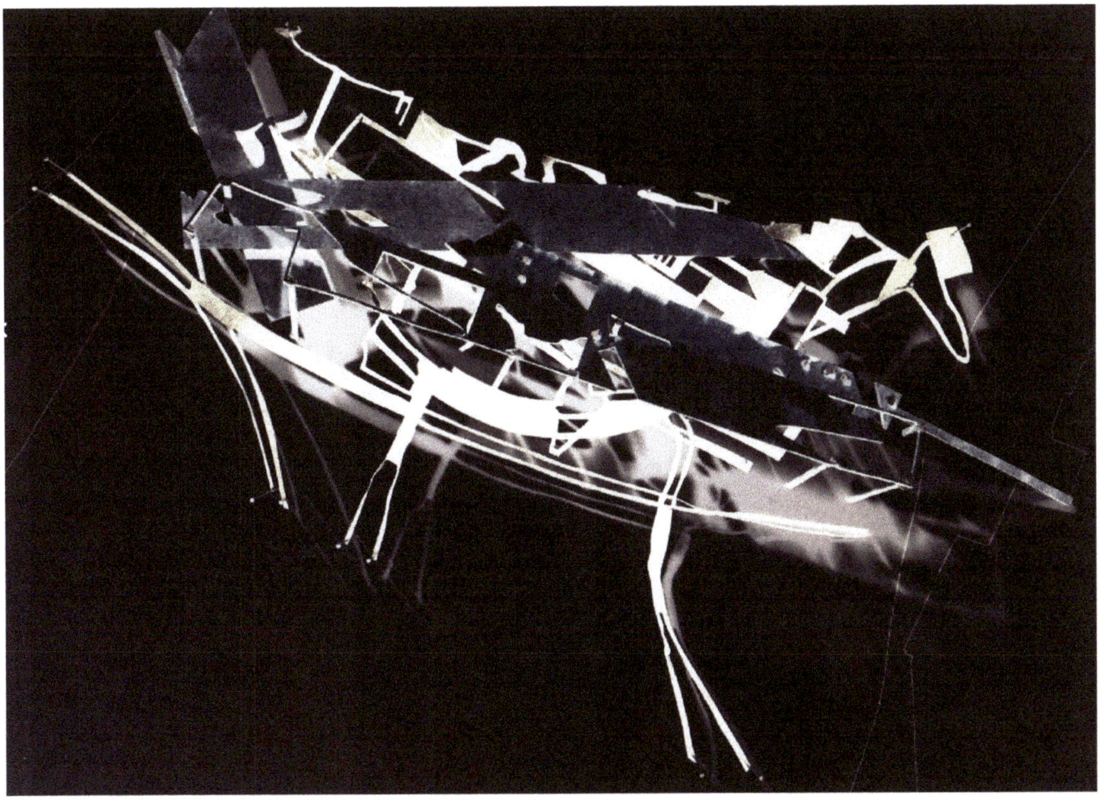

Works by Finola Simpson

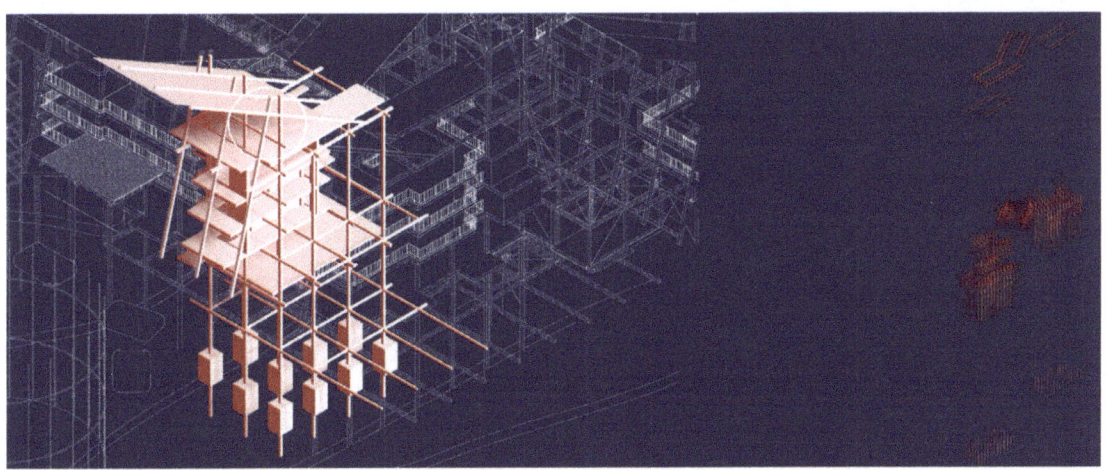
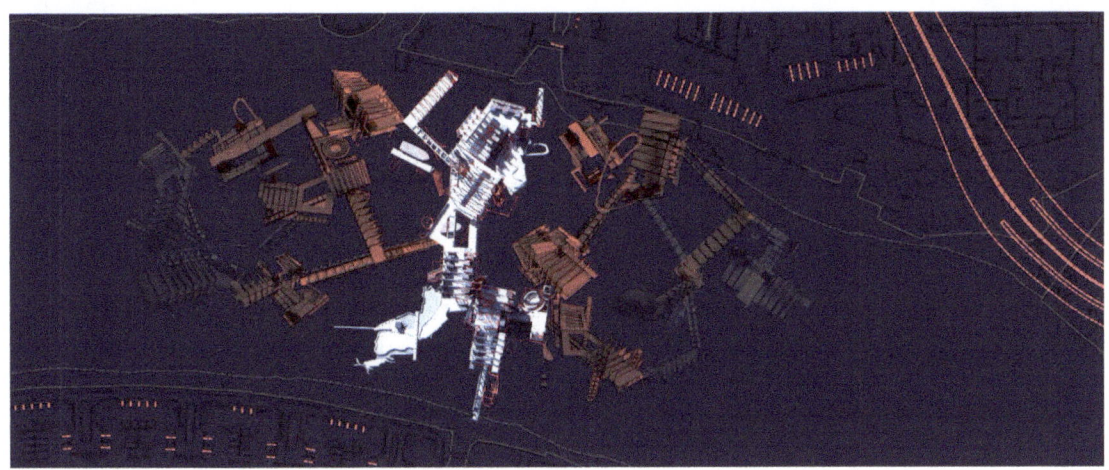

CASE STUDY BY ROWAN ISLES

'Neo-nostalgic Heterotopia: Deptford's Model Village'

The development of Convoys Wharf poses a massive change to the already gentrifying Deptford. The planned 2300 flats and their new residents, mostly young professionals working on the opposite river bank at Canary Wharf, will occupy a large portion of Deptford's river front. The site, with a history of cattle markets and naval shipyards, is currently a barren landscape owned by a Hong Kong investment firm. The residents of Deptford have already fought developers who have taken away vital community spaces. Tensions are high. Convoys wharf is Deptford's new battleground. In semester 1, the project conceived of an alien structure which would create a shield of fog to hide canary wharf, protecting Deptford from the incoming percolation of capitalist ideology which is driving the parasitic developments in Deptford. Protected in the cloud, a fragment of Deptford history is to be maintained. Ubiquitous in days gone by, pie and mash represents a London which is disappearing, being forgotten like the residents of Deptford. The site is proposed as a farm dedicated to providing the ingredients of pie and mash, not forgetting the jellied eels and liquor.

(right) Deptford Photo Series, Rowan Isles, DS3.1

Neo-nostalgic heterotopia: Deptford's model village, the semester two project, proposes a somewhat farcical polemic in two manifestations of nostalgia, a model village and a utopian settlement, both places approaching contrasting realisations of community and architecture.

The relationship between the two can be compared to Freud's theories surrounding the *Heimlich* (the familiar), and *Unheimlich* (the weird). The model village plays with *Heimlich* nostalgia in the form of capitalist tendencies, mirroring the Thatcherite ideal of Britain, which in reality is built on a façade of grand old Britain and the strength of its imperialistic past. The architecture samples from the vernacular of Deptford, neat little rows of terraced houses, a church, grassy parks and the pie and mash shop. Upon visiting Deptford model village all appears to be in-keeping with the idealistic image; however, behind the façade of some of the houses the *Unheimlich* world of a utopian settlement can be glimpsed, intriguing the visitors of the model village.

The utopian settlement originates from ideas of a nostalgia for the future, the *Unheimlich* of post war innovation and the socialist utopia posed by William Morris in *News from Nowhere*. (33) Here in this settlement people are free to live as they please, tending to the fields and milking the cows unencumbered by modern society but maintaining the ruse of the model village. Dressing up as a milkman for 5 minutes delivering fresh milk to the visitors of the model village, before returning through an unsuspecting door of a terrace house into the slaughterhouse hidden behind the façade. The architecture of the utopian settlement, inspired by the Smithsons, Buckminster Fuller and Archigram, is the epithet of *Unheimlich* nostalgia, the world we are supposed to be living in. The blend of the model village and utopian settlement form interstitial spaces, a moment where both groups of inhabitants have the ability to understand the convergence of the nostalgia of the *Heimlich* and *Unheimlich*, and question which side they would prefer to occupy.

(right) Model Houses, Rowan Isles, DS3.1

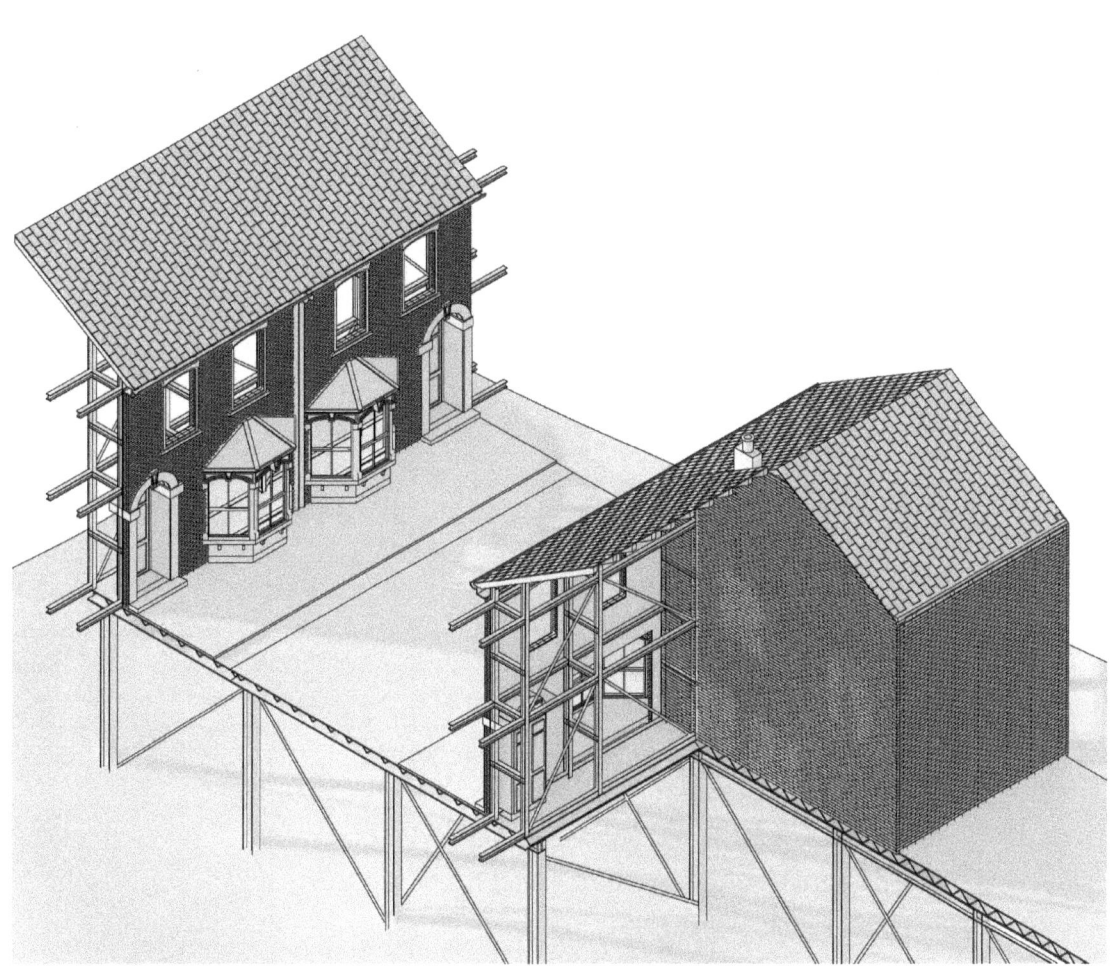

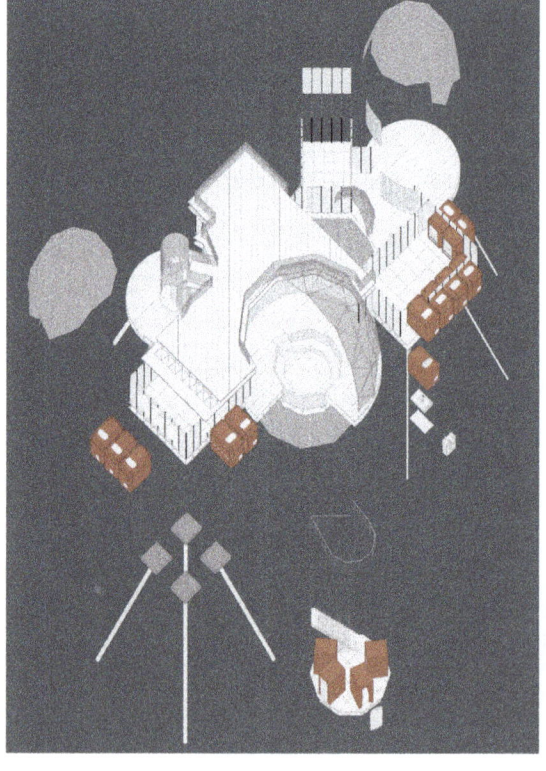

Works by Rowan Isles, DS3.1

CASE STUDY BY VICTORIA PEARCE

'The Thames as a Free Machine'

The film *Floating* by Richard Heslop (34) tells the story of a Docklands bus driver whose nervous breakdown is manifested in 'visions of a labyrinthine London about to be consumed by water'. As a reaction to his belief that a second great flood is about to descend upon the city, he begins to destroy his family's tower block flat in order to make room for an unlikely refuge in their front room and to construct an Ark to save both his family and humanity. Now over twenty years old, the anxieties of climate catastrophe and urban flooding experienced by the main character could never be more prevalent. Following on from his film, the project aids the main characters attempt to construct a protective space, one that welcomes all and creates an exchange between land and water. The project addresses our city's limited and exclusive access to the Thames and attempts to make *'use of the Thames as a free machine'*, accessible to all. Through critical analysis of those who live on the water and those who live behind the exclusive edge, the project considers how these two groups might be integrated and share a space through access to the river. Most would consider the Thames a public space and one to be enjoyed by all. The redevelopment of the Docklands has seen a huge rise in house prices, a complete demographic change and a resulting limited access to the Thames.

(top right) Landscape Test, Victoria Pearce, DS3.1   *(bottom right) Landscape Test, Victoria Pearce, DS3.1*

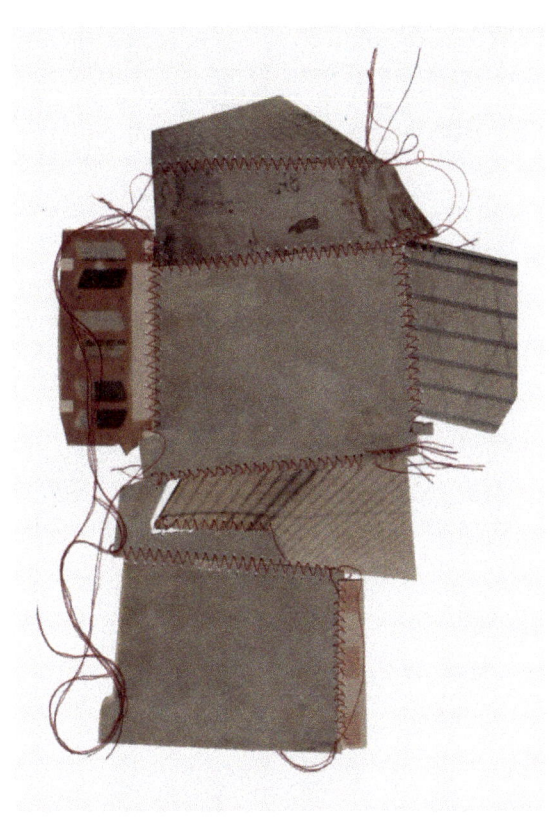
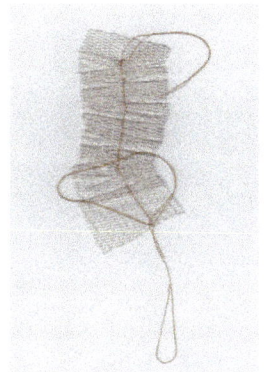

There are multiple access points to the river that have either been privatised or blocked off by construction works being carried out on private housing. In a census study, those closest to the water presented with the highest income; as you move further back the average income decreases, showing a correlation between low income and limited access to the river.

The project takes inspiration from the site's long history of industrialisation and technologies such as the rope and sail. It will also consider how we might use the Thames as a source of alternative energy. Structures such as the coracle boat and Cedric Prices adaptation of "The Red Sand Towers, as an alternative community." (35) These inspired a People's Parliament and meeting space for environmental research whilst simultaneously addressing free access to the Thames edge.

Inspired by the way sails harness the power of water and wind, the project begins to unravel the possibilities of the Thames to also be used as a 'free energy source'. Using 90% less material than wind turbines Kite Power will be the primary source of energy generation, spinning structures to generate electricity. These structures combined with the research into Frei Otto's retractable buildings initiated the development of a circular roof design. A community-led centre for environmental research and debate, the building design attempts to dismantle hierarchies with research education and political debate, all focused on climate change and all housed as part of a community exchange. The building is completely energy efficient with surplus being provided to local deprived communities. A zip up puffa jacket enclosure keeps the main hall warm and dry in the winter months, unzipping for air and light in the summer.

(bottom right) Inside the Free Machine, Victoria Pearce, DS3.1

Works by Victoria Pearce, DS3.1

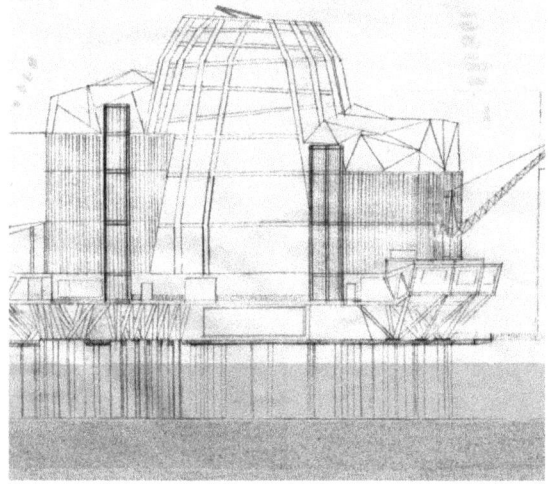
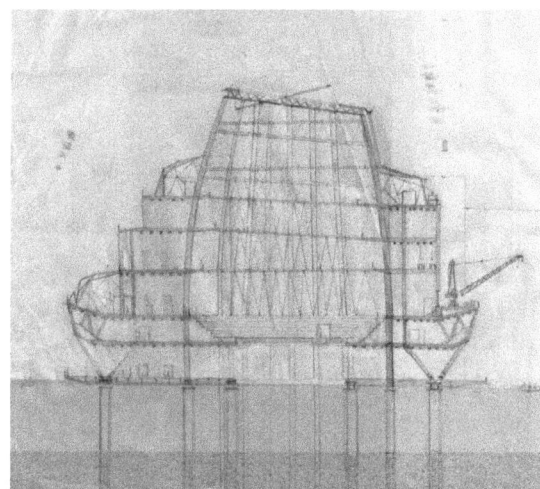

CASE STUDY BY MARK ROWE

'Ideal Home for a Serial Killer'

Produced in 1994, this was primarily a project searching for where the Architect had the authority that the profession often deluded itself it exercised universally.

The exterior surface, the façade, is part of the composite that is the city, itself democratically 'owned' by the gaze of everybody; the interior surface, the domestic, is seemingly private but, as Denis Neilson discovered on 8 February 1983, the apparatus of the state in its various guises can invade that space too; the only place we truly exercise significant control over, as Architects, is everything between those two surfaces, that is what we draw in sections and details, it is the materials and components which we oversee and certify on a building site for the duration of construction until those zones are sealed for posterity (or until a leak). Living now in an age of hyper-techno-surveillance, it feels even more like the interstitial spaces of our buildings may be our last sanctuary, and tellingly we discussed the *Diary of Anne Frank* as often as *Killing for Company* during this project's development. Obviously, it was also trying to shock, particularly in the context of the work of Tschumi and others, those who thought they were being transgressive but were only in fact disrespecting the narrow tenets of mid-century architectural modernism rather than wider contemporary culture in the late twentieth century.

(right) Psychopathic Element Design, Mark Rowe

Psychopathic Element Design

MARK ROWE

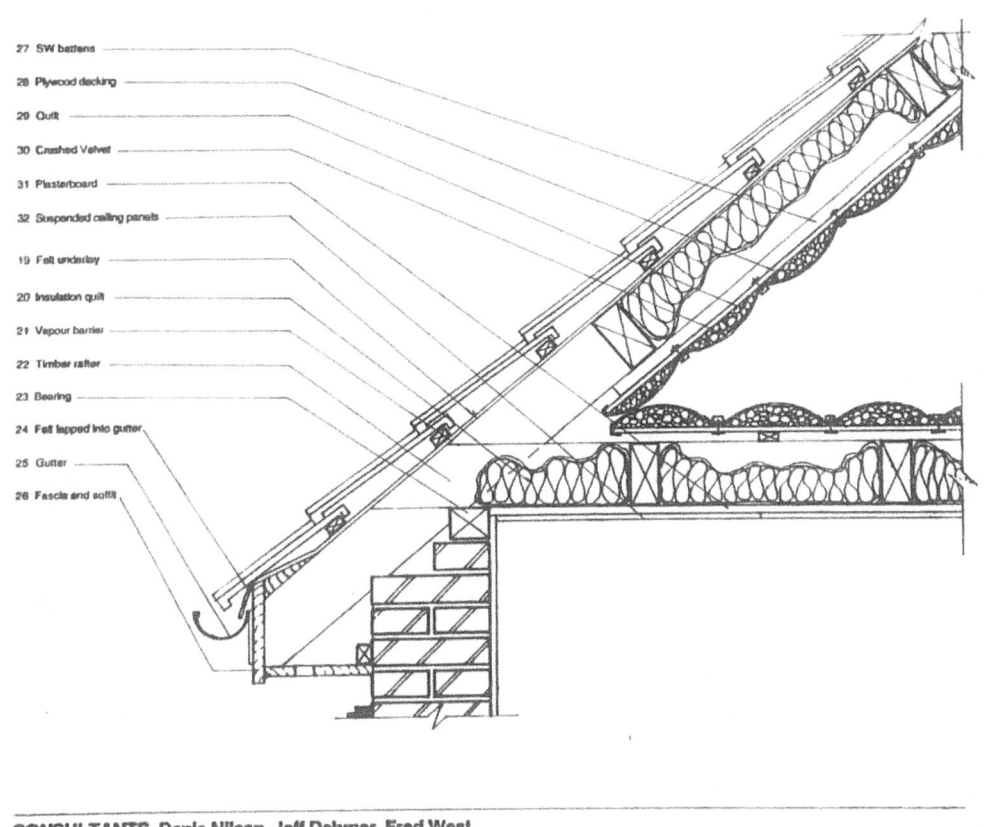

27 SW battens
28 Plywood decking
29 Quilt
30 Crushed Velvet
31 Plasterboard
32 Suspended ceiling panels
19 Felt underlay
20 Insulation quilt
21 Vapour barrier
22 Timber rafter
23 Bearing
24 Felt lapped into gutter
25 Gutter
26 Fascia and soffit

CONSULTANTS Denis Nilsen Jeff Dahmer Fred West

GEORGE GODWIN LIMITED

Tschumi's AA posters used dramatic images and language to ultimately inform architectural programmes and form only mildly grammatically deviant from their predecessors. This project wanted to run with the idea of needing *'to carry out murder to appreciate architecture'* to its natural unsavoury conclusion, letting form hide function rather than follow it. Following on from that premise, it also said something about the life and use of buildings that as designers we often facilitate but do not always want to acknowledge. The client always calls the shots and generally we provide for their needs rather than walking away from the commission; the prisons, asylum applicant detention centres, animal testing laboratories, abattoirs and worse of this country all need planning permission and building control approval. Communicating the project through the neutrality of a generic book of standard details, a typology prevalent in practice at the time, seemed like the most obvious way to manifest Arendt's banality of evil.

So, in every sense, although I maybe wasn't fully aware at the time, this project was about testing boundaries; the territory of an Architect's agency, who gets to define what that agency is deployed for (spoiler: whoever's paying), and the generally accepted limits of good taste. In professional practice these questions arise regularly, and my mind has strayed back to this exploration more often than you'd imagine!

(right) Psychopathic Element Design Poster, Mark Rowe

To really appreciate a murder, you may even need to commit architecture.

Architectural theory is merely rhetoric when a seductive image or notion is naively employed for shock value. If Murder in the Street differs from Murder in the Home how does this difference affect architecture ? Such an event is surely worth investigating. Radically.

Mark Rowe
Post Graduate Student of School of Architecture
South Bank University

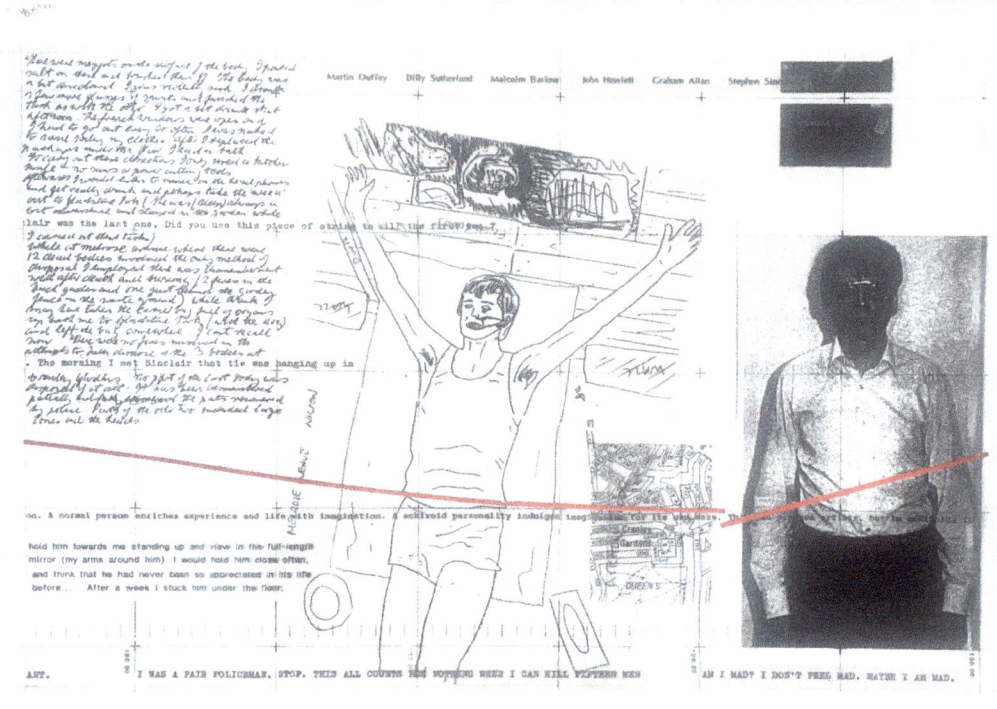

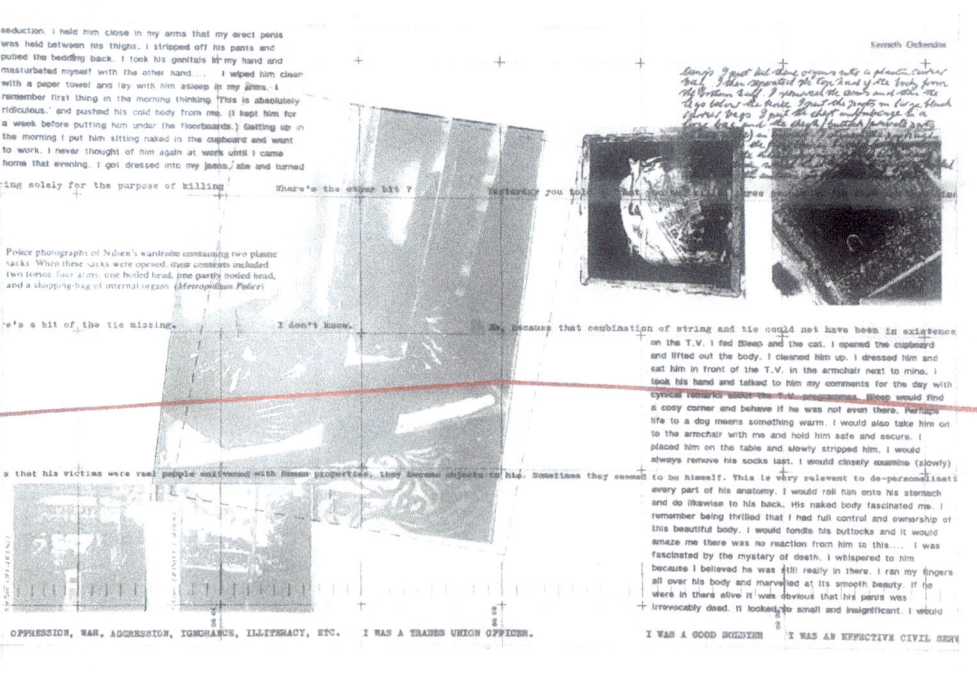

Works by Mark Rowe

Chimney storage spaces - typical detail

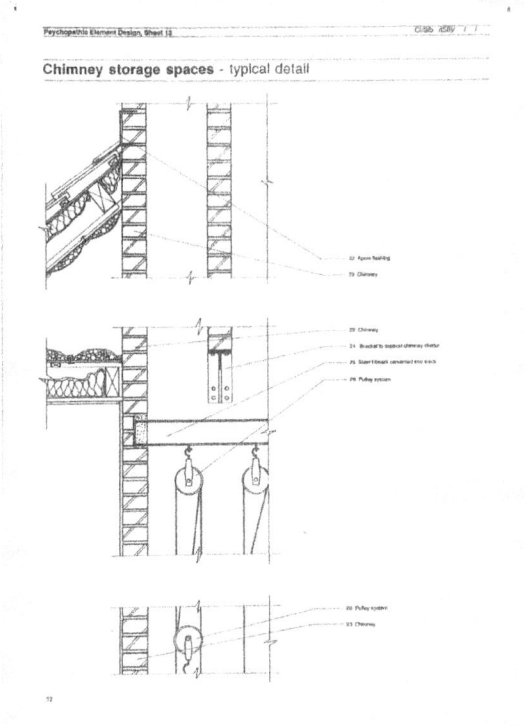

Refrigerated intermediate floors - key factors

Key factors	Action	Counteraction
Time	Decay of body parts	Refrigeration, Containment of parts
	Odour	Ventilation, Refrigeration
Gravity	Downward pull	Support
Society	Intrusion into private world	Disguise, Deception
Rain	Moisture deposition	Deflection, Impervious skin, Absorption and drainage
Police	Investigation	Disguise, Deception
Wind	Motive force (suction)	Rigidity, Resilience, Sealing
Schizophrenia	Concurrent realities	Separation of realities

Refrigerated intermediate floors - typical detail

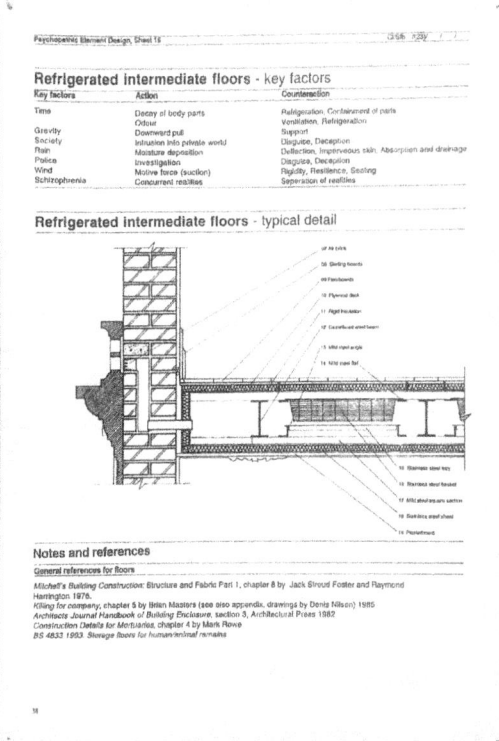

Notes and references
General references for floors
Mitchell's Building Construction: Structure and Fabric Part 1, chapter 8 by Jack Stroud Foster and Raymond Harrington 1976.
Killing for company, chapter 5 by Brian Masters (see also appendix, drawings by Denis Nilson) 1985
Architects Journal Handbook of Building Enclosure, section 3, Architectural Press 1982
Construction Details for Mortuaries, chapter 4 by Mark Rowe
BS 4833 1993. Storage floors for human/animal remains

Internal Inspection Manhole - typical detail

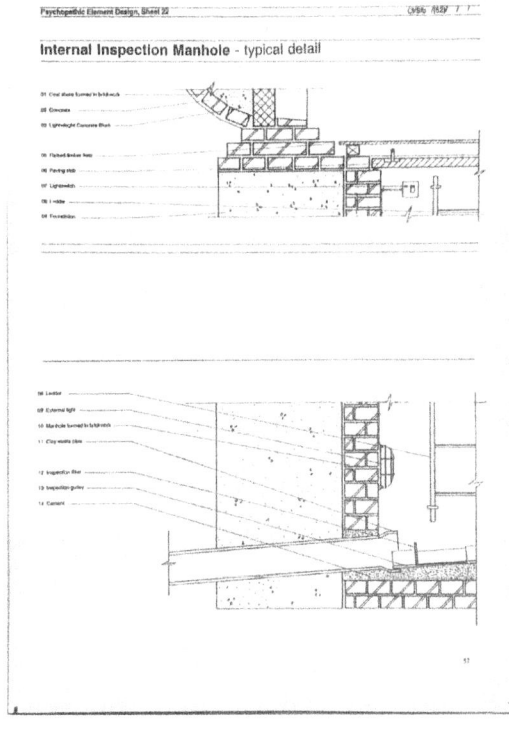

NOTES

(01) Kristin Ross, *Communal Luxury: The Political Imaginary of the Paris Commune* (London: Verso, 2015).
(02) Ibid.
(03) Karen Barad, *Meeting the Universe Halfway: Quantum Physics and the Entanglement of Matter and Meaning* (Durham: Duke University Press, 2007).
(04) bell hooks, *Ain't I a Woman: Black Women and Feminism* (Boston: South End Press, 1981).
(05) Audre Lorde, *Sister Outsider: Essays and Speeches* (Trumansburg, NY: Crossing Press, 1984).
(06) Bernard Tschumi, *Event-Cities* (Cambridge, MA: MIT Press, 1994).
(07) Anthony Vidler, *The Architectural Uncanny: Essays in the Modern Unhomely* (Cambridge, MA: MIT Press, 1992); Lebbeus Woods, *Radical Reconstruction* (New York: Princeton Architectural Press, 1997); Steven Holl, *Anchoring* (New York: Princeton Architectural Press, 1994).
(08) Holl, Ibid.
(09) Katherine Shonfield, *Walls Have Feelings: Architecture, Film and the City* (London: Routledge, 2000).
(10) Robin Evans, *Translations from Drawing to Building and Other Essays* (Cambridge, MA: MIT Press, 1997).
(11) Stephen Graham, *Vertical: The City from Skyscraper to Streetscape* (London: Verso, 2021).
(12) Louis Auguste Blanqui, *L'Eternité par les astres* (Paris: 1872).
(13) Edgar Allan Poe, *The Fall of the House of Usher*, in *Tales of Mystery and Imagination* (New York: Putnam, 1839).
(14) Ibid.
(15) Anthony Vidler, *The Architectural Uncanny* (Cambridge, MA: MIT Press, 1992).
(16) Kazimir Malevich, *The Writings on Art* (Moscow: Veshch, 1927).
(17) Archigram, *Walking City* (London: Studio Vista, 1964).
(18) Kristin Ross, *Communal Luxury*, Ibid.
(19) Wallace Shawn, *The Fever* (New York: Dramatists Play Service, 1990).
(20) Ibid.
(21) Walter Benjamin, *The Arcades Project*, trans. Howard Eiland and Kevin McLaughlin (Cambridge, MA: Harvard University Press, 1999).
(22) James Phillips Kay-Shuttleworth, *The Moral and Physical Condition of the Working Classes Employed in the Cotton Manufacture in Manchester* (London: Ridgway, 1832).
(23) Alexis de Tocqueville, *Voyage en Angleterre et en Irlande* (Paris: 1835).
(24) *The New Urban Formulary*, Ivan Chtcheglov, "Formulary for a New Urbanism" (Paris: Internationale Situationniste, 1953).
(25) Emily Davison archive, Royal Holloway University of London, *Suffragette Papers*.
(26) Ibid.
(27) Beatriz Colomina, *Sexuality and Space* (Cambridge, MA: MIT Press, 1992), chapter "The Split Wall."
(28) Adolf Loos, in Colomina, Ibid.
(29) *Cities of Sleep*, dir. Niraj Dinesh (documentary, 2016).
(30) Ibid.
(31) Situationist International, Ivan Chtcheglov, "Formulary for a New Urbanism," Ibid.
(32) Ernesto Mendez et al., *Organopónicos: Urban Agriculture in Cuba* (Havana: Instituto de Investigaciones Agropecuarias, 2015).
(33) William Morris, *News from Nowhere* (London: Longmans, Green and Co., 1890).
(34) Richard Heslop, *Floating* (film, UK, 2002).
(35) Cedric Price, *The Red Sand Towers*, architectural sketch archive (London: AA Publications, 1968).
(36) Situationist International, Ivan Chtcheglov, "Formulary for a New Urbanism," Ibid.

APPROPRIATE, RECONFIGURE, MAKE DO AND MEND

ALICIA PIVARO

APPROPRIATE, RECONFIGURE, MAKE DO AND MEND BY ALICIA PIVARO

'We asked the question what is 'allowed' as part of your architectural education? And we all looked elsewhere.'

"when education is used as a form of self-development, rather than a memory test, students realise that knowledge is power." (01)

Collaborating with Jane Tankard and the students of Studio 3.1 was a creative, dynamic and transformative experience. We informed our teaching with ideas from anarchism, Marxist urban theory and radical pedagogy as well as progressive politics, economics and art. Brazilian educational theorist and philosopher, Paolo Freire, saw education not as a 'banking system' of learning knowledge and facts but also the learning of how to think critically and creatively. *Pedagogy of the Oppressed* (01) is one of the foundational texts in the field of critical education, which seeks to help students question and challenge the beliefs and practices that dominate. Our students were encouraged to create, test and reflect on radical interventions in the city as pivots to create 'future-proof' microcosms of sustainable, propositional thinking. To be part of a movement of alternative visioning of the world that rejected the exploitative, extractive and competitive rules of neoliberalism for the collaborative, caring, co-operative strategies of eco-anarchism and post-capitalist thinking.

(right) Mayday Rooms, Rowan St John, DS3.1

This chapter highlights some of our sources of inspiration and how Appropriate, Reconfigure, Make Do and Mend were a loose collection of ideas, tools and tactics. These informed our joint working towards the idea of a co-produced city that was equitable, just and sustainable addressing the extreme climate and social inequalities we are faced with today. Our pedagogy jumped around histories and disciplines, from academia to activism. It operated in an expanded field of architectural practice.

APPROPRIATE, EVERYTHING, TOOLS, IDEAS, TACTICS, SPACES

"I only steal from art I can learn from." (02)

We asked the question, what is 'allowed' as part of your architectural education? And we all looked elsewhere. Students were encouraged to develop their own creative practices and outcomes by utilising ideas that might normally fall outside what is considered 'conventional'. This critical, socially-engaged, interdisciplinary practice blurred the boundaries between creative processes.

"A beached whale is a reference point for all the chapters, quite a good storyline, exploratory for the characters, straight, gay, dying, poor, and wealthy. Some are happy, some are sad. Jesus and Socrates, and Marx, they named it. They're our beached whale reference points. Django Reinhardt, Einstein, Edward Said, them too." (03)

Precedents included Dada, Situationists, Joseph Beuys' 'social sculpture' happenings, Matta Clark interventions and all used history, narrative, collage and montage to generate new configurations of meaning.

They sought to activate communities, raise awareness of social issues, create new knowledge, relationships and realities. Other disciplines and techniques we used were;

Film - idea of narrative, stories, time, histories, spatial manipulation
Theatre – choreography, drama, speed of change, audience and actor
Music – sampling, emotion, syncopation, harmony, event/performance
Protest – zines, posters, propaganda, squatting, take-overs
Art – techniques of communication and participation, use of space, installation.

Of particular interest to us were the Situationist International (1957 – 1972) – an organisation of social revolutionaries made up of avant-garde artists, intellectuals, and political theorists. Central to situationist theory was the concept of the spectacle, a critique of advanced capitalism with the primary concern of the increasing tendency towards the suppression and mediation of social relations through objects or consumption. Perhaps the most famous architectural project to come from Situationist thinking was New Babylon - the futuristic vision of Dutch artist and anarchist Constant Nieuwenhuys. New Babylon, an anti-capitalist city perceived and designed between 1959-74, was imagined to be architecture without an Architect where citizens themselves would determine the extension and uses of the spaces. The scale of New Babylon is what makes it a unique project that resonates with the civic agency and ambition in the work of, for example, Lina Bo Bardi.

(right) Regents Canal Whale, Malak Huseynova, DS3.1

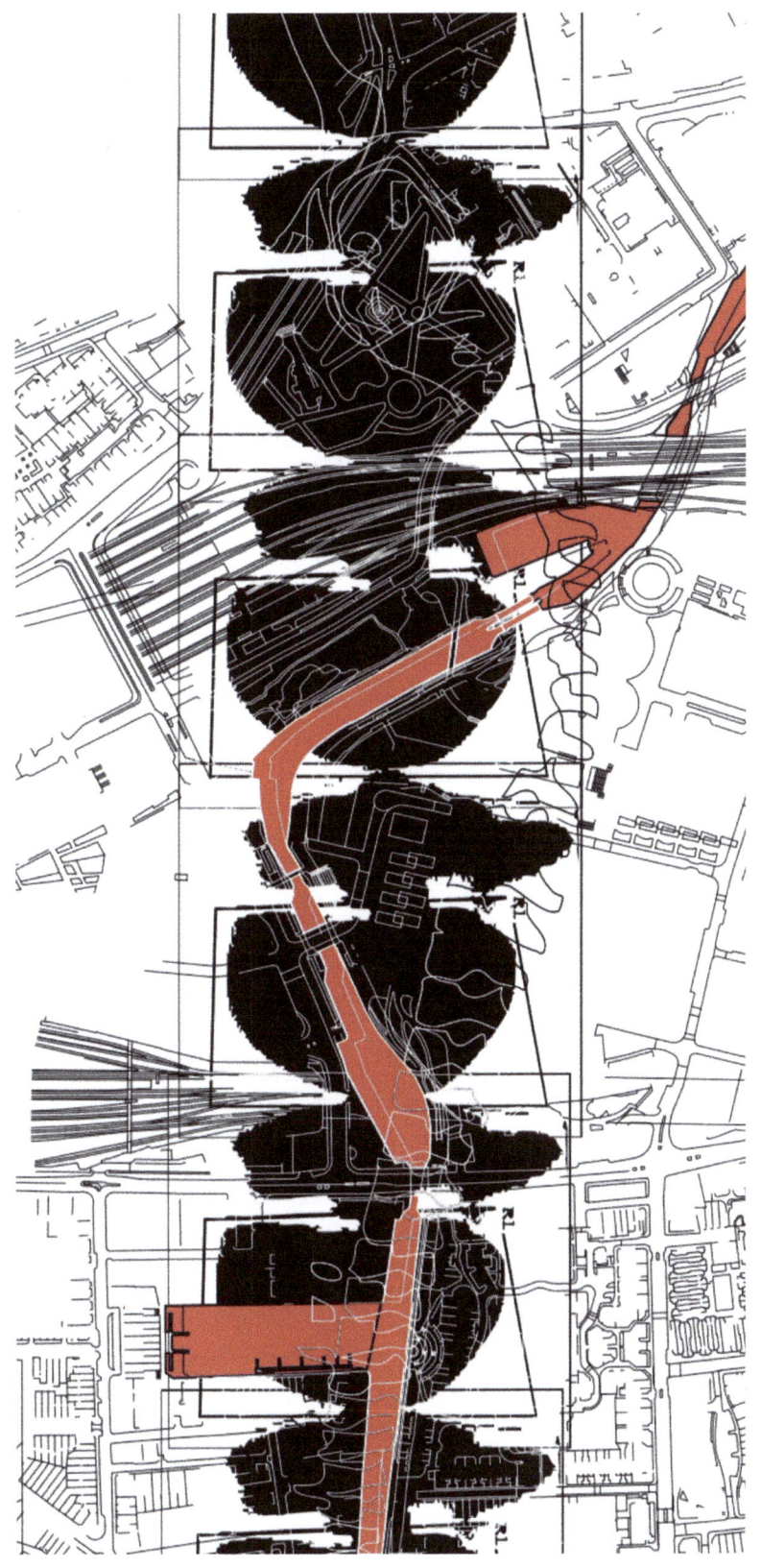

Lina Bo Bardi's work foregrounds the everyday and the creation of spaces that the community can use as they want. She also promoted the original mission of the Architect as an agent for social change, advocating for the necessity of political engagement. Socially-orientated projects of the 1990s to 2000s, as documented in *Living as Form*, (04) edited by Nato Thompson, can be traced back to the 1921 Paris Dada Season which involved citizens on the streets and included a mock trial. One of the first texts to address the political status of participation was by German theorist Walter Benjamin using the plays of Bertolt Brecht to explain the shift from mere spectators to collaborators. Through techniques of montage and juxtaposition, audiences are forced or provoked into taking a position on the action. These approaches include projects that de-authored lineage and embraced collective creativity, disruption and interventionism increasingly linking the idea of participation with political activism and belief.

"I went from an artist who makes things, to an artist who makes things happen." (05)

RECONFIGURE, EVERYTHING, SOCIAL RELATIONS, ECONOMIC AND POLITICAL CONSTRUCTS

"Be realistic, demand the impossible." (06)

In the studio, these methods were used as part of a participatory and collaborative approach to design linked to ideas of political empowerment, right to the city and deep and participatory democracy.

Marxist philosopher and sociologist, Henri Lefebrve contrasted the dominance of certain representations of space by scientists, planners and engineers over representational space that is the fluid and dynamic space of users. He revealed the ways which cultural and social life was vital to his concepts of 'Right to the City' and the 'Right to Difference'. Both these ideas were dependent on the diversity of population and activities in the city and the role of the public in the management and development of public space.

Lefebvre advocated for the messy, unplanned and constantly changing nature of urban culture that could allow for differences and create new practices and relationships. The right to the city is an idea and a slogan proposed by Lefebvre in his 1968 book *Le Droit à la Ville* (07) used by social movements, activists and progressive local authorities as a call to action to change the city as a co-created space.

In *Spatial Agency*, edited by Awan, Schneider and Till, they acknowledge that by making social space a social project:

"at a stroke Lefebvre wrestles the production of space from the clutches of specialists, most notably Architects and planners, and places it in a much broader context." (08)

In the book *Participation*, edited by Claire Bishop, she asks;

"So what are the connections between the earliest days of participatory art and practitioners today? [...]

(right) Studio Exploded, Isabella Testolin, DS3.1

Desire to create an active subject, one who will be empowered by participation [...] the idea of authorship where some or all of it is ceded to others which is seen as more egalitarian and democratic and also offer the benefits of greater risk and unpredictability. Collaborative creativity can be understood to emerge from and contribute to a more positive and non-hierarchical social model for society, even anarchic. [...] the third point is that of community cohesion and collective experience." (09)

Our post-capitalist economic thinking was informed by, amongst others, Kate Raworth's *Doughnut Economics: Seven Ways to Think Like a 21st Century Economist*, (10) which is a growingly successful counter-proposal to mainstream economic thinking. Drawing on insights from diverse schools of thought including ecological, feminist, institutional, behavioural and complexity economical thinking brings about the regenerative and distributive conditions for a sustainable economy.

Alternative economic models are being tested at local, regional and national levels, whether as versions of Kate Raworth's 'Doughnut economics' or variations of public, community owned, co-operative businesses, organisations and public systems for heating, banking, housing and transport, credit unions or community share or crowd-funded projects. We also shared the ideas of Colin Ward, a prolific anarchist author and teacher, who championed things and people on the margins, often hidden and undervalued, including community growers, self-builders, council estate kids and urban and rural squatters. He wrote about cities, education, housing, planning, nature, ecology and Utopia.

For him, Utopia wasn't some unobtainable fantasy but was happening all around us every day in the way people try to do things differently with care and respect, not profit. In his most famous book, *Anarchy in Action*, (11) Colin described these examples as 'seeds beneath the snow' and included spaces for small- scale mutual aid community groups, self-build and co-housing, Community Land Trusts, city farms and kitchens, community centres and bookshops.

All of these have either explicit or implicit anarchist tendencies.

"by counter-power I understand the capacity by social actors to challenge and eventually change the power relations institutionalised in society." (12)

MAKE DO AND MEND, EVERYTHING, CARE, REPAIR, ACCRETION, CHANGE, INTERVENTION

"Care is also a social capacity and activity involving the nurturing of all that is necessary for the welfare and flourishing of life." (13)

Our approach was rigorously informed by existing conditions, material, societal, historical, which we considered were pregnant with potential for intervention and considered change. Students undertook extensive action and creative research from which they developed their own briefs to a site or condition. Care and responses to the climate emergency were central to these investigations.

(right) Reparation, Sneha Sachin Shenoy, DS3.1

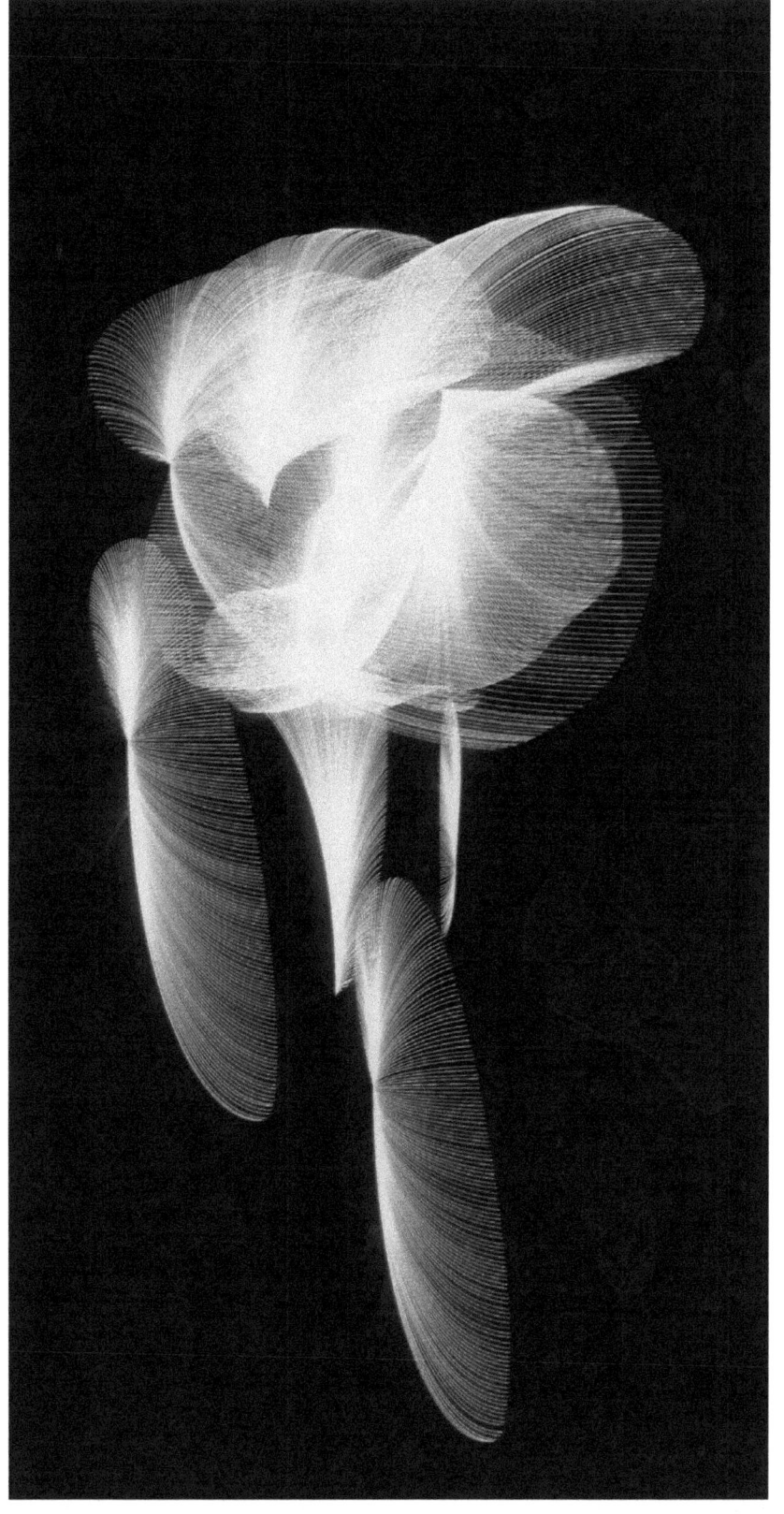

It is a practice of architecture that only changes what is necessary through tactics such as urban acupuncture, accretion, infill, intervention often small scale, ecologically responsible with a focus on recycling, re-use and sustainable materials and techniques. It reflects the techniques of squatters, DIYers, self-builders, eco-villages, global south communities and autonomous protest geographies. It looks to precedents outside the usual architectural canon including *Buildings without Architects* by John May, [14] Bernard Rudofsky's *Architecture without Architects* [15] and *Design Like you Give a Damn! Volume 1* [16] and *2* [17] by Architects for Humanity.

In *DIY Politics and World-making: Mutual Aid, Anarchism and Alternative Solutions*, [18] Ben Shepard places community gardening within a context of punks, poets, queers, feminists all building their own worlds in a search for new models of organisation and community development where the idea of DIY culture uses counter power to create new and alternative worlds.

Students created radical spaces which were less about a style and more about a propositional stance using spaces as a medium for cultural and political critique using alternative economics and politics where ownership, control, and management were part of a progressive vision of sharing, circular economics and mutual aid.

Key aspects of this approach included:

- rethinking how space is conceived, lived and changed - not just designed
- rejecting traditional typologies (house, museum, office) to blur the line between architecture, art, and performance
- creating sites of resistance and challenging power structures and suggesting more democratic, flexible, or utopian ways of inhabiting the world
- temporary spaces including installations, mobile shelters, refugee housing solutions
- flexible spaces that can be modified by their users, not just Architects/professionals
- ecological & multi-species experiments rejecting anthropocentrism and prioritizing symbiosis with nature.

UTOPIA IN THE HIGHGATE BOWL, 2016 – 17

Our site was a contested piece of land in North London. As one of the last areas of Drover's land, for centuries animals had been rested and fattened before their last trek into the meat markets of London. In the 20th century it was a market garden and until recently a garden centre. This space was a left-over, secret, ad-hoc world of nature and small scale, horticultural activity, a community amenity but also an ecologically rich landscape.

(bottom) Screening, Finola Simpson, DS3.1

Fifteen years ago, the site was sold to a developer who proposed three luxury houses and the community rallied to fight the proposals and created an alternative vision for the site. Due to delays, in 2016, the site and structures were inhabited by squatters who created an alternative, off-grid community of artists, eco-activists and others to restore and clear the site and buildings for growing and new activities. Many had come from the famous squat in Rochester Square, Camden. Our brief invited students to contribute ideas for the future of the Highgate Bowl.

They were asked to find a utopian or radical thinker from Highgate's history who could serve as both the starting point for their project and a collaborator from the past. The local utopian inhabitants had helped shape Highgate into what it became, a place of dreams, alternative political thought, intellectual radicalism, and a passion for a better world. In doing so, they collectively informed the culture and folklore of the village. Students were asked to manifest these utopian histories through acts of design, as museum, memorial, or alchemy.

Using artistic actions and personal responses to the site, they developed propositions for the complex landscape of the Highgate Bowl. Each project took the form of an installation or building conceived as a shrine or museum to the utopian ideals of their chosen Highgate inhabitant. Its location, form, and contents were all determined by their research and interpretation of their utopian figure.

CREATING RADICAL SPACES OF POTENTIAL.

Students were asked to develop their ideas into a building that proposed a pragmatic utopia. Each project included both permanent and temporary accommodation, spaces for those running the project as well as for visitors who would come to stay and learn. Every proposal also incorporated a 'place of exchange,' offering the potential for a different economic model or a closed-loop economy. The aim was for each design to propose a radical or alternative solution to a problem or condition the students had already identified. Student responses were wide-ranging, each reimagining the Highgate Bowl through distinct utopian propositions. Projects included an artists' collective with multigenerational living, a revolutionary commune, and an alternative self-sufficient settlement with a visitors' centre focused on anti-waste practices. Others proposed a wild animal sanctuary combined with a YMCA, a Coleridge-inspired literary and poetry centre, a contemporary convent, and a growing collective with residential and educational spaces. More speculative responses included New Atlantis, which explored ideas of dirt, germs, and productive waste; a spirulina production plant promoting alternative growing methods; and a fake passport processing centre offering refuge to those under threat of deportation. Additional proposals included a radical youth theatre with an outdoor stage, a women's refuge archiving invisible histories, a ceramics and craft centre using charcoal and brick, and a home for bees.

(right) Highgate Bowl Exhibition Poster, DS3.1

UTOPIA IN THE BOWL
A pop-up exhibition of students ideas for the Highgate Bowl

Exhibition open
2.30 - 4pm Saturday 8th and Sunday 9th July

At 10A Highgate Society, South Grove, N6

FINAL THOUGHTS

We hope we filled our students with radical optimism and awareness of their agency to make a difference. That they looked for inspiration from everything around them and were given permission to bring their own passions, knowledge, lived experiences and unique insights to their projects to disrupt the world of architectural academia. That they rejected the idea of single, architectural genius in favour of a practice of collaboration or co-production. To champion the often marginalised and hidden voices and communities, small moments and histories that need to be celebrated and given physical and political 'space' in our cities. And to have fun. All underpinned by a belief that teaching should challenge students to question and examine the dominant power structures and patterns of inequality that shape the world.

"Education, in the final analysis, is really about the production of agency. What kind of narratives are we going to produce that students can understand, that enlarge their perspective not only on the world but on their relationship to others and themselves? What is the basis for knowledge? In what way does it speak to a particular kind of future? Because all education is an introduction in some way to the future. It's a struggle over what kind of future you want for young people." (19)

(right) John Evelyn's Garden, Declan Slonim, DS3.1

NOTES

(01) Paulo Freire, *Pedagogy of the Oppressed* (New York: Continuum, 1970).
(02) David Bowie.
(03) Maria Faraone, *Studio Juggernaut*.
(04) Nato Thompson, ed., *Living as Form: Socially Engaged Art from 1991–2011* (Cambridge, MA: MIT Press, 2017).
(05) Jeremy Deller.
(06) "1968 Student Slogan."
(07) Henri Lefebvre, *Le Droit à la ville* (Paris: Anthropos, 1968). *The Right to the City*, translated edition.
(08) Nishat Awan, Tatjana Schneider, and Jeremy Till, eds., *Spatial Agency: Other Ways of Doing Architecture* (Abingdon: Routledge, 2011).
(09) Claire Bishop, ed., *Participation* (London: Whitechapel Gallery; Cambridge, MA: MIT Press, 2006).
(10) Kate Raworth, *Doughnut Economics: Seven Ways to Think Like a 21st-Century Economist* (White River Junction, VT: Chelsea Green Publishing, 2017).
(11) Colin Ward, *Anarchy in Action* (London: George Allen & Unwin, 1973).
(12) Manuel Castells, 2007.
(13) The Care Collective, *The Care Manifesto: The Politics of Interdependence* (London: Verso, 2020).
(14) John May, *Buildings without Architects: A Global Guide to Everyday Architecture* (New York: Rizzoli International Publications, 2010).
(15) Bernard Rudofsky, *Architecture without Architects: A Short Introduction to Non-Pedigreed Architecture* (New York: Museum of Modern Art, 1964).
(16) Architecture for Humanity, ed., *Design Like You Give a Damn! Architectural Responses to Humanitarian Crises*, vol. 1 (New York: Metropolis Books, 2006).
(17) Architecture for Humanity, ed., *Design Like You Give a Damn [2]: Building Change from the Ground Up*, vol. 2 (London: Thames & Hudson, 2012).
(18) Ben Shepard, "DIY Politics and World-Making: Mutual Aid, Anarchism and Alternative Solutions," last modified 2014, https://www.psa.ac.uk/sites/default/files/conference/papers/2014/DIY%20Politics%20and%20World%20Making.pdf.
(19) Henry Giroux.

MAKE DO AND MEND: ON TECHNOLOGY AND THE *UNHEIMLICH*

JANE TANKARD

MAKE DO AND MEND: ON TECHNOLOGY AND THE *UNHEIMLICH* BY JANE TANKARD

'A building that breathes through machines, that leaks light or radiation, that conceals its operations in ducts and joints, is at once reassuringly comfortable and disturbingly unfamiliar.'

In Terry Gilliam's film *Brazil*, [01] a retro-futurist world dominated by malfunctioning machines, endless bureaucracy and invasive, proliferating infrastructure, it is the service duct and its endless accumulations of amended and obsolete technology, bursting from every gap, tear and neglected building construction failure, that manifests our sense of unease. The malfunctioning service duct, laid bare, is a metaphor for technological anxiety; the duct is a controlled and hidden umbilical cord that if dismembered will cast us into chaos.

Twentieth century modernism displaced traditional vernacular's breathable materials (stone, cob, lime mortar, thatch), which allowed air and moisture to permeate building enclosures, with impermeable systems of enclosure. By the late twentieth century, the fully glazed, mechanically conditioned urban tower had become a global icon. Architect Ken Shuttleworth, reflecting on his own role in designing London's Gherkin, admitted that:

"lightweight fully glazed buildings with hermetically sealed curtain walls and huge reliance on mechanical systems make no sense anymore." [02]

(top right) Police Raid, Measured Survey, Brazil, Terry Gilliam, Arwa Al-Nasrawi + Fatima Salim, DS3.1

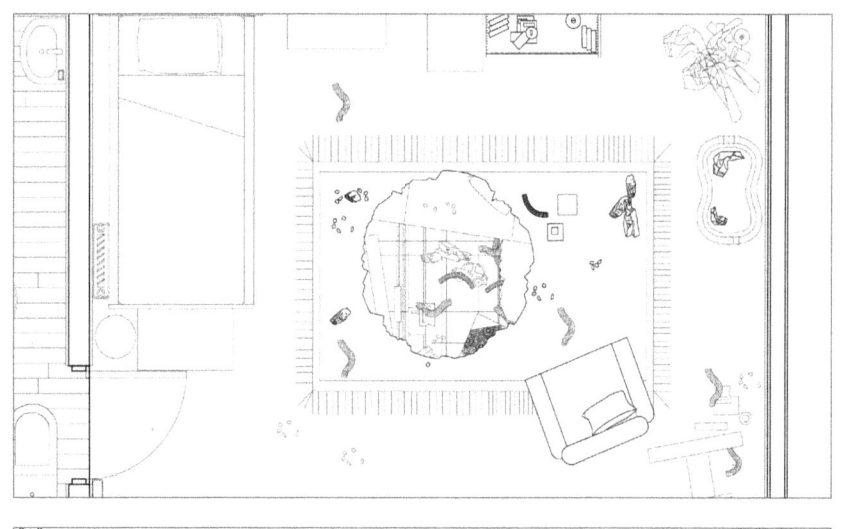

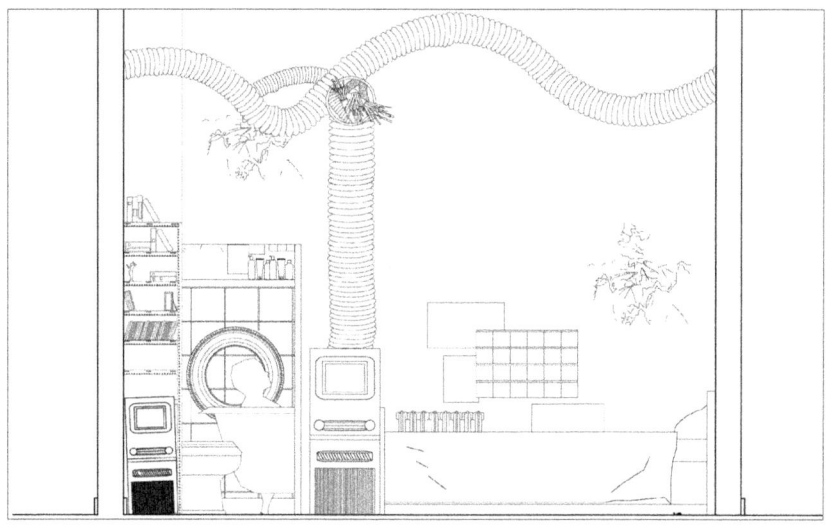

Since the early 20th century, modern architecture has obsessively pursued an aesthetic of seamlessness: curtain-walling, continuous planes and uninterrupted glazing with barely a whisper to hold it in place, appear frictionless and autonomous. Behind this apparent hyper-minimalism, as we have already explored in discussions of two of Mies van der Rohe's iconic projects, (03) lies a hidden technological underbelly. The apparent effortlessness of the seamless building is only possible through complex, concealed systems of HVAC, artificial lighting, damp-proof membranes and polluting synthetic coatings that maintain the illusion of purity at immense energetic, human health and environmental cost. Architecture conceived as a hermetic sealed box severs architecture from ecological exchange. Preventing the passage of air, water and sound, these building envelopes create interiors that are entirely reliant on mechanical regulation. The building, cut off from the environment, becomes a body on life support. Sylvia Lavin, Architect and writer, has suggested that modern architecture's technological aesthetic is one of disciplinary erasure: walls become blurred, surfaces liquid, atmospheres cultivated. (04) Yet this blurring is paradoxical for what looks continuous is, in reality, an architecture of concealment, of machines, systems and maintenance networks hidden in a building's plenums and ducts.

Louis Sullivan's extraordinary 1:1 Consultation Room Finish Detail drawings of the National Farmers' Bank in Minnesota, prints of which were discovered in 1991 in the Bank's basement, suggest the possibilities for a contemporary conception and design of an architecture at full scale.

The drawings, exhibited at the RIBA for the Desiring Practices symposium and exhibitions, (05) are beautiful, abstract and yet real, at the scale of the body and the city, although they belong to neither and can be read far beyond a contractor's instruction sheet. Readings of these drawings reveal a 'constructed' terrain, a topography, a surface of intersections and juxtapositions, a projected sequence of materiality and making. In her paper, published as part of the Desiring Practices Symposium publication, *Detailing* (06) Clare Cardinal-Pett quotes Marco Frascari:

"The joint, that is the fertile detail, is the place where both the construction and the construing of architecture takes place." (07)

Frascari positions the architectural joint as more than a structural element: it represents an intermediary pivot where the tangible act of construction intersects with the intangible process of conceptual meaning. In this sense, the joint becomes a liminal bridge between the physical and the metaphysical dimensions of architecture, where meaning is both made and apprehended. The space in-between, as described by Cardinal-Pett, suggests an overlap of the interstitial where the Owatonna Bank's body can be understood as ethereal and erotic. (08) Frascari's writings on the construction joint reveal the uncanny heart of this condition. (09) The joint is where materials meet, where a building's fragility is negotiated, where the repressed work of technology comes to the surface. From his perspective, the joint is never neutral: it embodies both a promise of continuity and a reminder of potential rupture.

(top right) Inflatable Model 1:1, Inaaya Amer, DS3.1

In the seamless architectures of modernity and contemporary developer-led commodified system building, joints are concealed and often disregarded, (out of sight, out of mind), yet it is precisely here, in the joining of the parts that the *Unheimlich* of technology resides; no one wants to think about maintenance, whether digital or analogue.

Emma Cheatle's 2008 photograph of Carolyn Butterworth licking Mies's Barcelona Pavilion (10) is an iconic image that reminds us of the cultural and symbolic ambiguities in Sullivan's details. Both unsettling and challenging, the image describes an embrace that is at once intimate and alien, an encounter between body and building that is both subtle and transgressionary. The image challenges how we think about the relationship between body and building and how as practitioners we measure, survey and record, site, material and physical engagement. (11) To lick a wall is to collapse the reassuring boundary between 'us' and 'it', blurring the neat categories of subject and object, surface and depth, asking us to consider notions of constructed terrain where the boundaries between the macro and the micro are embedded. In that gesture lies the spirit of what we've been exploring in the studio: porosity, liminality and the phenomenology of the marginal as central to architectural imagination. What happens when the city is no longer observed at a distance, but touched, licked, absorbed, into the body? How might porosity be understood at 1:1 when a building enclosure becomes a surface that embraces rainfall, only to release it as a humidifying agent, or at a scale of 1:5000 when thinking about the city as a sponge?

In *Walls Have Feelings,* Katherine Shonfield talks about the notion of smudging as a means to challenge modernist binary principles, a mechanism by which we can understand the messiness of everyday life and urban inhabitation. (12)

Smudging can be understood as a design mechanism which allows for this ambiguity, an action that recognises the complexity of human and non-human inhabitation of space and the notion of porosity. In this sense, the blurring of thresholds and the spaces between can be read as methodologies of literal and physical resistance to accepted power structures: instead of architecture enforcing discipline, it becomes a medium of negotiation, suggesting that boundaries are never absolute but always permeated by exchange. Technology has historically mediated porosity, through openings and ventilation systems, electrical conduits or digital networks that saturate buildings with invisible data streams. Yet the apparent fetishisation of minimalism has reconfigured porosity in uncanny forms. Sealed curtain walls and climate-controlled interiors erase porosity, whilst relying on complex technologies that create new, ever more sophisticated and impenetrable forms of digital permeability: systems that control energy, circulate air or maintain humidity.

Far from guaranteeing autonomy and neutrality, seamlessness renders architecture porous in conditions that are often toxic, unstable or unsettling, revealing a technological dependence, that is as much about microbial and toxic exchanges as it is about light and transparency.

(top right) Licking the Wall of the Barcelona Pavilion, Carolyn Butterworth, photograph by Emma Cheatle

A number of key thinkers and texts underpin the studio's approach to technology; framed by the unsettling notion of technological dependence as an uncanny space, we explore construction through compositional thinking and hybrid testing, navigating the space between the digital and the analogue.

The spectrum of architectural and cultural thinking that has enabled our studio-based discourse includes Sylvia Lavin's analyses of blurred disciplinary boundaries, (13) Richard Goodwin's work on porosity and parasitic public art, (14) Beatriz Colomina's research into the notion of 'sick' buildings (15) and Diller + Scofidio's Blur project. (16) A building that breathes through machines, that leaks light or radiation, that conceals its operations in ducts and joints, is at once reassuringly comfortable and disturbingly unfamiliar. The very technologies that sustain seamlessness reveal architecture's instability. Porosity is no longer just a material condition but a technological uncanny, surfaces that appear solid yet are perforated by leakage, boundaries that seem secure yet are constantly infiltrated.

In *X-Ray Architecture* (17) Beatriz Colomina argues that modern architecture has been profoundly shaped by early 20th century medical advances and technologies, particularly those evolved for the treatment of Tuberculosis, including radiography which dissolved the opacity of the body and, by extension, of architecture itself. Modernism's symbolic white walls, free plans and sunlight facing glazed screens functioned as medical prescriptions, enabling buildings to be flooded with light and air to combat disease.

But, when the home is infected with the qualities of the sanatorium, the domestic becomes a space of the uncanny, stripped of warmth and ornament in favour of clinical resolution. The glass wall, once celebrated as a symbol of transparency and liberation, also functions as a medical screen, turning inhabitants into patients constantly on display. The building itself becomes an X-ray apparatus, probing, ventilating and illuminating, leaving nothing hidden. Technology does not simply assist architecture but transforms it into an extension of the medical gaze, dissolving the boundaries and blurring the line between health and sickness, intimacy and surveillance. (18) While Colomina focuses on medical porosity, Sylvia Lavin addresses disciplinary porosity. In *Kissing Architecture (2011)*, (19) Lavin posits the notion that contemporary architecture is no longer an autonomous field, but one constantly contaminated by other media: art, film, sound and digital projection. She uses the metaphor of the kiss to describe moments of contact where architecture becomes porous to other disciplines, exchanging qualities and producing hybrid forms. This porosity is primarily technological: the use of projections, sensors and digital surfaces allows buildings to become screens, stages or interactive installations.

For Lavin, the notion of contamination does not signal the death of architecture but instead reveals its transformation into an affective medium. Buildings are no longer mute containers but participate in a network of images and sensations. Yet this porosity carries an uncanny dimension for if architecture traditionally provided stability and separation, its contamination with other media dissolves its identity, making it uncanny.

(right) Site: Palimpsest, Declan Slonim, DS3.1

A wall that doubles as a screen, a façade that flickers with projected images, unsettles expectations of solidity and permanence. Technology is undermining the boundary between surface and depth, building and media, creating porous thresholds that dissolve distinctions and create conditions of otherness. The logic of seamlessness persists here, but in altered form. A projection on a building surface appears seamless, but it depends on technological joints, cables, projectors, sensors all of which remain determinedly hidden. What seems like pure atmosphere is in fact a tightly engineered system and in this way, Lavin's disciplinary porosity echoes Frascari's insight: the uncanny resides not in the smooth surface itself but in the hidden technological apparatus that sustains it. And while Colomina and Lavin both remind us of Sullivan's 1:1 drawings and the molecular topography that is the construction joint, Richard Goodwin extends the idea of porosity into the urban and social realm, [20] developing porosity as a model for making architecture more open to public life. He critiques the sealed envelope of contemporary architecture and instead proposes interventions that render buildings permeable to flows of people, activities and art. For Goodwin, porosity is both spatial and political: it creates openings where public and private intermix, challenging the exclusivity of corporate or institutional structures.

Central to Goodwin's work also is the figure of the parasite. [21] Parasites, whether biological or architectural, live in relation to a host, attaching, and in the process altering, the holder's function.

Goodwin's parasitic art projects intervene in existing buildings, attaching installations or extensions that create new pathways and interactions. These parasitic architectures exemplify technological porosity: they infiltrate existing systems, redirect flows, and expose hidden possibilities. The parasite is inherently uncanny. It is neither fully inside nor outside, neither independent nor fully dependent. It destabilizes the identity of its host, making it other to itself. Goodwin harnesses this unsettling quality as a productive strategy for public art and urban design, demonstrating how porosity can produce encounters, disruptions and reconfigurations of the city.

The parasite also reveals what seamlessness tries to conceal: that no building is closed or autonomous. Every structure is constructed with joints, seams, and systems that connect it to wider networks of energy, capital and social interaction. Goodwin's parasitic interventions make visible the hidden infrastructures of the city. In this sense, his work extends Frascari's insight into the detail at an urban scale: the joint becomes the site of uncanny porosity, where technology and society infiltrate architecture. Perhaps the most literal exploration of architectural porosity is Diller + Scofidio's Blur Building, constructed for the Swiss Expo in 2002. [22] Rather than presenting architecture as a stable object, the Blur Building dissolves it into atmosphere. A mass of cloud-forming fog produced by computer-controlled nozzles, the pavilion appears and disappears depending on weather conditions and wind.

(bottom) Highgate Bowl Working Mens Club, DS3.1

(top right) Unfolding Plan, Olha Petrachkova, DS3.1

Visitors entering the building find themselves enveloped in mist, disoriented, with traditional markers of architectural solidity erased. In this context, technology is not hidden infrastructure but the medium of the architecture itself. Pumps, sensors and computational systems regulate the density of the fog, making porosity the building's defining condition. Boundaries between inside and outside collapse; one moves through gradients of visibility rather than through walls. The experience is profoundly uncanny: the visitor enters a building that cannot be seen, navigates spaces that continually dissolve and encounters architecture as an atmospheric prosthesis rather than a sheltering object. And yet, even here, the obsession with seamlessness persists. The mist appears natural, continuous, effortless. But this seamless fog is sustained by a dense technological infrastructure of pipes, nozzles and software that remains hidden beneath the surface. The uncanny experience of the Blur Building depends, once again, on the repression of the joint. The nozzles that produce fog are joints between water, air, and machinery, sites where technology makes atmosphere possible. The building reveals the atmospheric joint, where technology stitches climate, body and architecture together.

In technological terms, the notion of porosity emerges as a key mechanism in unlocking our understanding of how making and building transforms architecture through the lens of the uncanny. Porosity undermines the traditional promise of architecture as a secure refuge. Instead, technology renders buildings permeable, unstable and uncanny. Commodified, gentrifying seamlessness only intensifies this tension: the smoother the surface, the more hidden the technological joints that sustain it and the more uncanny their eventual revelation.

The construction joint, in Frascari's sense, becomes the emblem of this paradox: the invisible site where architecture both holds together and threatens to fall apart. Porosity, then, is not only about transparency or openness but about the ways buildings leak socially, environmentally, disciplinarily, atmospherically and chemically. [23] In an age of climate crisis and technological saturation, acknowledging the joint, rather than repressing it, might be a helpful condition of sustainability. The *Unheimlich* character of porous architecture may be showing us that buildings are never autonomous but always stitched and assembled. In the studio we are attempting to place the joint centre-stage, to embrace porosity as both an architectural reality and a cultural necessity, to help us rethink how we understand forms of structure, construction and enclosure.

(right) Unfolded Terrain, Inaaya Amer, DS3.1

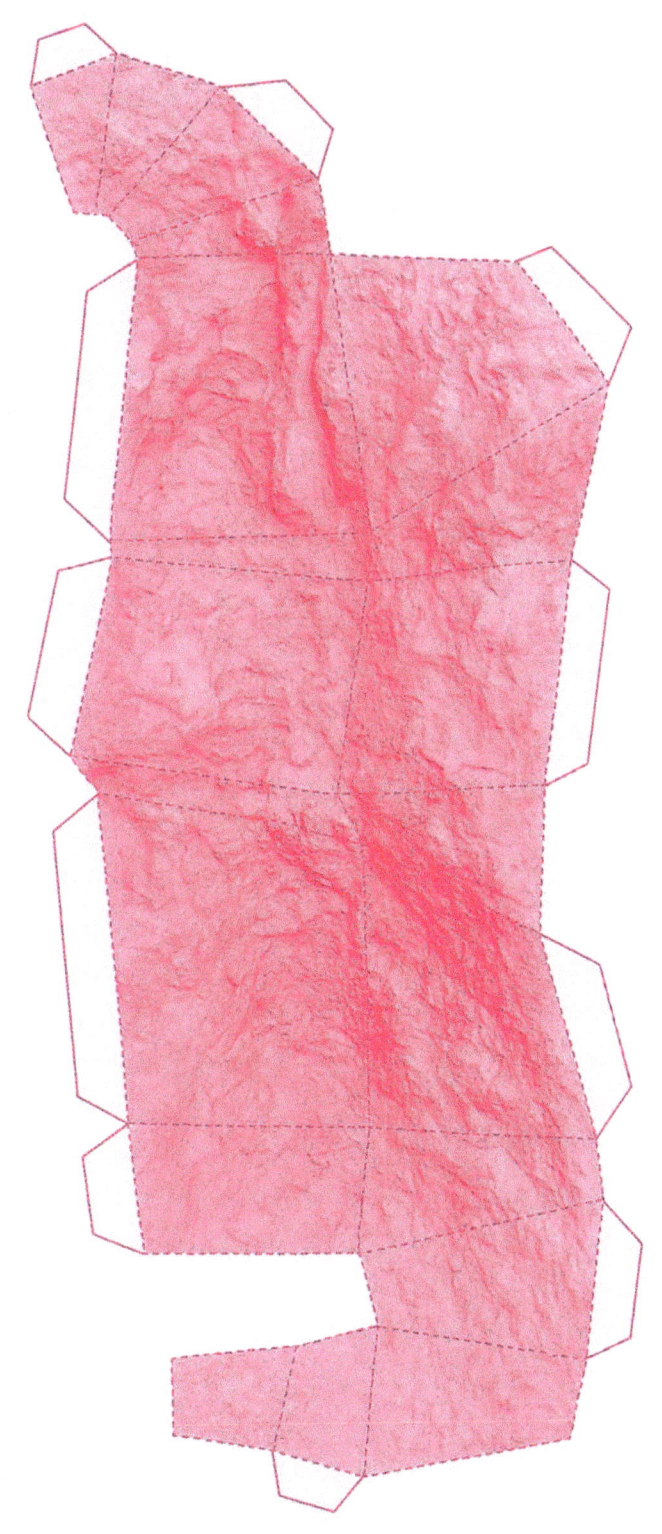

NOTES

(01) Terry Gilliam, dir., *Brazil* (UK/US, 1985), film.
(02) Merlin Fulcher, "Ken Shuttleworth on Glazed Buildings and Mechanical Systems," *Architects' Journal* (July 2010), https://www.architectsjournal.co.uk/archive/shuttleworth-calls-again-for-end-to-glass-binge.
(03) Jane Tankard, "Challenging the Tabula Rasa: In Search of the Unheimlich," in *Exploring the Unheimlich*, ed. Jane Tankard and Jake Parkin (London: University of Westminster, School of Architecture + Cities, 2025).
(04) Sylvia Lavin, *Kissing Architecture* (Princeton, NJ: Princeton University Press, 2011).
(05) Clare Cardinal-Pett, "Detailing," in *Desiring Practices: Architecture, Gender and the Interdisciplinary*, ed. Jane Rendell et al. (London: Black Dog Publishing, 1996).
(06) Sarah Wigglesworth, Duncan McCorquodale, Katerina Rüedi, et al., *Desiring Practices Project*, exhibitions, London, 1995.
(07) Cardinal-Pett, "Detailing."
(08) Marco Frascari, "The Tell-the-Tale Detail," *Via* 7 (1984), quoted in Clare Cardinal-Pett, "Detailing," in *Desiring Practices* (London: Black Dog Publishing, 1995).
(09) Cardinal-Pett, "Detailing."
(10) Frascari, "The Tell-the-Tale Detail," *Via* 7 (1984).
(11) Emma Cheatle, *Photograph of Carolyn Butterworth Licking Mies's Barcelona Pavilion*, 2008, reproduced in Carolyn Butterworth and Sam Vardy, "Site-Seeing: Constructing the 'Creative Survey'," *field* 2, no. 1 (2008): 125–138, https://feminist.ssoa.info/wp-content/uploads/2020/07/Site-Seeing_Constructing_the_Creative_Survey_Carolyn_Butterworth_and_Sam_Vardy.pdf.
(12) Ibid.
(13) Katherine Shonfield, *Walls Have Feelings: Architecture, Film and the City* (London: Routledge, 2000).
(14) Sylvia Lavin, *Kissing Architecture* (Princeton, NJ: Princeton University Press, 2011).
(15) Richard Goodwin, "Porosity: The Revision of Public Space in the City Using Public Art to Test the Functional Boundaries of Built Form" (PhD diss., University of New South Wales, 2007).
(16) Beatriz Colomina, Iván López Munuera, Nick Axel, and Nikolaus Hirsch, "Sick Architecture," *e-flux architecture*, 2022, https://www.e-flux.com/architecture/sick-architecture/360079/editorial.
(17) Elizabeth Diller and Ricardo Scofidio, *Blur: The Making of Nothing* (New York: Harry N. Abrams, 2002).
(18) Beatriz Colomina, *X-Ray Architecture* (Zürich: Lars Müller Publishers, 2019).
(19) Ibid.
(20) Sylvia Lavin, *Kissing Architecture* (Princeton, NJ: Princeton University Press, 2011).
(21) Richard Goodwin, *Porosity Games* (Snakes and Ladders, Hide and Seek, Jenga), Australian Research Council Discovery Grant project, University of New South Wales, 2003–2005.
(22) Richard Goodwin, *Parasite Roof*, Union Hotel, North Sydney, 1998, public art intervention.
(23) Elizabeth Diller and Ricardo Scofidio, "Blur Building," *Diller Scofidio + Renfro*, 2002, https://dsrny.com/project/blur-building.
(24) Walter Benjamin and Asja Lācis, "Naples," in *Illuminations*, ed. Hannah Arendt (New York: Schocken Books, 1968). (Original essay published 1925).

BROTHER HOUSES

ANESA CANA

BROTHER HOUSES BY ANESA CANA

'In parting, you are a well packed suitcase, with something missing as usual.'

Nestled within the verdant folds of Kosovo, across rural plains, at the foot of mountains and valleys, stand empty houses that speak more than one language; they whisper tales of an old world, an era draped in the traditions of the past, yet boldly streaked with the vibrant hues of the new. These structures, Brother Houses, affectionate siblings, stand as monuments to the unique interplay of local heritage, familial connections and the far-reaching influences of an expansive diaspora. Each house, a dream of familial reunion articulated in a foreign tongue, acts as a physical memorial to the life left behind; a life that, in the hearts of those who have ventured afar, remains frozen in time. Across the globe, are many little Kosovos encapsulated in the hearts of those in foreign lands, for whom these houses stand as loving tributes to the ongoing dance of parallel worlds, forever entwined yet distinctly separate. Fleeing war-torn Kosovo as a young child, I was thrust into a life of displacement, torn between two worlds. England became a refuge, but I lived in cultural limbo, a place where my heart and identity were constantly pulled in different directions. The trauma of war, of leaving home, created a deep fracture, where I never truly belonged in one place or the other. Caught between the memories of Kosovo's traditions, passed down through my parents and the unfamiliar realities of the host country, I became part of a permanent diaspora, a life shaped by nostalgia for a homeland I barely knew, and the challenges of forging a new identity in a foreign land.

(right) Brother Houses Photo Series by Anesa Cana

The weight of displacement left me floating between two cultures, one rooted in the pain of loss and another filled with the struggle for acceptance and belonging. This personal history is what inspired me to explore the concept of brother houses, an attempt to understand how migration, family, and cultural memory intertwine for those caught between worlds.

"In parting, you are a well packed suitcase, with something missing as usual. You are thousands of instructions to be fulfilled, you are your former self crying for you. You are the door closing with a cold creek, which seems to open a pit in your heart. And you become a hand raised in the air to say goodbye, a back turned so your tears do not show, even in parting you want to remain a desire. You are the impossible companionship of your brother, you are the absent presence of your father, the feel of his handshake. In parting, songs of silence are sung in honour of your step, and you become a foot pressed to the earth, leaving tracks; in earth's black flesh, in your misty fate, in the dreams of those you leave behind." (01)

For the Kosovar nation, emigration has been a persistent theme, with frequent migration waves driven by political, economic, and social pressures. These movements became ingrained in our collective identity, influencing family structures, community ties, and the built environment. As one account puts it, migration in the Kosovo context is:

"like a chain consisting of its own links, where each link is linked to another one. So, each citizen who has migrated before, after a period of time, has pulled away even other relatives, thus creating the diasporas in the world." (02)

The most dramatic wave of emigration occurred during the Kosovo War of 1998–1999, which led to widespread displacement. For the first time, whole family units left together. Nearly half of Kosovo's population was forced to flee, and many of those who settled abroad remained, further strengthening diasporic communities. (03) In the aftermath of the war, the region faced a severe housing crisis. Many homes had been destroyed, and international organisations rushed to provide emergency dwellings. These were small, standardised, and culturally indifferent, contrasting sharply with traditions of multigenerational living. Families accustomed to large, communal spaces suddenly found themselves in cramped, alien structures. (04)

Into this void stepped the diaspora. Remittances were sent, not just to rebuild but to expand, producing large and elaborate homes as symbols of dignity, success, and resilience. (05)

"Yes, around fifteen years ago. We always contributed money, sent it every month. So, my father started building our house for us, when he was ready to do it for all the brothers"

The resulting form was the row of Brother Houses, multi storey buildings constructed simultaneously, often identical in design, situated side by side in rural and suburban Kosovo. (06) These houses were shaped by the myth of return, a psychological state in which the migrant imagines one day going back to the homeland, preserving an image of it frozen in time. This mental construct resists acknowledgement of change, sustaining a conservative diaspora whose values remain fixed at the moment of departure.

(top right) Brother Houses Photo Series by Anesa Cana

(bottom left) Brother House Series Image by Jake Parkin

The houses became physical manifestations of this state, promising reunion while often remaining empty. (07)

The paradox is striking. In village after village, rows of monumental houses stand shuttered, occupied only in summer, or not at all. Their size and repetition embody a logic of multiplication, a doubling of houses for each brother, extending familial unity through architectural cloning. The uncanny dimension lies in their emptiness and their insistence on sameness, structures intended for reunion that echo instead with absence. Remittance financed construction transformed traditional dwellings of mud and stone into concrete Brother Houses. Driven by patriarchal customs, especially the Kanun, each brother was entitled to his own dwelling, and fairness demanded that the houses be built alike.

"It had the same architect, so the plans were the same, initially. We wanted it this way, my father was killed in the war and it was always his wish. So, we honoured it. On the outside they are identical." (08)

Rows of identical houses appear across Kosovo, uncanny in their multiplication. Their shutters are often closed, their interiors furnished but unused, their gardens untended. They stand as both monuments to memory and empty shells, uncanny precisely because they stage a reunion that never quite happens. The architecture of the brother houses embodies a language of multiples. Each unit is not singular but part of a set, each façade a mirror of its neighbour, every floor plan doubled, tripled, multiplied. The logic of repetition suggests permanence, yet also estrangement: to live in one is to live in all, to be absorbed into the series.

The uncanny arises when difference is erased, when the individuality of home dissolves into sameness. As one Architect observed:

"the concept is very simple, but it has resulted in the building of these large family houses where all the brothers are side by side, often identical, and each one attempts to be more monumental than the other." (09)

Such houses often remain unoccupied for most of the year, used only in August when families return from the diaspora. In their emptiness, they resemble ghost towns, entire streets where shutters remain drawn, windows dark. Children play in courtyards overgrown with weeds, yet the houses themselves remain mausoleums to a dream of reunion. The uncanny quality lies not just in their emptiness but in their excess, too large for present needs, too numerous for dwindling rural populations. The myth of return is therefore destabilised. While intended as bridges back to the homeland, the houses often stand as barriers instead, symbols of separation, architectural reminders that families are elsewhere.

The once tightly interwoven rural fabric is punctured by monumental, isolated houses, repeating endlessly but inhabited only intermittently. In this way the unhomely emerges when the house no longer performs its domestic function. The uncanny brother houses are not lived in homes but rather staged dwellings, frozen in anticipation. Their presence destabilises the familiar landscape of the village, rendering it strange. To walk among them is to feel both recognition and alienation, the homely transformed into its opposite. Generational shifts amplify this estrangement.

(right) Brother Houses Architectural Drawings, Photo Series by Anesa Cana

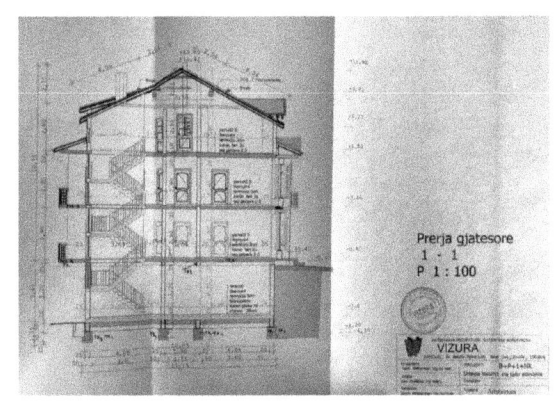
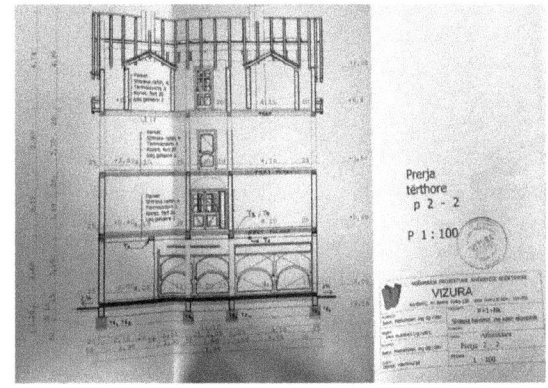
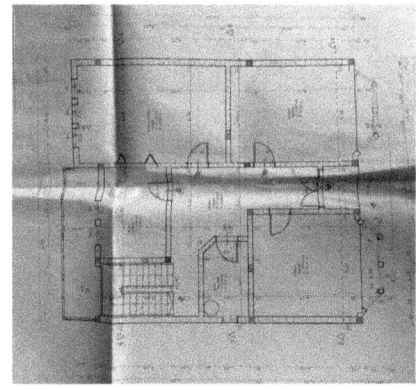
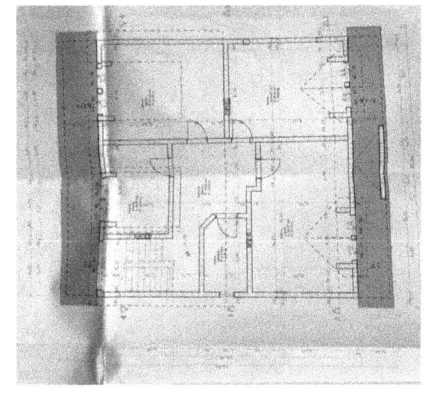

The first generation of migrants built brother houses out of duty and longing, but their children, born abroad, rarely use them. These younger generations identify less with the homeland and more with their adopted countries.

"We return once a year, sometimes not even that. The houses are there, but our lives are here,"

The uncanny gap widens: houses preserved as symbols by one generation become irrelevant to the next. The proliferation of empty brother houses across Kosovo forms a dispersed archive of absence. They are monuments to a familial ideal that falters in practice, repeated endlessly yet emptied of daily life. Their uncanny presence lies in this contradiction, familiar in form, estranged in function. The architecture itself enacts doubling and displacement. Built in concrete rather than stone, often with modern façades, they imitate urban villas while standing in rural settings. Their very hybridity renders them uncanny, neither traditional nor fully modern, neither village house nor urban palace. This ambiguity makes them hard to categorise, and thus unsettling. Photographs of rows of such houses underscore their repetition. In one village, five brothers' houses stand shoulder to shoulder, identical down to the balcony railings. In another, four multi storey villas form a row, each slightly more elaborate than the last.

The multiplication is relentless, suggesting both solidarity and competition, equality and rivalry. The uncanny arises precisely here, in the doubling that both unites and divides. In this context, the poetic passage on leaving resonates anew. The suitcase, the raised hand in parting, the absent presence of the father, all these gestures echo in the empty rooms of brother houses.

Architecture becomes the stage for longing and loss, the uncanny theatre of familial reunion that never fully occurs. The uncanny dimension is sharpened by the temporality of these houses. Built for permanence, they exist in a liminal state, suspended between absence and presence. They await inhabitants who rarely come, preserve traditions that fade with time, and embody returns that remain imaginary. In their repetition and vacancy, they expose the fissures of diasporic life. Brother houses also reflect the tension between individual identity and collective obligation. Each brother is entitled to his own dwelling, yet the houses must remain equal. This tension produces repetition, sameness as fairness. Yet the result is uncanny: to see five identical villas in a row is to feel estrangement, the familiar multiplied until it becomes strange.

In the end, the architecture of brother houses embodies the paradoxes of migration, presence and absence, reunion and separation, tradition and change. They are uncanny precisely because they insist on family unity while staging its impossibility. Their multiplication creates an eerie landscape of empty sameness, haunted by the memories of those who left and the silences of those who never returned.

(top) Gap Widens, Yi Shen, DS3.1

(right) Conflict Model, Yi Shen, DS3.1

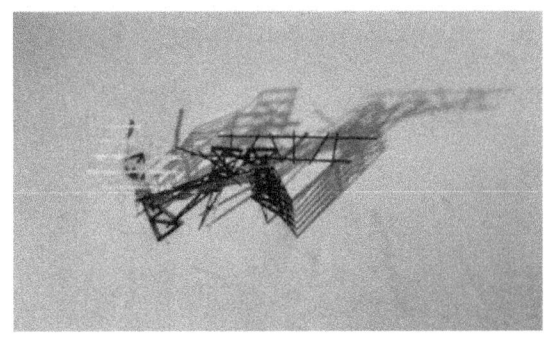

NOTES

(01) Anonymous, *Poetic Passage on Leaving*, cited in dissertation text.
(02) *Kosovo Migration Report* (Pristina: Government of Kosovo, 2008).
(03) UNHCR, *Kosovo Refugee Statistics 1999* (Geneva: UNHCR, 1999).
(04) International Crisis Group, *Post-War Housing in Kosovo* (Brussels: ICG, 2000).
(05) Besnik Gashi, *Remittances and Reconstruction in Kosovo* (Pristina: Kosovo Institute for Policy Research, 2004).
(06) Field Interview, Participant A, July 2022.
(07) Luljeta Brahimi, *Myth of Return and the Kosovar Diaspora* (Tirana: Albanian Migration Institute, 2010).
(08) Field Interview, Participant B, August 2022.
(09) Ardian Krasniqi, *Architecture of Brotherhood in Kosovo* (Pristina: Faculty of Architecture Press, 2015).

SERIES, EVENT

JAKE PARKIN

SERIES, EVENT BY JAKE PARKIN

'Original and copy collapse in an information space where everything is adjacent'

Architecture is often understood through its solidity, permanence, and formal authority, yet its meaning also emerges in the so-called 'interactive space' created by its distribution through drawings, photographs, films, performances, and narratives that extend far beyond the physical building. Distribution is generative because every duplication or reappearance produces new interactions and unexpected audiences. Familiarity achieved through circulation turns unfamiliar, eventually estranging what once seemed stable and producing what Anthony Vidler has described as the uncanny, where repetition displaces the ordinary and transforms it into something unsettling. (01) This text explores how distribution generates 'interactive space', how repetition produces uncanniness, and how authority is destabilised when objects, performances, and images are endlessly re-encountered. It does so not only in its content but also in its method. Composed as a series of eight short texts, each part is deliberately written to be read in any order. This exploration arises from interchangeability and the repetition of similar ideas in different registers, and does not depend upon a linear progression. This form of writing is itself an experiment in distribution, refusing the authority of the single ordered narrative. It mirrors the pedagogical processes of architectural studios, where work is tested in fragments, where drawings, models, and texts circulate and are reconfigured, and where meaning emerges through the repetition of attempts rather than through singular conclusions.

(top) Theatre Scan, AA Visiting School Los Angeles, Ali Jbil

(bottom) Theatre Scan, AA Visiting School Los Angeles, Davide Gualco

THE STAHL HOUSE

Designed in the late 1950s by Pierre Koenig with the Stahl family, the Stahl House was one of the Case Study Houses that sought to demonstrate new modes of modernist living. An elegant glass and steel structure perched in the Hollywood Hills, its significance for many lies less in the building itself than in the dissemination of its image. Julius Shulman's famous photograph of two women seated at the corner of the living room with the city glowing beneath them has been reproduced so extensively that it has become iconic in its own right, appearing in films, music videos, exhibitions, and advertisements. Even those unable to name the house often recognise the image. Walter Benjamin argued that:

"that which withers in the age of mechanical reproduction is the aura of the work of art." (02)

Andy Warhol, two decades later, embraced precisely this condition, treating serial reproducibility as both aesthetic and ethic. (03) The Stahl House sits between these positions. As a building, it has a precise site and singular presence, yet its fame is inseparable from Shulman's widely reproduced images.

Images do more than document this architecture: they manufacture its public aura by staging a view of Los Angeles life that could circulate anywhere, from magazines to posters to museum walls. In Benjamin's terms, aura should wither through reproduction, yet here reproduction generates a different aura belonging as much to the image as to the steel and glass on the hill. For Warhol, this logic holds: the house becomes legible through a repeatable image that anyone can recognise, much like a screen print designed to be seen again and again.

Benjamin's reflections on reproduction compared with Warhol's are instructive, for the photograph detaches the house from its specific site and produces a new aura based on distribution rather than uniqueness. While the design of the house may be understood simply, the repetition of its image layers it with cultural narratives that far exceed its material existence. Vidler's conception of the uncanny explains this effect, (01) as the house becomes both intimately familiar and strangely remote, encountered more in representation than in reality. Distribution transforms the Stahl House into an interactive cultural monument, significant not for its form alone but for its repetition and circulation.

(right) Anti-Assimilation School, Simi Oluwo, DS3.1

JOINERS

David Hockney's photographic 'joiners' series reveal another way in which distribution produces interactivity. In the late 1960s and 1970s many artists were experimenting with wide angle lenses to expand the visual field, yet Hockney found these results unsatisfactory, because they offered more vision at the cost of distortion, a distortion produced by technology rather than by conscious choice. In response he began assembling multiple Polaroids of his lounge, placing them side by side without intending a single composition, and in doing so realised that he was producing an interactive and narrative space, or 'joiner'. The viewer moved across the fragments as if walking through the room. From 1982, Hockney developed this into a deliberate and serialised method, distributing Polaroids in grids that captured pools, landscapes, and figures in motion. In his words:

"ten photographs means observing the same interaction ten times in different ways." [04]

This makes clear that repetition was central to the work. Roland Barthes's notion of the punctum, the piercing detail that fixes attention, is relevant here, as it is notably dissolved by Hockney into a field of competing details, so that the gaze never settles. [05] The familiar is fractured into multiplicity, producing an uncanny experience by which the ordinary becomes strange through its repetition. Hockney shows that distribution, far from diluting interaction, can heighten it, producing works that are both fragmented and immersive. The distribution of the body itself demonstrates how repetition unsettles identity.

MICHAEL JACKSON

In *Let's Entertain: Life's Guilty Pleasures* Akiko Busch writes:

"Michael Jackson, the apotheosis of such reinvention, has taken the split-screen self to new extremes. He excels not so much in inventing new identities but as in blurring them. Through surgery, lavish makeup, and alleged pigmentation, he has managed to put into question his race, his gender, and his age, all qualities that most people consider essential to their being. Jackson's identity is based on anti identity, making every effort to accommodate black and white, male and female, child and adult. [...] Indeed, there is an increasingly thin line between self-perfection and self mutilation, suggesting that the difference is sometimes clear only in the eye of the beholder." [06]

Jackson's self was never singular but endlessly distributed across disguises, performances, and appearances. On one occasion guards at an event failed to recognise him because he wore a wig, false teeth, blue contact lenses, and makeup, and only when he performed a moonwalk did they accept that he was authentic. Performance became the proof of identity, displacing appearance. Richard Serra's *List of Verbs* of 1967, with its catalogue of actions like layering, cutting, folding, and bending, offers an apt analogy as both sculptural practice and bodily transformation are processes of modification through repetition. [07] Jackson illustrates how distribution can destabilise authenticity, producing an uncanny self that is recognisable only through its iterations.

(top) Michael Jackson Statue at the Santarama Miniland in Johannesburg, South Africa, photograph by unknown

(bottom right) The Wrath of the Three Mighty Babas: London's Romanian Citizenship Application Centre, Adrian-Calin Paul, DS3.1

MISSILES

Oliver Laric's *Versions* film series demonstrates distribution in the digital age. Each video in the series carries the same title but with a different number, its images and references shifting with each mutation while the spoken text largely remains the same. Versions is simultaneously a sculpture, a talk, a video, a song, a novel, a recipe, a play, a dance, a routine, a feature film, a PDF, a form of merchandise. (08) It asks which transformation is real, best, or valid, and suggests that such distinctions do not matter. One section shows how an Iranian media outlet accidentally published a doctored photograph of a missile strike, later exposed by the public. The duplicated image spread rapidly online, spawning memes and countless adaptations, each adding to what Laric describes as a celebration of visual culture in a socially collective, internet-enabled present. (09) Laric's work thus constructs a field of digital events unfolding as a series of iterative translations, where authorship dissolves into circulation and meaning is continually reconstituted through the networked dynamics of reproduction and variation.

FAITH

Distribution at urban scale is exemplified by the Hawksmoor churches of the early eighteenth century. The New Churches Act of 1711 commissioned fifty new churches in London, eight of which were designed by Hawksmoor. (10) Later commentators traced geometries across their placement, interpreting them as occult patterns such as pentagrams. (11) Michel Foucault's notion of heterotopia clarifies the condition of the churches, for they are both everyday sites of ritual and estranged figures within a wider urban system. (12)

Distribution at this scale demonstrates how repetition produces interactivity, because the familiar ritual of worship acquires uncanny force when mapped across a city in the form of a hidden geometry. In this sense, the churches operate as a field of spatial and temporal events whose relational logic forms a series, a distributed network in which architectural repetition generates difference through contextual variation and collective urban memory. The same logic of transformation through iteration could be said about Madonna.

(middle left) Churches in the City of London, Jake Parkin
(bottom left) Betting shops in the City of London, Jake Parkin

(top right) Missile Launch, image created by Jake Parkin

THREE BALLS

John Baldessari transformed distribution into a form of play. His project *Throwing Three Balls in the Air to Get a Straight Line* of 1973 consisted of repeated attempts to achieve an impossible goal, each photograph showing three orange balls in the sky, never quite aligned. The series contained many variations, yet none resolved the task. The point was to insist, to generate meaning through repetition. Later, Baldessari obscured faces in photographs with coloured circles, shifting attention to other details and queering the act of recognition. In the same world as Ellsworth Kelly, Hal Foster has argued that repetition in postmodern art functions critically by revealing the instability of meaning. (13) Baldessari demonstrates this vividly, because the ordinary act of throwing a ball or identifying a face becomes strange when repeated or disrupted.

Distribution here is insistence, an active method of generating interactivity by refusing finality. The uncanny arises from the sense that repetition, far from clarifying, produces estrangement.

"That guy works in the vintage hardware store across the street... His eyes light up when he sees his wife." (14)

BAD COPY

In France, Philippe Parreno's 1994 performance at the inauguration of the Galeries Contemporaines des Musées de Marseille explored duplication. Olukemi Ilesanmi and Philippe Vergne recount:

"the audience recognised that this was theater and yet was totally enamoured by the impersonator and by the impersonation. The impersonator read a text written by Parreno and generally imitated a politician. It was a roaring and popular success. [...] so when he arrived ten minutes later for the official proceedings, the audience was kind of bored, because for them it had already taken place. The pre-performance was the spectacle, the real politician became not the bad copy, but the false copy of what happened ten minutes earlier." (15)

By placing the copy before the original, Parreno inverted the logic of authenticity. Derrida's concept of iterability is helpful here, for each repetition alters meaning and shows that no act can ever be pure. (16) The uncanny emerges from the collapse of authenticity, from the estrangement of a ritual that is both familiar and undermined. Distribution here is an act of timing and performance, a duplication that destabilises authority.

(top right) Terry's Hardware, photographs by Declan Slonim, DS3.1

(bottom) Deptford Smugglers Tunnel Under Terry's Hardware, Declan Slonim, DS3.1

FOLLIES

At the urban scale, Bernard Tschumi's Parc de la Villette demonstrates how distribution can generate interactivity through invisible systems. The park is structured around a grid of follies, each ten metres on each side, placed at intervals of 120 metres. The grid itself is not physically inscribed but is nevertheless operative, organising how visitors move across the site. Tschumi described the project as the encounter of three systems: objects, movements, and spaces. (17)

Rather than concentrating meaning in a central monument, the park distributes interaction evenly across multiple points. Visitors experience a sequence of encounters but never the totality of the grid. Vidler's notion of the uncanny applies here (01) because the park produces a sense of order that is everywhere active but nowhere visible. Interaction is dispersed, and the familiar idea of a park with a single focal object is estranged by the distributed repetition of follies.

The Stahl House shows how media circulation makes domestic space uncanny. Hockney demonstrates how fragmentation produces interactivity through multiplicity. Jackson reveals how the body becomes estranged when distributed across disguises and performances. Laric demonstrates how internet circulation produces infinite re-interactions. Hawksmoor illustrates how civic repetition generates both ritual and speculative geometry. Baldessari shows how repetition generates meaning through play. Parreno demonstrates how duplication destabilises authenticity. Tschumi illustrates how invisible grids distribute interaction across landscape. Vidler's account of the uncanny underpins the disparate parts, (01) in each case, where the familiar becomes strange through repetition, doubling, or displacement. From this exploration, distribution can produce multiplicity, generate uncanniness, and destabilise architectural norms. To teach, to write, and to analyse through repetition and interchangeability is to acknowledge that meaning resides in iteration, where the familiar is always estranged by its return.

(top) Parc de la Villette, Bernard Tschumi, photograph by Jake Parkin

(bottom left) Leeds Mosque Under Construction, photograph by Jake Parkin

NOTES

(01) Anthony Vidler, *The Architectural Uncanny: Essays in the Modern Unhomely* (Cambridge, MA: MIT Press, 1992).

(02) Walter Benjamin, "The Work of Art in the Age of Mechanical Reproduction," in *Illuminations*, ed. Hannah Arendt, trans. Harry Zohn (New York: Schocken, 1968), 221.

(03) Andy Warhol, *The Philosophy of Andy Warhol (From A to B and Back Again)* (New York: Harcourt Brace Jovanovich, 1975).

(04) David Hockney, *Cameraworks*, ed. Lawrence Weschler (New York: Alfred A. Knopf, 1984), 30.

(05) Roland Barthes, *Camera Lucida: Reflections on Photography*, trans. Richard Howard (New York: Hill and Wang, 1981).

(06) Akiko Busch, "Michael Jackson," in *Let's Entertain: Life's Guilty Pleasures*, ed. Philippe Vergne (Los Angeles: Museum of Contemporary Art, 2000), 122–23.

(07) Richard Serra, *Verb List Compilation: Actions to Relating to Oneself, Material, Place, and Process* (1967; repr. in *Richard Serra: Writings/Interviews* [Chicago: University of Chicago Press, 1994]).

(08) Oliver Laric, *Versions* (2009–ongoing), video series.

(09) Ibid.

(10) Kerry Downes, *Hawksmoor* (London: Thames and Hudson, 1979).

(11) Iain Sinclair, *Lud Heat: A Book of the Dead Hamlets* (London: Albion Village Press, 1975).

(12) Michel Foucault, "Of Other Spaces," *Diacritics* 16, no. 1 (Spring 1986): 22–27.

(13) Hal Foster, *The Return of the Real: The Avant-Garde at the End of the Century* (Cambridge, MA: MIT Press, 1996), 41–42.

(14) Maria Faraone, *Studio Juggernaut*.

(15) Olukemi Ilesanmi and Philippe Vergne, "Conversation," in *Philippe Parreno: Alien Seasons* (Minneapolis: Walker Art Center, 2001), 44–47.

(16) Jacques Derrida, *Limited Inc* (Evanston: Northwestern University Press, 1988).

(17) Bernard Tschumi, *Event-Cities* (Cambridge, MA: MIT Press, 1994).)

I FALL IN BETWEEN

CELO GRASSI (STUDIO JUGGERNAUT)

I FALL IN BETWEEN BY CELO GRASSI (STUDIO JUGGERNAUT)

'Slipping from either allegiance as I fail to fulfil, I fall in between'

Nonno only ever leaves keys in locked doors, the shadows of his fingertips visible as you approach. My grandmother's Madonna collection, 2194km away, likewise watch me from their perch. The mantlepiece alone displays five pairs of eyes. As I walk through rooms, wash up dishes, and sit at the edge of the bathtub, Madonna statues enclose me. Whilst unbound to any one place, I am made up of your inability to abandon, fifty five sets of eyes, and an inherited sense of misplacement.

Mainstream understanding of Travellers has been predicated on the White British experience of the culture. Fallacies afforded legitimacy, despite their deliberately limited interaction with the culture, have formed as the basis of these borders, drawn between me, you, half-yous and half-mes. Eclipsing the power of self-perception, Traveller identity was imposed, composed of pure blood and unpolluted cultural practices, all existing in the hegemon's imagination only. Defiance through non-confirmation, to neither your image or mine, becomes inevitable. Visibility alone violates the conditions set, as the myth of a detached and vanished Traveller culture crumbles in my lit and outstretched palms. Separation is essential in the perpetuation of the myth, planning permissions wielded as a weapon against the socio-spatial boundaries needed to guard all they know and understand. Separation and stigma dance round and round until their origins are unexaminable.

(top right) Untitled, Elizabeth Emmerson

(bottom left) (An Alternative) Public London Charter, Chloe Hudson

In this context, the immunity of community acts as the only salvation. A sanctum, within which bounds of membership are drawn from an echoed distinction between us and them. Inside, homogeneity is a necessity, lest I threaten this fragile place we call belonging. Slipping from either allegiance as I fail to fulfil, I fall in between. The discomfort is mutual, the uncategorised unnerve. Without a 'from', the line drawn to where I'll go becomes obscured and unpredictable. All words out of my tongue do not fit, they feel dishonest said in a language that's not mine. My language too has fallen through the gap, the void that resides in between all skins that I have tried to inhabit.

My accent is not mine, it never has been. I've tried on so many I no longer know the one I'm supposed to have. Dually-imposed thresholds of belonging have seeped into my self-perception, now precariously balanced on everything they think I'm not.

The space in-between. From this far into nowhere, everything has melted into the horizon, as your hand drawn borders fall off the edge of my world.

The myth of the monoculture, along with dreams of its refuge, are shattered, to my power and detriment. I can take your difference, squared, and wrap it out around me like a blanket. Shared humanity peaks through and takes my hand, as we exchange lenses. Seeing double turns into seeing triple, quadruple, the scarred residual of a boundary between us becoming increasingly powerless. Unable to find myself on a map, I must trust I have a home here.

OUTSIDE THE PANOPTICON ANTI-TRAVELLER RHETORIC IN THE UK THROUGH A FOUCAULDIAN LENS.

The passing of the *Police, Crime, Sentencing and Courts Act* [01] received significant backlash [02] for its authoritarian expansion of police powers, most notably in respect to protesting laws. A less scrutinized aspect, however, has been the criminalisation of unauthorised encampments, explicitly targeting Gypsy, Roma, Traveller, (GRT) communities.

Under section 60C-E, [03] individuals that are residing or intend to reside on land with a vehicle can be asked to leave in the event they have caused, or are likely to cause, 'significant damage, disruption, or distress'. Failure to comply results in arrest and the seizing of property (homes), those found guilty can be imprisoned for three months and may face a fine of £2500. Placed in the context of chronic national shortages [04] of stopping sites, with discriminations in the planning system resulting in the overwhelming rejection of Traveller site applications, the anti-nomadic sentiment and accompanying active discrimination against GRT communities, is explicit. In understanding its widespread endorsement, Foucault's account of disciplinary power is instrumental. [05]

Anti-Gypsyism and Anti-Traveller rhetoric permeates our culture; it infiltrates media outlets, creeps into conversations, and unsurprisingly materialises as some of the highest rates of racially motivated abuse, with 62% of Gypsies and Travellers having experienced racial abuse and 47% of Roma people had been racially assaulted.

(upper left) Untitled, Elizabeth Emmerson
(bottom left) What do you think? Amy Wallace, DS3.1

(top right) Untitled, Elizabeth Emmerson

The stigmatisation of GRT groups coincides with the highest levels of deprivation, low educational attainment, and poor health outcomes, and yet, as opposed to locating disadvantage in systematic racism, culpability is often linked to lack of integration within wider society. Attempts at assimilation strategies through welfare conditionality, permanent sites, even re-defining the bounds of Traveller identity, (06) through a Foucauldian lens resembles disciplining via examination for 'truth' in response to nomadism's threat to the power knowledge apparatus of the Panopticon. That is, surveillance requires registration, documentation, the assignment of a 'true' name and place, most of which nomad lifestyles subvert.

Embedded within British societies' rejection, stigmatization and abuse towards un-assimilated groups, are ongoing attempts to discipline GRT communities, contemporarily upheld by gross misrepresentations that coincide with hegemonic interests. For example, shows such as *My Big Fat Gypsy Wedding*, (07) or the over-reporting of Travellers alleged environmentally destructive (08) tendencies, forge fabricated identities justifying intervention, and consequently guide the norms informing civilian surveillance, i.e., at what point you feel distressed, or suspicious that anti-social behaviour may occur.

The criminalization of GRT communities is both a product and a means of sustaining panopticism. Those who cannot be 'corrected' must be misrepresented, punished and omitted, without which onlookers may not so easily digest our political representatives referring to a protected ethnic minority group as a 'disease', (09) or openly expressing contempt towards legal settlements near residential areas. (10)

Success of the Panopticon can be seen in claims that 'Travellers have preferential treatment' (11) a demonstration of a self-governing body in action; internalising surveillance and norms to the extent that they become self-enforced, on ourselves and others. The origins of a coerced binary between the normal/abnormal, nomadic/settled, delinquent/civilised become un-examinable once collectively automised, enabling the low-cost implementation of Draconian laws upon marginalised populations.

(top left) Untitled, Elizabeth Emmerson
(middle left) Untitled, Elizabeth Emmerson

(bottom right) Battle of Orgreave (re)enactment, Vanessa Assaf, DS3.1

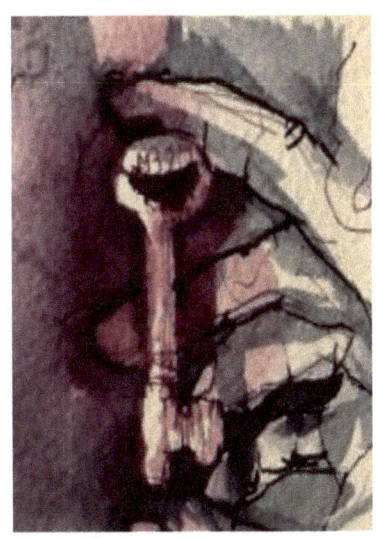
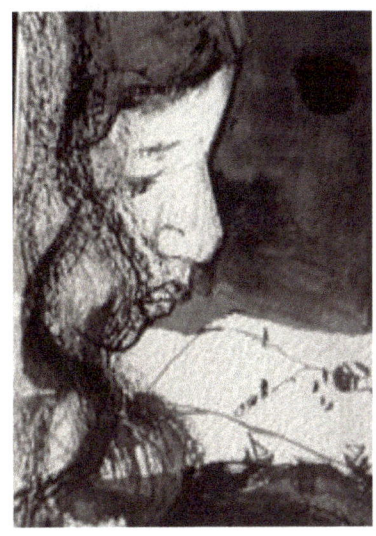
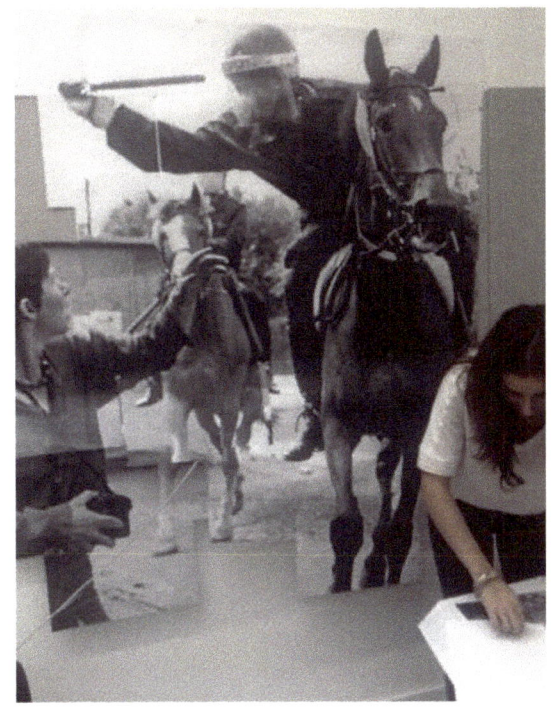

NOTES

(01) *legislation.gov.uk*, "Criminal Justice and Public Order Act 1994, Section 60C," legislation.gov.uk/ukpga/1994/33/section/60C; Michel Foucault, "Docile Bodies," "The Means of Correct Training," and "Panopticism," in *The Foucault Reader*, ed. Paul Rabinow (London: Penguin, 1986), 179–213.

(02) *The Justice Gap*, "New Public Order Bill Branded as Authoritarian by Critics," thejusticegap.com/new-public-order-bill-branded-as-authoritarian-by-critics/.

(03) UK Government, "Police, Crime, Sentencing and Courts Bill 2021 Factsheets: Unauthorised Encampments Factsheet," gov.uk/government/publications/police-crime-sentencing-and-courts-bill-2021-factsheets/police-crime-sentencing-and-courts-bill-2021-unauthorised-encampments-factsheet.

(04) *Gypsy-Traveller*, gypsy-traveller.org.

(05) Michel Foucault, "The Subject and Power," *Critical Inquiry* 8, no. 4 (1982): 777–795, jstor.org/stable/1343197.

(06) Ibid.

(07) *The Irish Times*, "Big Fat Gypsy Wedding Campaign Ruled Offensive," irishtimes.com/news/big-fat-gypsy-wedding-campaign-ruled-offensive-1.546695.

(08) *Friends of the Earth UK*, "Out of Site: Britain's Nomadic People," friendsoftheearth.uk/system-change/out-site-britains-nomadic-people.

(09) *Hansard*, "Travellers in Mole Valley," House of Commons Debate, 25 April 2019, hansard.parliament.uk/Commons/2019-04-25/debates/368D852C-9209-497B-B510-032F0ABDEA34/TravellersInMoleValley#contribution-3B9BA008-FFF3-4D8D-88E0-1E869E51F378.

(10) *The Telegraph*, "Tory MP Accused of Fanning Flames of Racism over Traveller Site," 1 March 2024, telegraph.co.uk/politics/2024/03/01/tory-mp-accused-fanning-flames-of-racism-traveller-site/.

(11) *Hansard*, "Planning System: Gypsies and Travellers," House of Commons Debate, 29 January 2020, hansard.parliament.uk/commons/2020-01-29/debates/6C426CC1-F880-4415-ADFA-2393F47A5AE8/PlanningSystemGypsiesAndTravellers.

ACKNOWLEDGEMENTS

JANE TANKARD + JAKE PARKIN

JANE TANKARD + JAKE PARKIN

Acknowledgements

Farid Abdalla, Jasmine Abu Hamdan (Zaha Hadid Architects), Alessandro Ayuso, Maria Bahrim, Michelle Barratt, Peter J. Baldwin, Will Barty, Maria Bessarabova (Wilkinson Eyre), Kishan Bhopal, Simon Bowden Architects, Steve Bowkett, Ben Brakspear, Lindsay Bremner, Carlos Villanueva Brandt (AA), Henry Burns (FA.E: Collective), Kitty Byrne (Hopkins Architects), Anesa Cana, Deniz Cetin, Reece Davey (V+A Museum), Andrew Dawes (Zoda), Georgie Day, Kevin Driver (Turner Studio), EA.F. Collective, Rauiri Fallon, Maria Faraone (Oxford Brookes University), Ali Glover (F.A.I: Collective), Thomas Grove (Adam Architects), Celo Grassi, William Handyside (RSH+P), Christopher Hartiss (Modulous), Hanna Henrikkson Rebizant (Bartlett), Chloe Hudson (AA), Christos Kakouros, Ben Kearns (Creative Giants), Maria Kramer, Andreas Lang (Public Works), Zineb Lemseffer (Ben Adams), Cameron McKay, Henry Cameron McKay (LSA), Tyen Masten (Tyen Masten Studio), Inigo Minns (AA), Cati Miralles, Paul Monaghan (AHMM), Ali Montero (Ali Montero Architecture), Henry Morgan, Trevor Morriss (SPPARC Architects), Daniele Natale (DBLO Associates Architects), John Naylor (Grimshaw Architects), Olivia Neves Marra (AA), John Ng (RCA), Lucy O'Riley, Cagda Ozbecki, Chris Pierce (AA), Alicia Pivaro, Kevin Rhowbotham, Mark Rowe (prev. Perkins+Will), Tim Rowson, Mike Russum (Birds Portchmouth Russum), Martin Sagar, Tetsuya Saito (AA), Luke Sanders (Sheppard Robson), Sarmad Suhail (Michaelis Boyd), Aleks Stankovic (Studio Marsa), Hafsa Syed, Allen Sylvester (Ullmayer Sylvester), Dean Van der Vord (Red Deer), Manijeh Verghese (Open City), Amy Wallace, Victoria Watson, Aoi Phillips Yamashita (Clementine Blakemore Architects), Luka Ziobakaite.

(right) La Jetee Choreography, Beth Allen, DS3.1

(bottom right) Spica's World, Ben Daughtrey, DS3.1

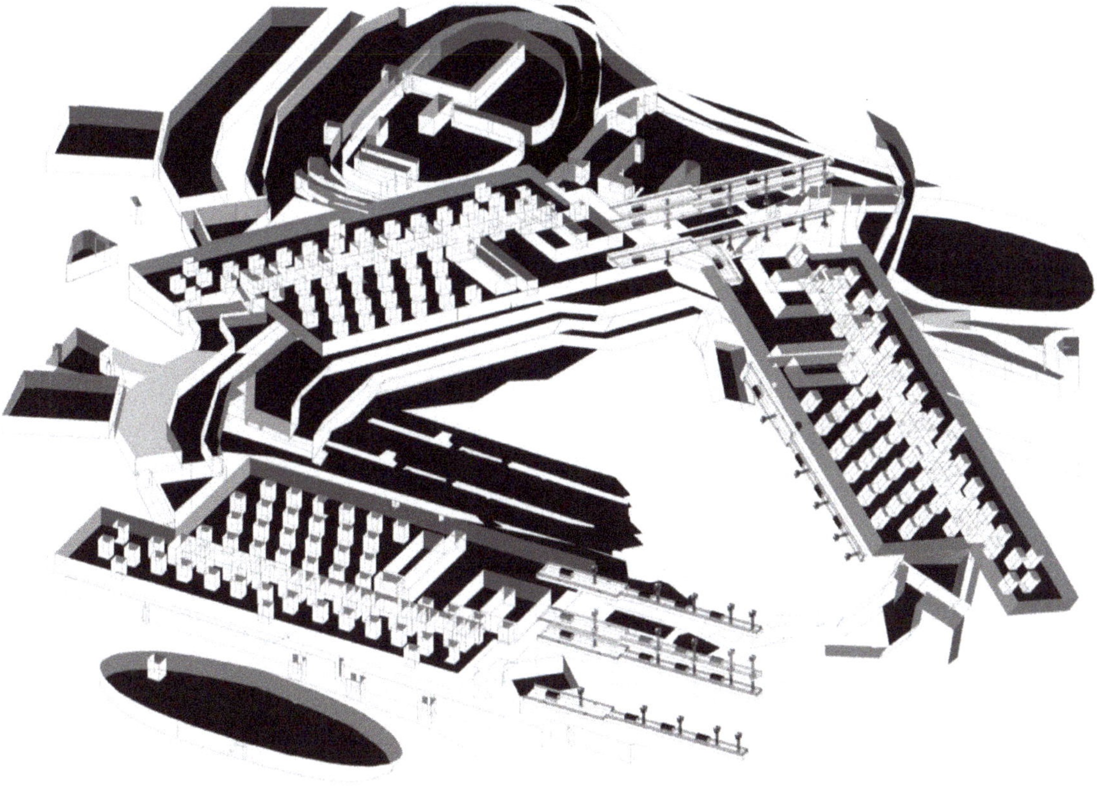

2015/16
Farid Abdulla, Vanessa Assaf, Michelle Barratt, Mahmoud Chehab, Giacomo Brusa, Hanna Furey, Javier Garcia-Navarro, Sofie Hald, Jamie Hedgecock, Rim Kalsoum, Joey Khan, Tahmid Miah, Eira Mooney, Eline Putne, Giulia da Lorenzo Bellacci, Denise Carcangiu, Flavia Cerasi, San Martino, Lilac Shahed, Maria Yli-Slippola

2016/17
Jadene Aguilar, Sheikh Tanim Ahmed, Ziadoon Azeez, Veronica Cappelli, Lai Chan, Simrath Diocee, Ioana Dumitrasc, Alison Edwards, Daniel Gee, Abdul Rahman Hassan, Ronahi Kaplan, Myungin Lee Eleanor Lucock, Ani Markova, Katia Petsali, Maria Ribalaygua, Amirah Suhaimy, Janice Yee Tai, Fiona Tmava

2017/18
Arwa Al-Naswari, Vicky Carillo Mullo, Jeffrey Chan, Samiye Cifci, Ben Daughtry, Faustine Ghislain, Adam Kramer, Unnati Mankad, Federico Minieri, Muhtasim Mojnu, Teodora Neagoe, Setareh Nosrati, Elena Ryskute, Fatima Salim, Amy Wallace, Luka Ziobakaite

2018/19
Leen Ajlan, Beth Allen, Estera Badelita, Polina Bouli, Katie Brown, Daria Donovetsky, Kevin Ferenzena, Hanane Ferraz, Kate Hubert, Areesha Khalid, Ugne Kiseliovaite, Cameron McKay, Aya Mousa, Sulaman Muhammad, Aamirah Munshi, Simi Oluwo, Natalia Orzel, Adrian-Calin Paul, Darina Procopciuc, Kenza Salmi el Idrissi, Yara Samaha, Zsuzsanna Szohr

2019/20
Hana Alsaai, Pietro Asti, Ioshua Bulman, Esther Callinawan, Sarah Daoudi, Aleksandar Donov, Julia Gromny, Aissam Hachemi, Kirill Menshikov, Suzana Meziad, Alicia Montero, Henry Morgan, Sebastian Mortimer; Nabiha Qadir; Ecaterina Reabov, Rowan St John, Hafsa Syed, Bradley Welch

2020/21
Hicham Abari, Mohamed Alkhaja, Saya Agha, Sarah Al Matrook, Maria Bahrim, Mathew Bailey, Stephanie Grange, Gabriela Mac'Allister, Vlad-Ilie Necula, Riane Oukili, Naran Oyuntsetseg, Aikaterini Pechynaki, Mario Priore, Eleni Savvaidi, Yael Shnitzer, Daniel Smith, Maisie-Ann Spencer, Sumaita Zaman

2021/22
Lamisah Abdal, Rima Almesri, Giorgia Bresciani, Nina Busz, Brandon Clark, Maja Dworak-Kula, Mateusz Gliniewicz, Halima Haq, Anna Ludmann, Sam McMahon, Aidan McMillan, Naran Oyuntsetseg, Julia Pastor, Anastasia Plahotniuc, Glena Sabri, Feriel Siad, Saba Torabi, Shakira Willingale-Hayes

2022/23
Wizana Ahmed, Sara Anwar, Monica Basta, Salaheldeen Elnour, Amelia Gavina, Vinya Kerai Julia Lassota, Harry Mellor, Victoria Pearce, Darya Prokopets, Yasmin Sattar, Finola Simpson, Maryam Syed, Isabella Testolin, Sofia Whilby, Annie Williams, Zahra Zougari

2023/24
Souleymane Avice, Gabriella Abbott, Fajer Alasfour, Andrea Betteridge, Asya Caiado, Kyrah Copeland-Thompson, Gemma Daniel, Hanaan Eggay, Rowan Isles, Ekta Jadeja, Vinaya Kerai, Sofia Najy Mezdagat, Areebah Nagi, Maria Ruano Delgado, Declan Slonim, Jerrell Singh, Camilla Nuñez Suarez, Jessica Tofan, Zsiriah Thomas, Abigail Williams

2024/25
Rachele Airighi, Inaaya Amer, Nico de la Flor Rey, Angela de la Vega, Rania Elkharim, Munira Osman, Olha Petrachkova, Aa'ishah Boutrig, Malak Huseynova, Ozlem Incedal, Namar Nazer, Bhakti Patel, Sneha Sachin Shenoy, Sarina Sheikhmohammadi, Yixiao Shen Ermis Tsolos

(bottom) Morpheus Neighbourhood, Cally Road, Christos Kakouros, DS3.1

FROM JANE

I would like to give special thanks to: Steve Bowkett, Tonia Carless, Paul Monaghan, Kevin Rhowbotham, Kath Shonfield and of course Alicia, Thomas and Jake.

FROM JAKE

I would like to give special thanks to: Alessandro Ayuso, Susan Bone, Chloe Hudson, Diony Kypraiou, Jimenez Lai, Sarah Mills, Tyen Masten, Inigo Minns, John Ng, Carlos Villanueva Brandt, Paolo Zaide and Jane!

(right) OPEN Westminster Show, DS3.1, photograph by Jake Parkin

Exploring the *Unheimlich*

DS3.1
Edited by Jane Tankard and Jake Parkin

A University of Westminster,
School of Architecture + Cities Publication

Designed by Mark Boyce

All texts ©2025 the authors

This work is licensed under a CC BY-NC 4.0 license

ISBN 978-1-7385696-2-5

Books in the Studio as Book series are available to purchase via OpenStudioWestminster here:
http://www.openstudiowestminster.org/studio-as-book/
or from online book stores.

The editors have attempted to acknowledge all sources of images used and apologise for any errors or omissions.

School of Architecture + Cities
University of Westminster
35 Marylebone Road
London
NW1 5LS

www.ingramcontent.com/pod-product-compliance
Lightning Source LLC
Chambersburg PA
CBHW061139230426
43663CB00024B/2973